Introduction to Human-Computer Interaction

Introduction to Human-Computer Interaction

Daniel Moore

www.willfordpress.com

Published by Willford Press,
118-35 Queens Blvd., Suite 400,
Forest Hills, NY 11375, USA

ISBN: 978-1-64728-030-7

Cataloging-in-Publication Data

Introduction to human-computer interaction / Daniel Moore.
    p. cm.
Includes bibliographical references and index.
ISBN 978-1-64728-030-7
1. Human-computer interaction. 2. User-centered system design. 3. Human computation.
4. User interfaces (Computer systems). I. Moore, Daniel.
QA76.9.H85 I58 2022
004.019--dc23

For information on all Willford Press publications
visit our website at www.willfordpress.com

Table of Contents

Preface

It is with great pleasure that I present this book. It has been carefully written after numerous discussions with my peers and other practitioners of the field. I would like to take this opportunity to thank my family and friends who have been extremely supporting at every step in my life.

Human-computer interaction deals with the research of the design and use of computer technology that is focused on the interfaces between people and computers. It observes the ways in which humans interact with computers. It also designs computer technologies that enable humans to interact with computers in new ways. The field of human-computer interaction combines the areas of design, media studies, computer sciences and several other fields. It primarily focuses on the methods of designing and implementing new computer interfaces. It also delves into methods for studying human computer use and its sociocultural implications along with methods for determining if the user is a human or a computer. This book presents the complex subject of human-computer interaction in the most comprehensible and easy to understand language. Some of the diverse topics covered in this book address the varied branches that fall under this category. It will provide comprehensive knowledge to the readers.

The chapters below are organized to facilitate a comprehensive understanding of the subject:

Chapter – What is Human-Computer Interaction?

Human-Computer interaction is concerned with the researches in the design as well as the utilization of computer technology, primarily focusing on the interfaces between users and computers. This is an introductory chapter which will introduce briefly all the significant aspects of human-computer interaction as well as its importance.

Chapter – Fundamental Concepts of Human-Computer Interaction

Some of the fundamental concepts of human-computer interaction are interaction technique, human-centered computing, mobile interaction, mobile computing, user experience design, computer accessibility, computer user satisfaction, banner blindness, etc. This chapter has been carefully written to provide an easy understanding of these key concepts of human-computer interaction.

Chapter – User Interface: Types of Elements

In human-computer interaction, the space where the interactions between humans and machines occur is referred to as user interface. The two main types of user interface are natural user interface and graphical user interface. The topics elaborated in this chapter will help in gaining a better understanding about these types of user interface as well as the user interface tools.

Chapter – Interface Design Methods

The design of user interfaces for machines and software such as mobile devices and computers, with a focus on maximizing the user experience and usability, is known as user interface design. Common types of interface design methods are user-centered design and ecological interface design. This chapter discusses in detail these methods of interface design.

Chapter – Human-Computer Interaction: Models and Laws

The main models of human-computer interaction are Keystroke-level model and GOMS. Some of the various laws of human-computer interaction are Fitts' law, Steering law and Hick's Law. This chapter closely examines these models and laws of human-computer interaction to provide an extensive understanding of the subject.

Chapter – Applications of Human-Computer Interaction

Human-computer interaction is applied in various fields such as game design, vehicles, wrist watch, etc. It is also used in virtual reality and augmented reality. These diverse applications of human-computer interaction have been thoroughly discussed in this chapter.

Daniel Moore

1

What is Human-Computer Interaction?

Human-Computer interaction is concerned with the researches in the design as well as the utilization of computer technology, primarily focusing on the interfaces between users and computers. This is an introductory chapter which will introduce briefly all the significant aspects of human-computer interaction as well as its importance.

Human-Computer Interaction focuses on the interactions between human and computer systems, including the user interface and the underlying processes which produce the interactions. The contributing disciplines include computer science, cognitive science, human factors, software engineering, management science, psychology, sociology, and anthropology. Early research and development in human-computer interaction focused on issues directly related to the user interface. Some typical issues were the properties of various input and output devices, interface learn ability for new users versus efficiency and extensibility for experienced users, and the appropriate combination of interaction components such as command languages, menus, and graphical user interfaces (GUI). Recently, the field of human-computer interaction has changed and become more devoted to the processes and context for the user interface. Functionality of a system is defined by the set of actions or services that it provides to its users. However, the value of functionality is visible only when it becomes possible to be efficiently utilized by the user. Usability of a system with a certain functionality is the range and degree by which the system can be used efficiently and adequately to accomplish certain goals for certain users. The actual effectiveness of a system is achieved when there is a proper balance between the functionality and usability of a system.

The rapid growth of computing has made effective human-computer interaction essential. HCI (human-computer interaction) is the study of how people interact with computers and to what extent computers are or are not developed for successful interaction with human beings. Utilizing computers had always begged the question of interfacing. The methods by which human has been interacting with computers has travelled a long way. The journey still continues and new designs of technologies and systems appear more and more every day and the research in this area has been growing very fast in the last few decades. The growth in Human-Computer Interaction (HCI) field has not only been in quality of interaction, it has also experienced different branching in its history. Instead of designing regular interfaces, the different research branches have had different focus on the concepts of multimodality rather than unimodality, intelligent adaptive interfaces rather than command/action based ones, and finally active rather than passive interfaces.

Gustav Evertsson describes Human-Computer Interaction is about designing computer systems so the user can carry out their activities productively and safely. It is not how easy something is to use, it is about how usable it is. Or, a broader definition of HCI is; Human-Computer Interaction is a discipline concerned with the design, evaluation and implementation of interactive computer systems for human use and with the study of major phenomena surrounding them.

> "It is a wide variety of different kind of people and not just technical specialists as in the past, so it is important to design HCI that supports the needs, knowledge and skills of the intended users".

As its name implies, HCI consists of three parts: the user, the computer itself, and the ways they work together.

User: By "user", we may mean an individual user or a group of users working together. An appreciation of the way people's sensory systems (sight, hearing, touch) relay information is vital. Also, different users form different conceptions or mental models about their interactions and have different ways of learning and keeping knowledge. In addition, cultural and national differences play an important part.

Computer: When we talk about the computer, we're referring to any technology ranging from desktop computers, to large scale computer systems. For example, if we were discussing the design of a Website, then the Website itself would be referred to as "the computer". Devices such as mobile phones or VCRs can also be considered to be computers.

Interaction: There are obvious differences between humans and machines. In spite of these, HCI attempts to ensure that they both get on with each other and interact successfully. In order to achieve a usable system, you need to apply what you know about humans and computers, and consult with likely users throughout the design process. In real systems, the schedule and the budget are important, and it is vital to find a balance between what would be ideal for the users and what is feasible in reality. Human-Computer Interaction studies how people design, implement and use computer interfaces. HCI has become an umbrella term for a number of disciplines including theories of education, psychology, collaboration as well as efficiency and ergonomics.

Some of the disciplines involved in the field of Human-Computer Interaction Recent developments in the area of HCI have shown an interest in adaptive interfaces, speech recognition, gestures and the role of time.

Having these concepts in mind and considering that the terms computer, machine and system are often used interchangeably. In this context, HCI is a design that should produce a fit between the user, the machine and the required services in order to achieve a certain performance both in quality and optimality of the services. Determining what makes a certain HCI design good is mostly subjective and context dependant. For example, an aircraft part designing tool should provide high precisions in view and design of the parts while a graphics editing software may not need such a precision. The available technology could also affect how different types of HCI are designed for the same purpose. One example is using commands, menus, graphical user interfaces (GUI), or virtual reality to access functionalities of any given computer.

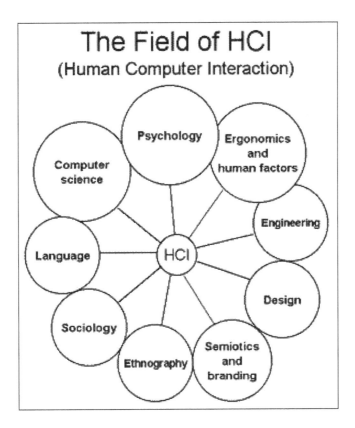

The Goals of HCI

The goals of HCI are to produce usable and safe systems, as well as functional systems. Usability is concerned with making systems easy to learn and easy to use. In order to produce computer systems with good usability developers must attempt to:

- Understand the factors that determine how people use technology.

- Develop tools and techniques to enable building suitable systems.

- Achieve efficient, effective and safe interaction.

- Put user first.

Underlying the whole theme of HCI is the belief that people using a computer system should come first. Their needs, capabilities and preferences for conducting various tasks should direct developers in the way that they design systems. People need not change themselves in order to fit in within the system. Instead, the system should be designed to match their requirements.

HCI Technologies

Gustav Evertsson describes HCI design is about designing the computer system for the people and not the people for the computers. There are a lot of important factors that have to be considered by designers. Example of factors is:

- Physiology such as the human behavior and mental processes.

- Organizational such as the influence of one individual in a group with the other member as attitude and behavior.

- Ergonomics such as how people interact with different artifacts.

HCI design should consider many aspects of human behaviors and needs to be useful. The complexity of the degree of the involvement of a human in interaction with a machine is sometimes invisible compared to the simplicity of the interaction method itself. The existing interfaces differ in the degree of complexity both because of degree of functionality/usability and the financial and economical aspect of the machine in the market. For instance, an electrical kettle need not to be sophisticated in interface since its only functionality is to heat the water and it would not be cost-effective to have an interface more than a thermostatic on and off switch. On the other hand, a simple website that may be limited in functionality should be complex enough in usability to attract and keep customers. Therefore, in design of HCI, the degree of activity that involves a user with a machine should be thoroughly thought. The user activity has three different levels: physical, cognitive, and affective. The physical aspect determines the mechanics of interaction between human and computer while the cognitive aspect deals with ways that users can understand the system and interact with it. The affective aspect is a more recent issue and it tries not only to make the interaction a pleasurable experience for the user but also to affect the user in a way that make user continue to use the machine by changing attitudes and emotions toward the user.

The existing physical technologies for HCI basically can be categorized by the relative human sense that the device is designed for. These devices are basically relying on three human senses: vision, audition, and touch. Input devices that rely on vision are the most used kind and are commonly either switch-based or pointing devices. The switch-based devices are any kind of interfaces that use buttons and switches like a keyboard. The pointing devices examples are mice, joysticks, touch screen panels, graphic tablets, trackballs, and pen-based input. Joysticks are the ones that have both switches and pointing abilities. The output devices can be any kind of visual display or printing device.

The recent methods and technologies in HCI are now trying to combine former methods of interaction together and with other advancing technologies such as networking and animation. These new advances can be categorized in three sections: wearable devices, wireless devices, and virtual devices. The technology is improving so fast that even the borders between these new technologies are fading away and they are getting mixed together. Few examples of these devices are: GPS navigation systems, military super-soldier enhancing devices (e.g. thermal vision, tracking other soldier movements using GPS, and environmental scanning), radio frequency identification (RFID) products, personal digital assistants (PDA), and virtual tour for real estate business. Some of these new devices upgraded and integrated previous methods of interaction. As an illustration, there is the solution to keyboarding that has been offered by Compaq's iPAQ which is called Canesta keyboard. This is a virtual keyboard that is made by projecting a QWERTY like pattern on a solid surface using a red light. Then device tries to track user's finger movement while typing on the surface with a motion sensor and send the keystrokes back to the device.

Importance of Human-Computer Interaction

HCI is extremely important when designing clear intuitive systems which will be usable for people with a varied range of abilities and expertise, and who have not completed any formal training. HCI takes advantage of our everyday knowledge of the world to make software and devices more understandable and usable for everyone. For example, using a graphic of a miniature folder in a computer's interface helps the user understand the purpose of the folder, as everyone has experience with real paper folders in their everyday lives. Ultimately, if a system is well designed with HCI techniques, the user should not even have to think about the intricacies of how to use the system. Interaction should be clear, intuitive, and natural.

Daily Life

Today computers permeate every aspect of our daily lives. Even if a person does not directly own or use a computer, their life is affected in some way by computing. ATM machines, train ticket vending machines, and hot drinks dispensing machines are just a few examples of computer interfaces a person can come into contact with daily without needing to own a personal computer. HCI is an important factor when designing any of these systems or interfaces. Regardless, if an interface is for an ATM or a desktop computer, HCI principles should be consulted and considered to ensure the creation of a safe, usable, and efficient interface.

Business and Industry

HCI is an important consideration for any business that uses computers in their everyday operation. Well designed usable systems ensure that staff are not frustrated during their work and as a result are more content and productive. HCI is especially important in the design of safety critical systems, such as, for example, those found in power plants, or air traffic control centers. Design errors in these situations can have serious results, possibly resulting in the death of many people.

Accessibility

HCI is a key consideration when designing systems that are not only usable, but also accessible to people with disabilities. The core philosophy of HCI is to provide safe, usable, and efficient systems to everyone, and this includes those with different sets of abilities and different ranges of expertise and knowledge. Any system properly designed with HCI user-centeed techniques and principles will also be maximally accessible to those with disabilities.

Software Success

Good use of HCI principles and techniques is not only important for the end user, but also is a very high priority for software development companies. If a software product is unusable and causes frustration, no person will use the program by choice, and as a result sales will be negatively affected.

Untrained Users

Today, very few computer users actually read the manual accompanying the software, if one exists. Only very specialised and advanced programs require training and an extensive manual. Computer users expect to understand the main functionality of an average program within a few minutes of interacting with it. HCI provides designers with the principles, techniques, and tools necessary to design effective interfaces that are obvious and easy to use, and do not require training.

Design Principles of Human-Computer Interaction

"The most important thing to design is the user's conceptual model. Every thing else should be subordinated to making that model clear, obvious, and substantial. That is almost exactly the opposite of how most software is designed." By a conceptual model is meant:

A description of the proposed system in terms of a set of integrated ideas and concepts about what it should do, behave and look like, that will be understandable by the users in the manner intended.

To develop a conceptual model involves envisioning the proposed product, based on the user's needs and other requirements identified. To ensure that it is designed to be understandable in the manner intended requires doing iterative testing of the product as it is developed. A key aspect of this design process is initially to decide what the user will be doing when carrying out their tasks. For example, will they be primarily searching for information, creating documents, communicating with other users, recording events, or some other activity? At this stage, the interaction mode that would best supports this need to be considered. For example, would allowing the users to browse be appropriate, or would allowing them to ask questions directly to the system in their native language be more affective? Decision about which kind of interaction style use (e.g., whether to use a menu-based system, speech inputs, commands) should be made in relation to the interaction mode. Thus, decision about which mode of interaction to support differ from those made about which style of interaction to have; the former being at a higher level of abstraction. The former are also concerned with determining the nature of the users' activities to support, while the later are concerned with the selection of specific kinds of interface.

Once a set of possible ways of interacting with interactive system has been identified, the design of the conceptual modal then needs to be thought through in term of actual concrete solution. This entail working out the behavior of the inter face, the particular interaction style that will be used, and the "look and feel" of the interface. At this stage of "fleshing out," it is always a good idea to explore a number of possible designs and to assess the merits and problems of each one.

Another way of designing an appropriate conceptual model is to interface metaphor this can provide a basic structure for the conceptual model that is couched in knowledge users are familiar with. Examples of well-known interface metaphors are the desktop and search engines.

Software has a behavioral face it shows to the world that is created by the programmer or designer. This representation is not necessarily an accurate description of what is really going on inside the computer, although unfortunately, it frequently is. This ability to represent the computer functioning independent of its true actions is farmore pronounced in software than in any other medium. It allows a clever designer to hide some of the more unsavory facts of how the software is really getting the job done. This disconnection between what is implemented and what it offered as explanation gives rise to a third model in the digital world, the designer's represented model--the way the designer chooses to represent a program's functioning to the user. Donald Norman refers to this simply as the designer's model.

The closer the represented model comes to the user's mental model, the easier he will find the program to use and to understand. Generally, offering a represented model that follows the implementation model too closely significantly reduces the user' sability to learn and use the program, assuming that the user's mental model of his tasks differs from the implementation model of the software.

We tend to form mental models that are simpler than reality; so if we create represented models that are simpler than the actual implementation model, we help the user achieve a better understanding. Pressing the brake pedal in your car, for example, may conjure a mental image of pushing a lever that rubs against the wheels to slow you down. The actual mechanism includes hydraulic cylinders, tubing, and metal pads that squeeze on a perforated disk, but we simplify all that out of our minds, creating a more effective, albeit less accurate, mental model. In software, we imagine that a spreadsheet scrolls now cells into view when we click on the scrollbar. Nothing of the sort actually happens. There is no sheet of cells out there, but a tightly packed data structure of values, with various pointers between them, from which the program synthesizes a new image to display in real-time.

Another important thing is that there are several gulfs that separate mental states from physical ones. Each gulf reflects one aspect of the distance between the mental representation of the person and the physical components and states of the environment. And these gulfs present major problems for users.

The Gulf of Execution

Does the system provide actions that correspond to the intentions of the person? The difference between the intentions and allowable actions is the gulf of execution. One measure of this gulf is how well the system allows the person to do the intendedactions directly, without extra effort: do the action provided by the system match those intended by the person?

The Gulf of Evaluation

Does the system provide a physical representation that can be directly perceived and that is directly interpretable in terms of the intentions and expectations of the person? The Gulf of evaluation reflects the amount of effort that the person must exert to interpret the physical state of the system and to determine how well the expectations and intentions have been met. The gulf is small when the system provides information about its state in a form that is easy to get, is easy to interpret, and matches the way the person thinks of the system.

The Seven Stages of Action as Design Aids

The seven-stage structure can be a valuable design aid, for it provides a basic checklist of questions to ask to ensure that the Gulfs of evaluation and execution are bridged. In general, each stage of action requires its own special design strategies and, in turn, provides its own opportunity for disaster. It would be fun were it not also so frustrating, to look over the world and gleefully analyze each deficiency. On the whole, as you can see in figure the questions for each stage are relatively simple. And these, in turn, boild own to the principles of good design. Principles of good design are discussed below.

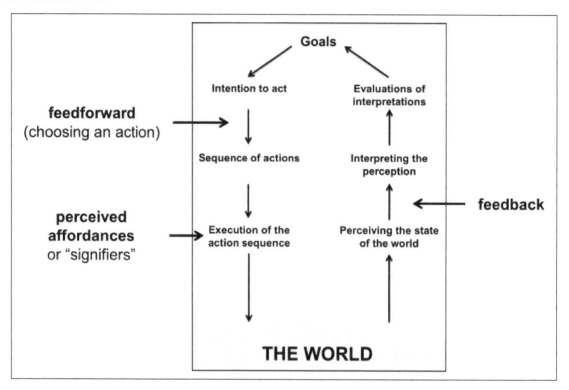

Design Principles

A number of design principles have been promoted. The best known are concerned with how to determine what users should see and do when carrying out their tasks using an interactive product.

- Visibility

- Affordance

- Constraints

- Mapping

- Consistency

- Feedback

Visibility

The more visible functions are, the more likely users will be able to know what to do next. In contrast, when functions are "out of sight," it makes them more difficult to fit and knows how to use. Norman describes the controls of a car to emphasize this point. The controls for different operations are clearly visible (e.g., indicator, headlights, horn, hazard warning lights), indicating what can be done. The relationship between the way the controls have been positioned in the car and what they do makes it easy for the deriver to find the appropriate control for the task at hand. For example, one problem that you often encounter, in word processing software you often needed to set the properties of a word document.

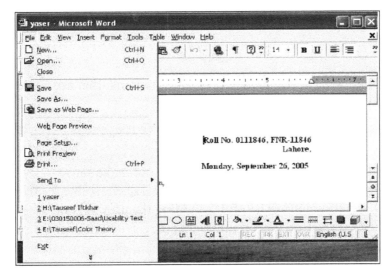

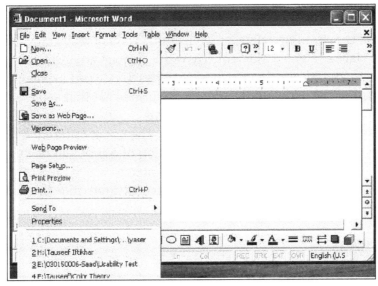

Affordance

Affordance is a term used to refer to an attribute of an object that allows people to know how to use it. For example, a mouse button invites pushing by the way it is physically constrained in its plastic shell. At a very simple level, to afford means "to give a clue." When the affordances of a physical object are perceptually obvious it is easy to know how to interact with it. For example, a door handle affords pulling, a cup handle affords grasping, and a mouse button affords pushing. Norman introduced this concept in the late 80s in his discussion of the design of everyday objects. Since then, it has been much popularized, being what can be done to them. For example, graphical elements like button, icon, links, and scroll bars are talked about with respect to how to make it appear obvious how they should be used, icons should be designed to afford clicking, scroll bars to afford moving up and down, buttons to afford pushing.

There are two kind of affordance:

- Perceived
- Real

Real

Physical objects are said to have real affordances, like grasping, that are perceptually obvious and do not have to be learned.

Perceived

User interfaces that are screen-based are virtual and do not make sense to try to design for real affordances at the interface, except when designing physical devices, like control consoles, where affordance like pulling and pressing are helpful in guiding the user to know what to do. Alternatively screen based interfaces are better conceptualized as perceived affordances, which are essentially learned conventions.

Constraints

The design concept of constraining refers to determining ways of restricting the kind of user interaction that can take place at a given moment. There are various ways this can be achieved. A common design practice in graphical user interfaces is to deactivate certain menu options by shading them, thereby restricting the user to only actions permissible at that stage of the activity. One of the advantages of this form of constraining is it prevents the user from selecting incorrect options and there by refuses the chances of making a mistake. The use of different kinds of graphical representations can also constrain a person's interpretation of a problem or information space. For example flow chart diagram show which objects are related to which thereby constraining the way the information can be perceived. Norman classified constraints into three categories: physical, logical, and cultural.

Physical Constraints

Physical constraints refer to the way physical objects restrict the movement of things. For example, the way a external disk can be placed into a disk drive is physically constrained by its shape and size, so that it can be inserted in only one way. Likewise, keys on a pad can usually be pressed in only one way.

Logical Constraints

Logical constraints rely on people's understanding of the way the world works. They rely on people's common-sense reasoning about actions and their consequences. Picking up a physical marble and placing it in another location on the phone would be expected by most people to trigger something else to happen. Making actions and their effects obvious enables people to logically deduce what further actions are required. Disabling menu options when not appropriate for the task in hand provides logical constraining. It allows users to reason why (or why not) they have been designed this way and what options are available.

Culture Constraints

Culture constraints rely on learned conventions, like the use of red for warning, the use of certain kinds of signals for danger, and the use of the smiley face to represent appy emotions. Most cultural constraints are arbitrary in the sense that their relationship with what is being represented is abstract, and could have equally evolved to be represented in another form (e.g., the use of yellow instead of red for warning). Accordingly, they have to be learned. Once learned and accepted by a cultural group, they become universally accepted conventions. Two universally accepted interface conventions are the use of windowing for displaying information and the use icons on the desktop to represent operations and documents.

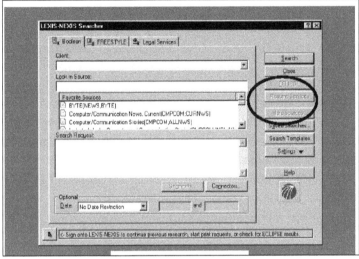

Example of logical constraints.

Mapping

This refers to the relationship between controls and their effects in the world. Nearly all artifacts need some kind of mapping between controls and effects, whether it is a flashlight, car, power plant, or cockpit. An example of a good mapping between controls are effect is the up and down arrows used to represent the up and down movement of the cursor, respectively, on a computer keyboard. The mapping of the relative position of controls and their effects is also important. Consider the various musical playing devices. How are the controls of playing rewinding, and fast for ward mapped onto the desired effects? They usually follow a common convention of providing a sequence of buttons, with the play button in the middle, the rewind button on the left and the fast-for wardon the right. This configuration maps directly onto the directionality of the actions.

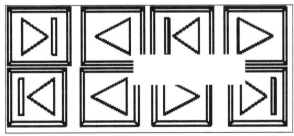

Imagine how difficult it would be if the mapping were used.

Consistency

This refers to designing interfaces to have similar operations and use similar elements for achieving similar tasks. In particular, a consistent interface is one that follows rules, such as using the same operation to select all objects. For example, a consistent operation is using the same input action to highlight any graphical object at the interfaces, such as always clicking the left mouse button. Inconsistent interfaces, on the other hand, allow exceptions to a rule. An example of this is where certain graphical objects (e.g., email messages presented in a table) can be highlighted using the right mouse button, while all other operations are highlighted using the left button. A problem with this kind of inconsistency is that is quite arbitrary, making it difficult for users to remember and making the users more prone to mistakes.

On of the benefits of consistent interfaces, therefore, is that they are easier to learn and use. Users have to learn only a single mode of operation that is applicable to all objects. This principle worked well for simple interfaces with limited operations, like mini CD player with small number of operations mapped onto separate buttons. Here all the user has to do is learn what each button represents and select accordingly. However, it can be more problematic to apply the concept of consistency to more complex interfaces, especially when many different operations need to be designed for. For example, consider how to design an interface for an application that offers hundreds of operations. There is simply not enough space for a thousand buttons, each of which maps onto an individual operation. Even if there were, it would be extremely difficult and time consuming for the user to search through them all to find the desired operation.

A much more effective design solution is to create categories of commands that can be mapped into subsets of operations. For the word-processing application, the hundreds of operation available are categorized into subsets of different menus. All commands that are concerned with file operations are placed together in the same file menu.

Another problem with consistency is determining what aspect of an interface to make consistent with what else. There are often many choices, some of which can be inconsistent with other aspects of the interface or ways of carrying out actions. Consider the design problem of developing a mechanism to let users lock their file son a shared server. Should the designer try to design it to be consistent with the way people lock things in the outside world (called external consistency) or with the way they lock objects in the existing system (called internal consistency)? However, there are many different ways of locking objects in the physical world (e.g., placing in a safe, using a padlock, using a key, using a child safety lock), just as there are different ways of locking electronically. The problem facing designer is knowing which one to be consistent with.

Human-Computer Interaction Factors in Technology Enhanced Learning

Advances in technology in recent years has meant that a wide variety of technology such as PCs, laptops, the Internet, mobile devices, tablets, smart phones are becoming embedded into our everyday lives and the modern society today. Web 2.0 has brought not just technological advances but social changes. Student experience with mobile devices such as smart phones, tablet devices and laptops means that they are often familiar with instant access to online resources and expect to be able to use them as part of their own individual learning.

Recently, there has been increased interest in the importance of HCI in learning sciences. Learning Sciences ICLS 2012, Pierre Dillenbourg made the case that many of the important problems of learning / education are not primarily addressed through innovations in learning theory but by addressing important problems through useful, usable, perhaps innovative designs (a particular emphasis in HCI).

HCI is very much a multi-disciplinary study of how humans interact with technology. Many of these disciplines, such as cognitive psychology, sociology, computing, artificial intelligence and linguistics all have a direct bearing on learning. HCI provides a number of relevant theories of memory, attention, perception, and knowledge that are particularly significant when it comes to the acquisition, storage and retrieval of knowledge – particularly heuristic knowledge gained through experience – learning by doing.

The learning society is often referred to a society that is "founded on the acquisition, renewal and use of knowledge" (emphasis by author) moving the focus from teaching/teacher to learning/learner and from formal to a much more self-directed form of "learning throughout life experiences". In this context, acquiring knowledge is not the same as acquiring information. The role of computing technology in a knowledge based society has become increasingly important by providing easy access to data, facts, and information as well as helping the learner transform information into knowledge. The individual is becoming much more responsible for developing his/her own skills. Knowledge about facts is becoming less important than learning how to access, analyse and exploit information and transform it into new knowledge.

HCI has long been concerned with accessibility and principles for designing interactive technologies for diverse users. Aspirations of overcoming the Digital Divide, through providing universality and accessibility for all, have become major concerns in HCI.

Many tools we are familiar with today may be enhanced to provide advanced data services. A good example of this is the newspaper, which in the future may have flexible content which can present data, information and knowledge in many innovative forms, for example, virtual reality, 3D, 4D and multiple dimensions of visualization. These advanced capabilities will have the power to transform the way we currently view teaching and learning into a much more flexible, tailored, customizable set of tools to improve the engagement of students. The more "fun" an interface is the more likely the student is to engage successfully with their own learning.

There are many opportunities to investigate this area further with HCI principles in mind. The way humans use memory and how this further influences learning is crucial when researching how students might gather and store new facts, information and knowledge. The active learning approach is based to a large extent on a social constructionist view of learning and in particular much of the work of Biggs on constructive alignment.

According to Biggs, "The teacher's task is not to transmit correct understandings but to help students construct understandings that are more or less acceptable". Geoff Petty described this as learning by doing. He stated, "Research shows that active learning is much better recalled, enjoyed and understood. Active methods require us to 'make our own meaning', that is, develop our own conceptualizations of what we are learning". During this process, we physically make neural connections in our brain, the process we call learning. Passive methods such as listening do not require us to make these neural connections or conceptualizations. Active methods also develop thinking skills such as analysis, problem solving, and evaluation and are more fun.

HCI influences on Pedagogies Relevant to Online Learning

Two pedagogies influential in online teaching and learning that are relevant to this discussion are social constructivism and connectivism. Social constructivism, particularly based on the work of Vygotsky emphasises the social aspects of learning. Put simply, this involves students constructing their own knowledge through discussion or collaboration and ideas being constructed from experience to have a personal meaning for the student. Vygotsky's theory involves learning contexts in which students play an active role in learning. Siemen's theory of connectivism on the other hand, is concerned with learning through our connections and by making connections, tapping into networks, accessing resources, connecting ideas. This leads logically to knowing where to find information being more important than what we know. This is particularly relevant in the Internet age. Today, Siemens suggested, "The pipe is more important than the content within the pipe". These pedagogies require supporting opportunities for collaboration, interaction, discussion and finding resources.

Learning and Technological Changes

Over the past twenty years or so, technology has transformed how we live our lives, how we communicate, and how we learn. Advances in technology in recent years has meant that a wide variety of technology such as PCs, laptops, the Internet, mobile devices, tablets, smart phones are becoming embedded into our everyday lives and the modern society today. These technologies have become so embedded that changes to the technology results in changes to society. The move from Web 1.0 to Web 2.0 has changed the way many users interact with technology. They are no longer merely passive recipients but have become active content creators. Web 2.0 has brought not just technological advances but social changes. These changes present challenges for Web-based education, including how, where, and when learning happens. Student experiences with these types of devices means that they are often familiar with instant access to online resources and expect to be able to use them as part of their own individual learning. It is reasonable therefore that learning needs and theories that describe learning principles and processes should reflect those of underlying social environments.

In The Learning Society, the author suggested, the future of education is networked. Using the full power of video and mobility, people can collaborate to create and share knowledge as well as develop new ways of teaching and learning that captures the attention and imagination of learners anywhere, anytime on any device.

The report goes on to highlight significant developments in learning research:

- Learning is an active, social process: Learners learn new knowledge, principles, and concepts for themselves through dialogue and interaction with others, such as teachers and peers, as well as interacting with their learning environment.

- Motivation is critical to effective learning: Levels of motivation and emotional states, positive or negative, can be critical in effective learning.

- Learners bring different knowledge to a new learning challenge: Learners have prior knowledge no matter how inaccurate or narrow. Effective learning builds on this, engages with it and progressively moves towards new understanding, step-by-step. This highlights the role of formative assessment in establishing current levels of understanding in order to be able to monitor progress.

- Learners start from different places and take different routes to the learning outcome.

- To be effective, knowledge should be discovered as an authentic, integrated whole.

Technology Enhanced Learning

JISC defined a technology enhanced learning culture where a wide range of learners (e.g., full-time, part-time, professionals, overseas) is provided with a robust technology environment that provides the learning opportunities wherever the learner chooses.

Goodyear and Retalis used the term to cover all those circumstances where technology plays a significant role in making learning more effective, efficient or enjoyable. They included both hardware – such as interactive whiteboards, smart tables, handheld technologies, tangible objects – and software, e.g., computer-supported collaborative learning systems, learning management systems, simulation modelling tools, online repositories of learning content and scientific data, educational games, web 2.0 social applications, 3D virtual reality, etc.

Learning, Technology and Cognitive Aspects

There have been many innovative philosophies such as those proposed by Maria Montessori in the late 20th century. Her educational approach encourages experimentation and independent thinking rather than the more mainstream pre-determined textbook curriculum. HCI can contribute greatly in this area since there is a recognition and acceptance of human differences and diversity that education needs to take account of.

Dror said:

> "Learning means that the cognitive system acquires information and stores it for future use. If these processes do not occur properly, then the learners will not initially acquire the information, and even if they do, then they will not be able to recall it later, or/and the information will not be utilized and behaviour modified".

He described how training (whether traditional, e-learning, or blended learning) is inextricably linked to connections and dependence on the human cognitive system. Research, including work on making training and technology interactive, has found that when users are properly-cognitively involved, engaged, and challenged the outcomes are better.

Technology can be made more Effective by Making it Interactive

The challenge is to create mental representations that are long lasting and effect behaviour, something best done by creating memorable learning experiences targeting specific brain structures. Patricia Chalmers described the difficulty of learning and remembering information merely presented on a computer screen, for example, on a website, asking "Where am I?" or "Where was I?" or "Where am I going?" She explained this as understanding where new knowledge fits into "the big picture."

Technologies: An example - Clickers

Clickers are an example of how I have recently used innovative technologies in an attempt to improve student engagement in some classes. Clickers are small handheld devices that allow students/audiences to answer questions by pressing buttons on the handset in a "Who Wants to be a Millionaire" style of participation. There are many researchers who have contributed to this field. Bruff found that Clickers were less effective if merely used for tracking and evaluation, but were of particular benefit for use in class as well as small group discussions making classes more fun and providing opportunities for "teachable moments."

Other researchers have focused on the quality of class interaction and cognitive processing. Duncan, Plant and Stowell and Nelson have researched student satisfaction, and Pileggi and O'Neill looked at teamwork.

HCI Experiment: Memory Enhancement using Visualisation

One example taken from a recent HCI class is to investigate improving memory. Students are asked to supply ten objects from their possessions. These ten objects are then visualised interacting with objects linked to the numbers 1 to 10. One links with bun (visualise any form of bun, e.g., burger bun or sticky bun with white icing), two is shoe, three is tree, four is door, five is hive, six is sticks, and so on for all ten numbers. Students then visualise one of the volunteered objects interacting with one of these items. Particularly memorable examples include: lip gloss interacting with eight gate – in this case a student suggested a cow looking over the gate with sticky, glossy lips – the lip gloss – an unforgettable image. Another student suggested handbag as the item interacting with two shoe – their comment was girls always carry spare shoes in their handbag. Ten weeks later the class could remember all ten random items.

The expression, "A picture is worth a thousand stories," refers to the concept that a complex idea can be simplified with an image. This method takes advantage of a fact about human memory: most people remember images better than verbal or written information. Images are concrete, while raw information is often abstract. The goal of visualisation is to present large amounts of data easily and understandable. This has implications for online learning since there are many innovative, creative ways of using visualisation to assist in the learning process by providing opportunities for improving memorability. HCI provides much research on memory and how we use it. With advances in human-focused technology and design, memory aids are progressing from simple strategies, such as mnemonics and visual associations, towards workstations and wearable computer systems that actively augment the user's memory.

Lessons from Gaming and HCI

Lessons can be learned from the computer games community. There is great learning potential in the virtual environments of gaming. Computer games are problem-solving spaces described as situated learning since the player is situated in an actual problem-solving space. Education can learn a lot from computer games about effective ways to teach. For example, games provide information when it is needed, instead of all at once in the beginning, when it is usually forgotten by the time it is needed. Assessment is another area for improvement. In games, assessment and learning are tightly aligned; games constantly assess player performance and provide feedback. Most games are engaging and addictive with every success bringing another new challenge. Once you start playing, it is difficult to stop.

Engagement is an important concept in HCI, not only for informing the design and implementation of interfaces, but also for enabling more sophisticated interfaces capable of adapting to users. Engagement has often been described as occurring when the brain is rewarded, and that for something to be perceived as rewarding, it must evoke positive emotions. Two essential components to the perception of something being rewarding are wanting and liking. Dix, Finlay, Abowd and Beale in their HCI textbook, describe reward as essentially positive reinforcement of desired or good behaviour. This could be through providing explicit praise (used frequently in educational systems when a correct answer is given) or through more implicit elements that engage or entertain the user. Novelty, social interaction, feedback and surprise are all potentially rewarding to the user. For example, seeing a direct relationship between action and effect (feedback) can be rewarding. Rodgers, Sharp, and Preece in Interaction Design: Beyond HumanComputer Interaction discuss affective learning as a way to design systems to elicit positive responses from users (feeling at ease, being comfortable, enjoying the experience) and topics such as user frustration caused by an interface and how interface agents (anthropomorphism) and synthetic characters affect us. Brave and Nass also examine the effects of emotions during HCI and how emotions tend to alter attention and memory, bias judgment and motivate behaviour.

HCI is often focused on software interfaces; however, the principles of good interface design can be applied in many situations, for example, creating a website, a mobile phone, or an intelligent fridge. Intuitive design relies on understanding human psychology. Usability is a measure of the effectiveness, efficiency and satisfaction with which specified users can achieve specified goals in a particular environment. By following these principles, it is possible to create systems where the relationships between the user's goals, the required actions, and the results are sensible, meaningful and not arbitrary. Feedback is deemed to be essential in HCI in a useable interactive interface.

Donald Norman defines three principles of interactive design in his book 'The Design of Everyday Things'. These are:

- Visibility: It should be obvious what a control is used for. Good visibility allows the user to easily translate goals into actions.

- Affordance: It should be obvious how a control is used. A button affords (suggests) pushing, a lever affords pulling, etc. The user should know how to operate a control just by looking at it.

- Feedback: It should be obvious when a control has been used. This relates to the information sent back to the user about what has been achieved, e.g., sound, highlighting, animation etc.

Another feature of gaming that could apply to education is the practice of modification or customisation. Many game developers encourage players to modify their products and encourage users to create things like new maps or scenarios. In HCI, it is recognised that users are different, hence a diverse, inclusive, individualised environment will have many benefits. Dyck, Pinelle, Brown, and Gutwin analysed several current game interfaces looking for ideas that could be applied more widely including the suggestion that games allow:

- Effortless community: Easy to form, join, and participate in communities of users.

- Learning by watching: 'Over the shoulder' of more experienced users as they work.

- Deep customizability: Allow users to modify interfaces and share these with others.

- Fluid system-human interaction: Communicate information to users in ways that do not demand the user's attention and do not interrupt the flow of work.

These ideas have arisen in games because of their focus on user performance and user satisfaction, and we believe that they can help to improve the usability of other types of applications.

3D PRINTING FOR HUMAN-COMPUTER INTERACTION

A common misconception is that 3D printing is limited to the plastic extrusion process seen on today's popular consumer devices such as the MakerBot. In this process, plastic is extruded through a hot nozzle and deposited voxel by voxel (a physical pixel), layer by layer onto a build platform until the 3D object is complete. This is called *fused deposition modeling* (FDM).

The reason FDM technology entered the consumer market first is that its patents expired first: 3D printing is a technology developed in the 1980s with a variety of different processes and materials. In 2009, the first FDM patent ran out; only a few months later, the MakerBot Cubcake CNC appeared on the market. However, many more advanced technologies still have active patents and thus right now are available only in industry.

Another recently expired patent is that of *stereolithography* 3D printing, a process used, for example, in the Form2 3D printers. A liquid resin is poured into a tank. Then a laser (SLA 3D printing) or a projector (DLP 3D printing) selectively shines light onto the resin, which hardens it in these locations. Many other 3D-printing techniques will be available for startups soon. For instance, in inkjet 3D printing, an inkjet head releases a binder that selectively hardens powder in a powder bed. At the end of the process, users remove the object in a process that resembles an archaeological excavation. Metal printing works similarly: A laser selectively melts and fuses metal powder in a powder bed. Finally, layered-object manufacturing (LOM) can process materials that cannot be extruded, bound, or sintered. It takes entire sheets of material, such as a roll of fabric, cuts each sheet into a shape using a laser or other cutting device, and then stacks each layer to create the 3D object. Many more processes and materials exist, from machines that 3D print with felt to create entirely soft objects such as Teddybears, to 3D printers that can print glass.

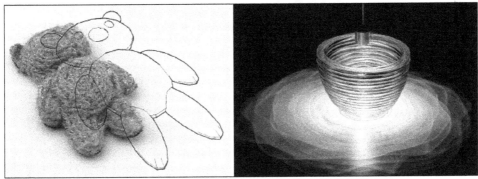

D printing with different materials: (left) a 3D-printed soft teddy bear; (right) a 3D-printed glass vase.

The words 3D printing and additive manufacturing are often used interchangeably; however, they are not the same. 3D printing is a subcategory of additive manufacturing. Additive manufacturing is any process that creates objects by iteratively adding material until the object is finished. 3D printing is a specific additive manufacturing process in that it has full control over the placement of every voxel in the 3D object, which lends it unlimited degrees of freedom and thus unlimited complexity in the objects it can build. This makes it a very powerful tool.

The Process for Creating Physical Objects using 3D Printing

The traditional workflow consists of three steps: 3D modeling, slicing (preparing a model for fabrication), and 3D printing.

3D modeling: There are many different 3D editors with different modeling processes. The most accessible ones for novice users, such as TinkerCAD, use a process called *solid modeling*, in which users combine primitive shapes, such as cubes and spheres, and use Boolean operations, such as intersect, join, and subtract, to create a 3D model.

SketchUp, use a process called *surface modeling*, in which users manipulate the faces, edges, and vertices of a 3D model. This allows for more expressive free-form shapes but, there is a drawback: Users can accidentally create invalid geometry, for instance, by creating a hole in the surface geometry, which goes against the watertight requirement of 3D printing (i.e., the geometry needs to be "manifold"). In solid modeling, water-tightness is always guaranteed, as it is an inherent property of the modeling process. Many tools exist to help analyze 3D models for defects and repair them for 3D printing, either as additional plugins for 3D editors such as the SketchUp Manifold plugin, or as separate programs, the most popular one being Autodesk Meshmixer.

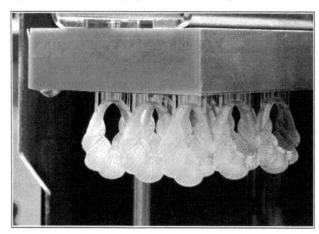

Slicing: To prepare a model for 3D printing, users have to open the 3D model in a separate program called a slicer. Preparing a model for 3D printing includes steps such as generating the support material that is printed below the model geometry that has nothing underneath it (called an overhang), splitting the model into layers that the 3D printer will print one at a time, and selecting the materials with which the object will be printed. Each of these attributes has additional parameters. For instance, there are different types of support structures for different use cases: Each layer consists of not only a height but also a number of outlines (so-called shells) and the percentage of infill, a honeycomb pattern used inside the object instead of solid infill to save printing time. The slicer typically imports the 3D model in .stl file format (but other formats, such as the recently developed .amf, exist). For most 3D editors that do not have an .stl export built in, there are additional plugins that can be installed (e.g., Sketchup provides an .stl extension plugin).

Fabrication: The slicer exports instructions to the 3D printer in so-called G-Code, which is the machine language for 3D printers. G-Code tells the print head where to move, how much material to extrude along the way, and how fast to move. Similar commands exist for leveling the print bed, warming up the extruder nozzles, and other parts of the printing process. Regular users will not have contact with low-level G-Code; however, many HCI research projects such as WirePrint leverage custom G-Code commands for their applications. Before printing, users typically must load the right materials into the 3D printer and level the printing platform to be the right distance from the extruder nozzle. However, more and more of these routines are becoming automated to make the process easier (e.g., via auto-leveling of the print bed).

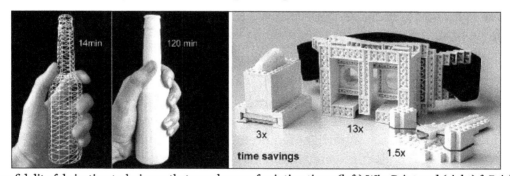

Two low-fidelity fabrication techniques that save hours of printing time: (left) WirePrint and (right) faBrickation.

Optional: finishing and post-coloring. To give the object a higher-quality appearance, finishing can be applied to the 3D-printed objects. Depending on the material and process used, different finishing steps are suitable, such as using sandpaper or acetone to smooth the surface. Besides polishing the surface, additional color can be added, for instance, via hydrographic printing, in which the object is dipped into a water bath with a custom-color film floating on its surface that subsequently adheres to the object.

Challenges with 3D Printing

Despite the amazing potential of 3D printing technologies, there remain some sticky problems that must be solved. Here are some of the key challenges we face in the coming years.

Speed: One challenge with 3D printing is that the process is relatively slow. For instance, printing an object the size of a head-mounted display takes around 15 hours on a plastic extrusion printer. When designing a new object that requires many iterations, the long fabrication time slows down the design process. To allow for faster iteration, *low-fidelity fabrication* can print intermediate versions of a design as fast as low-fidelity versions. Only the final version will be printed as slow high-fidelity. The low-fidelity version preserves the key aspect that is currently being tested, such as the shape of an object. Figure also shows faBrickation, another implementation of the low-fidelity fabrication concept that focuses on modularity by combining off-the-shelf Lego bricks with 3D-printed parts.

Interaction model: Researchers have also questioned whether the current interaction model with 3D printers in which users use a *digital* editor to create a *physical* object is the best workflow. With *interactivefabrication*, researchers have instead proposed that users work hands on with the physical workpiece, as in traditional crafting, providing physical feedback after every editing step. Figure (left) shows such a system: Users touch the screen and see the physical output in the form of foam drops as they appear on the platform underneath after a few seconds. Because fast physical output is challenging, researchers have also built intermediate systems toward this vision based on augmented and mixed reality.

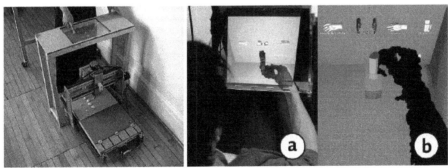

(left) Interactive fabrication with Shaper. (right) MixFab: a mixed-reality modeling environment that allows users to embed real-world objects.

Sustainability: With 3D printing hardware becoming more and more available, a future in which everyone can produce physical objects is getting closer. However, in contrast to digital design, physical objects require actual materials and produce actual physical waste. Personal fabrication is currently a one-way process: Once an object has been fabricated with a 3D printer, it cannot be changed. Any alteration requires printing a new version from scratch. Instead of reprinting the entire object, Patching Physical Objects proposes to change the existing object: Users mount the object into the 3D printer, then load both the original and the modified 3D model into a piece of software, which in turn calculates how to patch the object. After identifying which parts to remove and what to add, the system locates the existing object in the printer using the system's built-in 3D scanner. After calibrating the orientation, a mill first removes the outdated geometry, and then a print head prints the new geometry in place.

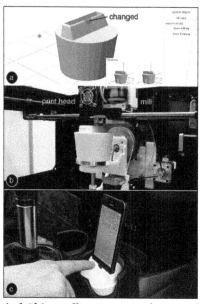

Patching Physical Objects allows users to change existing physical
objects to minimize waste and printing material.

Intellectual property: Once an object is available as a digital 3D model, users can fabricate it on their 3D printers for only the cost of the material, bypassing the cost that normally compensates the designer for his or her work. A recent survey found that 80 percent of top 3D designers don't share their designs for fear of theft. Thus, securing intellectual property rights might close the content gap that is currently delaying further adoption of personal fabrication devices.

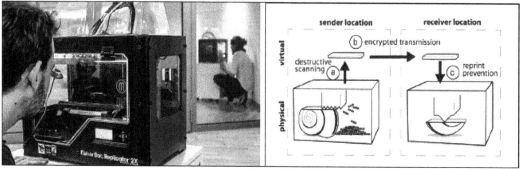

Scotty allows the relocation of physical objects while preserving
intellectual property, i.e., keeping the object unique.

Scotty is an appliance that allows users to send objects to distant locations while maintaining copyright. For the object transfer not to interfere with intellectual property—that is, to keep the object unique and to not produce illegal copies in the process—the object needs to disappear at the sender location and reappear at the receiver location. Scotty achieves this by (1) Destroying the original during scanning by shaving off one layer at a time with the built-in milling machine. Each layer is captured with the built-in camera. (2) During transmission, Scotty prevents "men-in-the-middle" from fabricating a copy of the object by encrypting the object using the receiver's public key. (3) Finally, during refabrication, Scotty prevents the receiver from making multiple copies by maintaining an eternal log of objects already fabricated.

What is Down the Road?

On the technology side, we are seeing rapid progress every year. For instance, the 3D-printing company 3D Systems stated that 3D printing speed on average has doubled every 24 months over the past 10 years. Similarly, we see new 3D-printing materials coming out in short intervals. Material science journals, such as *Advanced Materials*, can provide HCI researchers with insights on what is coming out soon. Printing new functional materials with properties such as light-activated shape changing will allow for new types of sensors and actuators that will enable completely new interactive applications. On the other hand, there are many open research questions concerning the workflow with 3D printers. They include how to provide the necessary domain knowledge and machine knowledge required to produce physical objects and how to make the process more interactive with a tighter feedback cycle.

2
Fundamental Concepts of Human-Computer Interaction

Some of the fundamental concepts of human-computer interaction are interaction technique, human-centered computing, mobile interaction, mobile computing, user experience design, computer accessibility, computer user satisfaction, banner blindness, etc. This chapter has been carefully written to provide an easy understanding of these key concepts of human-computer interaction.

Interaction Technique

One enduring trait of computing systems is the presence of the human operator. At the human-computer interface, the nature of computing has witnessed dramatic transformations from feeding punched cards into a reader to manipulating 3D virtual objects with an input glove. Yet technology must co-exist with the human interface of the day. Not surprisingly, themes on keeping pace with advances in technology in the human-computer interface.

To place input devices in perspective, we illustrate a classical human factors interpretation of the human-machine interface. Figure simplifies the human and machine to three components each. The internal states of each interact in a closed-loop system through controls and displays (the machine interface) and motor-sensory behaviour (the human interface). The terms "input" and "output" are, by convention, with respect to the machine; so input devices are inputs to the machine controlled or manipulated by human "outputs". Traditionally human outputs are our limbs the hands, arms, legs, feet, or head but speech and eye motions can also act as human ouput. Some other human output channels are breath and electrical body signals (important for disabled users).

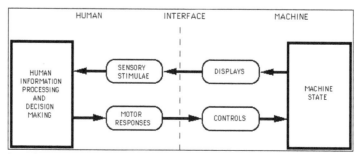

The human-machine interface. Input devices are the controls humans manipulate to change the machine state.

Interaction takes place at the interface through an output channel--displays stimulating human senses--and the input channel.

Two broad themes are interaction and technology. A familiar message is that interaction is the key to pushing the frontier and that technology should evolve and bend to serve interaction, rather than interaction conforming to technology. This is a contestable viewpoint. Advances in technology are often independent of the consequences or possibilities for human-computer interaction or other applied disciplines. Basic research fields such as materials science or semiconductor physics push the boundaries of science, addressing fundamental questions and spawning "low-level deliverables". Through engineering and design, deliverables eventually filter up into commercial products. As human factors researchers or human-machine system designers, we should fully expect to mold interaction scenarios within a given resource base today's technology. Although technological constraints tend to vanish simply by waiting for new advances, interaction problems persist since their solution requires multidisciplinary research and design efforts that are often ill-defined and qualitative. This is where the greatest challenges lie.

In advanced virtual environments, goals are to empower the user, to instrument all or part of the body, and to force the machine to yield to natural dialogues for interaction.

Technology

We focus on technological characteristics of present and future input devices. While specific devices are cited, the intent is not to list and categorize the repertoire of devices.

Transducers

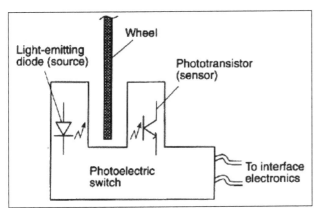 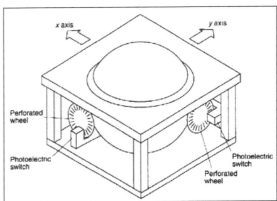

A photo-electric switch as an input transducer. (a) A light-emitting diode provides a source of light and stimulates a phototransistor sensor, switching it on and off. The light beam is interrupted by a rotating perforated wheel. (b) Two photo-electric switches sense x and y motion of a rolling trackball.

The most simplistic, technology-centered view of input and output devices is at the electro-mechanical level of the transducer. Transducers are energy converters. For input devices the conversion is usually from kinetic energy (motion) or potential energy (pressure) to electric energy (voltage or current). By far the most common input transducer is the switch. The hardware supporting mouse buttons and alphanumeric keys is the most obvious example. Motion applied to the switch opens or closes a contact and alters the voltage or current sensed by an electronic circuit. Many "high-level" devices are an aggregate of switches. The x-y pointing capability of mice and trackballs, for example, is often implemented by photo-electric switches. A beam of light is interrupted by perforations in a rotating wheel driven by the mouse ball or trackball. Light pulses stimulate phototransistors that complete the conversion of kinetic energy to electric energy.

Joysticks are commonly available in two flavors. Displacement or isotonic joysticks move about a pivot with motion in two or more axes. The 544-G974 from Measurement Systems, Inc., for example, is a three axis displacement joystick sensing x and y pivotal motion as well as twist. Deflection is +/-15° about the x and y axes and +/-10° of twist.

(a) A three-axis displacement joystick senses tilt about the base and twist about the vertical axis.
(b) A four-axis isometric joystick senses force in the x, y, and z axes, and torque in the twist axis.

Force sensing or isometric joysticks employ resistive strain gauges which undergo a slight deformation when loaded. An applied force generates compression or tension in a wire element bonded to a load column. The wire element undergoes compression or tension which changes its resistance. This effects a change in voltage or current in the interface electronics. An example is the *426-G811*, also from Measurements Systems, Inc. This four-axis joystick senses x, y, and z force, and torque about the twist axis. Up to 10 lbs of force is sensed in the x and y axes, and 20 lbs in the z axis. Torque up to 32 in.-lbs is sensed in the twist axis. Deflection is slight at 0.65 in. for the x and y axes, 0.25 in. for the z axis, and 9° for the twist axis.

Although most input devices are manually actuated, we should acknowledge the microphone as an important input device. Converting acoustic energy to electric energy, microphones are the transducers that permit us to talk to our computer.

Gloves, 3D Trackers and Body Suits

The technology underlying many successful input devices, such as the mouse or QWERTY keyboard, is mature and stable. Juggling or conducting an orchestra are human activities with the potential of entering the world of human-machine dialogues; yet, significant inroads--on purely technological grounds--must be achieved first. Applications such as these do not exist at present. A challenge for researchers is to get the technology into the mainstream as an entertainment medium or a means of performing routine tasks in the workplace.

Devices such as gloves and body suits are really a compliment of transducers working in unison to deliver fidelity in the interface. Most gloves combine a single 3D tracker and multiple joint sensors. The *DataGlove* by VPL Research, Inc. is a thin lycra glove with a magnetically coupled 3D tracker mounted on it. Bending in the two proximal joints is measured by the attenuation of a light signal in each of two fiber optic strands sewn along the fingers and thumb. Position and orientation measurements are accurate to 0.13 inches RMS and 0.85° RMS at 15 inches. Data are transfered over RS232 or RS422 links at rates up to 38.4 kilobaud. Sampling rate is 30 Hz or 60 Hz. The *DataGlove*, first introduced at *CHI '87* by Zimmerman, Lanier, Blanchard, Bryson, and Harvill, was the first input glove to gain widespread use in the research community. Options are available for abduction sensing (on the thumb, index, and middle fingers) and force feedback.

The *DataGlove* has been criticized because of its non-linear mapping between joint movement and the intensity of the reflected light. As well, the lack of abduction sensing (on the standard model) limits the number of hand positions that can be detected, for example, in gesture recognition tasks.

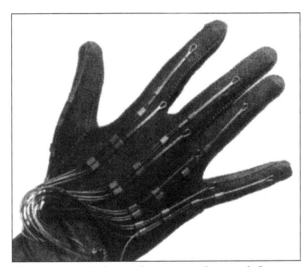

The VPL DataGlove. Two optical strands are sewn along each finger to sense bend in two joints. A single strand sewn on the thumb senses single joint motion.

The CyberGlove by Virtual Technologies includes 22 resistive-strip sensors for finger bend and abduction, and thumb and pinkie rotation. The mapping is linear with 8 bits of resolution per sensor. A force feedback option is available. The strip sensors are a more natural transducer for sensing bend and abduction than the optical fibres in the VPL Data Glove. Their presence is less apparent, more comfortable, and easily extends to applications beyond the hand. Complete body instrumentation is possible through custom sewn suits covering the torso or limbs. The stip sensors can be added in the suit's material at any anatomical position where bend is to be sensed.

An inexpensive input glove is the *Power Glove* by Mattel, designed as an input device for the Nintendo Entertainment System (videogame). It was used in a low-end system known as *Virtual Reality on Five Dollars a Day*. *x*, *y*, and *z* location, and wrist rotation are determined using ultrasonic receivers (two on the glove) and transmitters (three, wall-mounted). Bend in the thumb and first three fingers is detected to 2 bits of resolution via strain gauges. Seventeen buttons on the forearm padding provide various select functions.

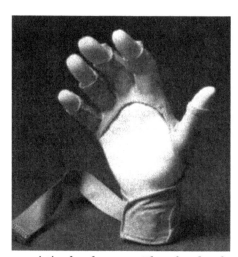

The Virtex *CyberGlove* includes 22 resistive-bend sensors. Three bend and one abduction sensor are used for each finger and thumb. Thumb and pinkie cross-over and wrist rotation are also sensed.

There are several 3D trackers in current use, including the Polhemus *Isotrack*, the Ascension Technology Corp. *Bird* and the Logitech *2D/6D Mouse*. A transmitter or source mounted in the vicinity of the user generates an electromagnetic or ultrasonic field that is picked up by a sensor mounted on the glove (or torso, head, etc.). A cable from the sensor to the interface electronics completes the loop permitting six degree-of-freedom localization of hand position and orientation. The six degrees of freedom are the spatial coordinates with respect to the x, y, and z axes, and the angular orientations around each axis, known as pitch, roll, and yaw. The cable is sometimes called a "tether" since it confines body motion near the interface electronics. A problem with the widely used Polhemus device is that nearby metallic objects interfere with the source/sensor signal. This has inspired some alternate technologies such as optical tracking using infra-red transmitters and receivers or ceiling-mounted video cameras.

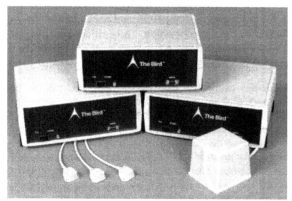

The Ascension *Bird* 3D electromagnetic tracker includes a sensor
(bottom center), a source (right), and interface electronics.

Device Properties

Input devices possess numerous properties and parameters which can enhance or limit performance., "properties" are the qualities which distinguish among devices and determine how a device is used and what it can do. They place a device within a "design space"--a framework for comparison and analysis.

Device properties cannot be adjusted or optimized. For example, cursor positioning is relative using some devices, but absolute with others. There is no middle ground. In relative positioning, motion (or force) applied to the device influences the motion of the cursor relative to its current position. In absolute positioning, the cursor position on the display maps to specific, absolute spatial coordinates on the device. This property distinguishes among device and determines the sorts of actions that may be easier on one device but harder on another.

"Clutching" is an interaction property inherent in tablets, mice, and other devices using relative positioning. Clutching is the process of disengaging, adjusting, and re-engaging the input device to extend its field of control. This is necessary when the tracking symbol, whether a cursor on a planar CRT or a virtual hand in 3-space, cannot move because the controlling device has reached a limit in its physical space. The most obvious example is lifting and repositioning a mouse when it reaches the edge of the mouse-pad; however, many input devices for virtual environments require constant clutching to allow the user to attain new vantages in a potentially huge task space. In such situations, clutching is implemented through a supplemental switch or through gestural techniques such as grasping. Characteristics such as this affect performance, but quantitative distinctions are difficult to measure because they are highly task dependent.

Device Models

A model is a simplified description of a system to assist in understanding the system or in describing or predicting its behaviour through calculations. The "system" in this sense is the set of input devices. Models can be broadly categorized as descriptive or predictive. Several ambitious descriptive models of input devices have been developed. One of the earliest was Buxton's taxonomy which attempted to merge the range of human gestures with the articulation requirements of devices. In Figure, devices are placed in a matrix with the primary rows and columns (solid lines) identifying what is sensed (position, motion, or pressure) and the number of dimensions sensed (1, 2, or 3). For example, potentiometers are 1D (left column) but a mouse is 2D (center column); trackballs are motion sensing (center row) but isometric joysticks are pressure sensing (bottom row). Secondary rows and columns (dashed lines) delimit devices manipulated using different motor skills (sub-columns) and devices operated by direct touch vs. a mechanical intermediary (sub-rows). For example, potentiometers may be rotary or sliding (left sub-columns); screen input may be direct through touch or indirect through a light pen (top sub-rows).

		Number of Dimensions						
		1		**2**				**3**	
Position	Rotary Pot	Sliding Pot	Tablet & Puck	Tablet & Stylus	Light Pen	Floating Joystick	3D Joystick	**M**
			Touch Tablet		Touch Screen			**T**
Motion	Continuous Rotary Pot	Treadmill	Mouse			Trackball	3D Trackball	**M**
		Ferinstat				X/Y Pad		**T**
Pressure								**T**
	Torque Sensor					Isometric Joystick		

Buxton's taxonomy places input devices in a matrix by the property sensed (rows), number of dimensions sensed (columns), requisite motor skills (sub-columns), and interaction directness.

Foley, Wallace, and Chan provided a two-tiered breakdown of graphics tasks and listed devices suited to each. Seven main tasks were identified: *select, position, orient, path, quantify,* and *text entry*. Within each category a complement of sub-tasks was identified and appropriate device mappings offered. For example, two of the position sub-tasks were "direct location" and "indirect location". The touch panel was cited for the direct location task and the tablet, mouse, joystick, trackball, and cursor control keys were cited for the indirect location task. Foley et al.'s taxonomy is useful because it maps input devices to input tasks; however, it does not provide a sense of the device properties that generated the mappings. The strength of Buxton's taxonomy is its focus on the these properties.

Researchers at Xerox PARC extended the work of Buxton and Foley et al. into a comprehensive "design space" where devices are points in a parametric design space. Their model captures, for example, the possibility of devices combining position and selection capabilities with an integrated button. (Selection is a discrete property outside the purview of Buxton's taxonomy.)

The models above are descriptive. They are useful for understanding devices and suggesting powerful device-task mappings; but they are not in themselves capable of predicting and comparing alternative design scenarios. Their potential as engineering (viz., design) tools is limited.

The point above surfaced in a workshop on human-computer interaction (HCI) sponsored by National Science Foundation. The participants were leading researchers in human-computer interaction. Among other things, they identified models that are important for the future of HCI. These were organized in a matrix identifying scientific vs. engineering models as relevant to human vs. machine characteristics. In Figure, the device models are found at the intersection of machine characteristics and descriptive scientific models. Interesting in the figure is the relative paucity of models cited as useful engineering tools, at both the human or machine level (right column). Three engineering models were cited: the Keystroke-Level (KL) model of Card, Moran, and Newell; the Programmable User Model (PUM) of Young, Green, and Simon; and Fitts' law. These models are all predictive. They allow performance comparisons to be drawn before or during the design process. The idea is that interface scenarios can be explored a priori with performance comparisons drawn to aid in choosing the appropriate implementation. A challenge for HCI researchers, therefore, is to bring basic research results to the applied realm of engineering and design--to get the theory into the tools. Newell & Card elaborate further on this point.

Table: Models for human and machine characteristics of importance to human-computer interaction.

	Science		Development Technique (engineering)
Human Characteristics	Normal 4-stages Normal slips (perceptual Models) (Cognitive Psychology) Egan et al. user abilities	Routine cognitive skill GOMS, NGOMS, CCT Unified cognitive models HMP, Soar, ACT* ETIT Fitts' Law	KL Model PUMS Fitts' Law
Machine	Input device taxonomies Buxton et al.; Foley et al.; Mackinlay et al.	State-transitions (CSP, CCS,ES-TEREL). Squeak, PIE, Alexander PAC, PPS Grammar Models BNF, CLG TAG, ETAG, DTAG fitts' Low	Fitts'Low

Device Parameters

A parameter is any characteristic of a device or its interface which can be tuned or measured along a continuum of values. Input parameters are the sorts of features controlled or determined one way or another by designers or by system characteristics. Output parameters are the dependent variables or performance measures commonly studied in research by, for example, manipulating "device" or an input parameter as an experimental factor. Presumably a setting exists for each input parameter that yields optimal performance on the range of output parameters.

Some parameters, such as mass, resolution, or friction, are "in the device" or its electronics, and can be designed in, but cannot be tuned thereafter. Others exist in the interface software or system software. Examples are sampling rate or the control-display (C-D) relationship. Still others exist through a complex weave of transducer characteristics, interface electronics, communications channels, and software. Lag or feedback delay is one such example.

Although some parameters can be adjusted to improve performance, others are simply constraints. Resolution, sampling rate, and lag are parameters with known "optimal" settings. Resolution and sampling rate should be as high as possible, lag as low as possible. Obviously, these parameters are constrained or fixed at some reasonable level during system design. Although typical users are quite unconcerned about these, for certain applications or when operating within a real-time environments, limitations begin to take hold.

Resolution

Resolution is the spatial resolving power of the device/interface subsystem. It is usually quoted as the smallest incremental change in device position that can be detected; however, alone the specification can be misleading. This is illustrated in figure, showing device position (input) vs. the position reported (output) over a spatial interval of 10 arbitrary units. (a) The resolution is 1 unit and it is reported in precise, equal steps over the range of device movement. In (b) *non-linearity* is introduced. Resolution in the middle of the field of movement is very good (~0.25 units at 5 units input), but it is poor at the extremes (~1.5 units output at 1 unit input). Another important trait is *monotonicity*. Positive changes in device position should always yield positive changes in the output; however, this is often not the case as illustrated in (c). Other non-ideal characteristics (not shown) are *offset*, which results if the step function shown in (a) is shifted up or down; and *gain*, which results if the slope of the step function differs from unity. In the interface electronics, temperature sensitivity is the main culprit compromising performance. It must be remembered that the number of steps is usually quite large and resolution spec's must be met for each degree of freedom. Very small changes in voltage or current must be sensed in the interface electronics on multiple input channels. If the transducers are magnetically-coupled, then interference or noise may be the main cause of poor resolution, non-linearity, etc.

Touch screens, tablets, and other devices using finger or stylus input have apparent resolution problems since it is difficult to resolve finger or stylus position to the same precision as the output display (a single pixel). In fact, the resolving power of the input device often exceeds that of the output device; however the input/outut mapping is limited by the contact footprint of the input device (e.g., the width of the finger tip).

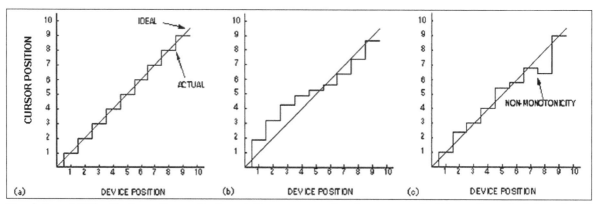

Resolution: (a) The ideal case for 1 unit of resolution over 10 units of movement. In (b) non-linearity is introduced showing degraded resolution at the extremes of movement than in the center. (c) Non-monotonicity occurs when the output fails to increase uniformly with the input.

3D trackers have resolution better than 1 inch and 1 degree; but this varies with the proximity of the sensor to the source and other factors. Resolution often sounds impressive in specification sheets; but when application demands increase, such as widening the field of use or combining two or three trackers, limitations become apparent. The specification sheets of 3D trackers are surprisingly sparse in their performance details. Is the resolution cited a worst-case value over the specified field of use, or is it "typical"? How will resolution degrade if two or more trackers are used? What is the effect of a large metal object five meters distant? These questions persist.

Resolution will constrain a variety of applications for 3D virtual worlds. The motions of a dancer are difficult to capture with any justice because of the large expanse of movements required. Sensing the common action of tying one's shoelaces would be a formidable task for a pair of input gloves controlling virtual hands in a simulated environment. Resolution is one constraint in this case because the movements are extremely intricate.

Sampling Rate

Sampling rate is the number of measurements per unit time (e.g., samples per second) in which the position of the input device is recorded. It is the input analog of the refresh rate for updating the output display. The rate of sampling begins to constrain performance when input or output motion is quick. Typical rates are from 10 to 100 samples per second. This is fine for many applications, but may be inadequate for real-time 3D environments which must sense and respond to the natural, sometimes rapid, motions of humans. Acts such as tying one's shoelaces or juggling involve a series of quick, intricate, coordinated hand motions that would require, among other things, a high sampling rate. In the more common application of capturing temporal cues in gestures for a sign language, sampling rate has been cited as a constraint.

Sampling rate is illustrated in figure below (a) and (b). A mouse can be wiggled back-and-forth easily at rates up to about 6 Hz. Figure shows this as a sinusoid with the back-and-forth motion of the hand on the vertical axis and time on the horizontal axis. If the mouse position is sampled at 60 Hz (every 16.7 ms) with immediate updates of the screen, there will be about 10 updates of the cursor for each back and forth motion of the mouse. Cursor motion will appear as in Figure. The loss of fidelity is obvious.

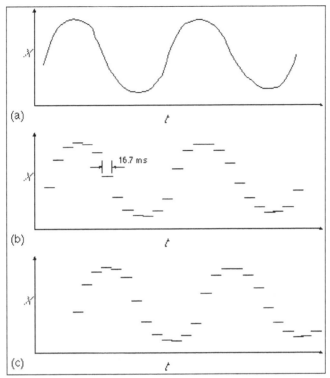

Sampling rate and lag. Sinusoidal back-and-forth motion of a mouse at 6 Hz is shown in (a). At 60 Hz sampling, the cursor appears as in (b). With three samples of lag, cursor motion is delayed as in (c).

A high sampling rate is essential in 3D virtual worlds because of spatial dynamics. In the mouse example above, the back-and-forth motion of the the hand and cursor will not exceed about 10 cm. If the controlling device is a 3D tracker attached to the head, similar back-and-forth motion (a few cm at the nose) will translate into very large movements in the visual space in very small time intervals. Smooth viewing motion necessitates a high sampling rate with immediate display refreshes.

Lag

Lag is the phenomenon of not having immediate updates of the display in response to input actions. High sampling and refresh rates are wasted if the re-drawn viewpoint does not reflect the immediately preceding sample, or if the sample does not capture the immediate habit of the user. One reason this may occur is the drawing time for the scene. If the image is complex, then drawing time may take two or three (or more) sampling periods. Green and Shaw describe a client-server model which lessens this effect.

If updates are delayed by, say, three samples, then the cursor motion for our earlier example is degraded further. Lag leads to a variety of non-ideal behaviours, even motion sickness. All current 3D trackers have significant lag, in the range of 30 ms to 250 ms (depending on how and where measurements are made). Furthermore, the source of the lag is not always obvious and is difficult to measure. The sampling rate for input devices and the update rate for output devices are major contributors; but lag is increased further due to "software overhead" a loose expression for a variety of system-related factors. Communication modes, network configurations, number crunching, and application software all contribute.

Significant lags occur in most teleoperation systems, whether a remote microscope for medical diagnosis or a space-guided vehicle. Evidently, lags more than about 1 s force the operator into a move-and-wait strategy in completing tasks. Since lag is on the order of a few hundred milliseconds in virtual environments, its effect on user performance is less apparent.

In one of the few empirical studies, Liang, Shaw, and Green measured the lag on a Polhemus *Isotrak*. They found lags between 85 ms and 180 ms depending on the sampling rate (60 Hz vs. 20 Hz) and communications mode (networked, polled, continuous output, direct, and client-server). Although the software was highly optimized to avoid other sources of lag, their results are strictly best-case since an "application" was not present. Substantial additional lag can be expected in any 3D virtual environment because of the graphic rendering required *after each sample*. Liang et al. proposed a Kalman predictive filtering algorithm to compensate for lag by anticipating head motion. Apparently predictive filtering can obviate lags up to a few hundred milliseconds; however, beyond this, the overshoot resulting from long-term prediction is more objectionable than the lag.

In another experiment to measure the human performance cost, lag was introduced as an experimental variable in a routine target selection task given to eight subjects in repeated trials. Using a 60 Hz sampling and refresh rate, the minimum lag was, on average, half the sampling period or 8.3 ms. This was the "zero lag" condition. Additional lag settings were 25, 75, and 225 ms. Movement time, error rate, and motor-sensory bandwidth were the dependent variables. Under the zero lag condition (8.3 ms), the mean movement time was 911 ms, the error rate was 3.6%, and the bandwidth was 4.3 bits/s. As evident, lag degraded performance on all three dependent variables. At 225 ms lag (compared to 8.3 ms lag), movement times increased by 63.9% (to 1493 ms), error rates increased by 214% (to 11.3%), and bandwidth dropped by 46.5% (to 2.3 bits/s). Obviously, these figures represent serious performance decrements.

Table: Motor-sensory performance in the presence of lag. The dependent variables movement time, error rate, and bandwidth are all degraded as lag is introduced. Performance degrades dramatically at 225 ms of lag.

Measure	Lag (ms)				Performance Degradation at Lag = 225 ms[a]
	8.3	25	74	225	
Movement Time (ms)	911	934	1058	1493	63.9%
Error Rate (%)	3.6	3.6	4.9	11.3	214.0%
Bandwidth (bits/s)	4.3	4.1	3.5	2.3	46.5%
[a] relative to lag = 8.3 ms					

The communication link between the device electronics and the host computer may prove a bottleneck and contribute to lag as the number of sensors and their resolution increases. The *Cyber-Glove* by Virtual Technologies provides greater resolution of finger position than many gloves by including more sensors up to 22 per glove. However, correspondingly more data are required. At the maximum data rate of 38.4 kilobaud, it takes about 5 ms just to relay the data to the host.

Alone this is trivial, however a tradeoff is evident between the desire to resolve intricate hand formations and the requisite volume of "immediate" data. If we speculate on future interaction scenarios with full body suits delivering the nuances of complex motions a common vision in VR, then it is apparent that lag will increase simply due to serial bias in the communications link. Since technological improvements can be expected on all fronts, lag may become less significant in future systems.

Optimality and Control-Display Gain

Unlike resolution, sampling rate, and lag, some parameters are "tunable" along a continuum. Presumably, a setting exists which leads to optimal human performance. This is an elusive claim, however, because no clear definition of "optimal" exists. How does one measure optimality? Quantitative measures such as task completion time or error rate are commonly used, but are narrow and do not capture important qualitative aspects of the interface. Ease of learning, skill retention, fatigue, effort, stress, etc., are important qualities of an optimal interface, but are difficult to measure. This idea has been studied extensively in an area of human factors known as *human engineering*. As a brief example, if a relative positioning system is employed, the nuisance of clutching may go unnoticed in an experiment that only required a narrow field of motion. If frequent clutching results in a subsequent application of the same technology, then frustration or stress levels may yield highly *non-optimal* behaviour which eluded measurement in the research setting.

Even though task completion time and error rate are easily measured in empirical tests, they are problematic. Getting tasks done quickly with few errors is obviously optimal, but the speed-accuracy tradeoff makes the simultaneous optimizing of these two output variables difficult. This is illustrated by considering control-display (C-D) gain. C-D gain expresses the relationship between the motion or force in a controller (e.g., a mouse) to the effected motion in a displayed object (e.g., a cursor). Low and high gain settings are illustrated in figure below.

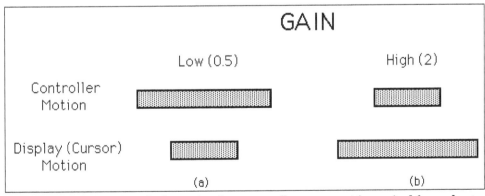

Contol-display (C-D) gain. (a) Under low gain a large controller movement is required for moderate cursor movement. (b) Under high gain a slight controller movement yields significant cursor movement.

Although, a common criticism of research claiming to measure human performance on input devices is that C-D gain was not (properly) optimized, close examination reveals that the problem is tricky. Varying C-D gain evokes a trade-off between gross positioning time (getting to the vicinity of a target) and fine positioning time (the final acquisition). This effect, first pointed out by Jenkins and Connor, is illustrated in figure.

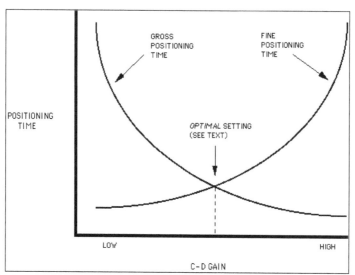

Low and high gains evoke a trade-off between gross positioning time and fine positioning time. Total positioning time is minimized at the intersection of the two.

Presumably, the optimal setting is at the intersection of the two curves in figure above, since the total time is minimized. However, minimizing total target acquisition time is further confounded by a non-optimal (viz., higher) error rate. This was illustrated in an experiment which varied C-D gain while measuring the speed and accuracy of target acquisitions. Twelve subjects performed repeated trials of a routine target acquisition task while C-D gain was varied through LOW, MEDIUM, and HIGH settings. As expected, the total target acquisition time was lowest at the MEDIUM setting. However, the error rate was highest at the MEDIUM setting. So, the claim that an optimal C-D gain setting exists is weak at best. Other factors, such as display size (independent of C-D gain setting), also bring into question the optimality of this common input device parameter.

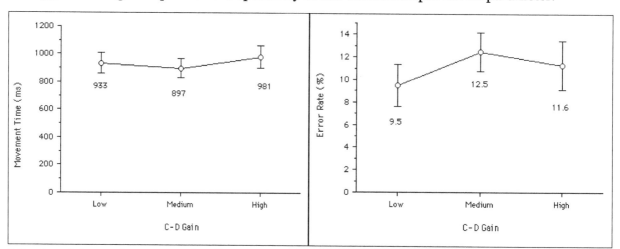

C-D gain and the speed-accuracy trade-off. Positioning time is lowest under MEDIUM gain, but error rates are highest.

The linear, or 1st order, C-D gain shown in figure maps controller displacement to cursor (display) displacement. In practice, the C-D gain function is often non-linear or 2nd order, mapping controller velocity to some function of cursor velocity. Examples include the Apple *Macintosh* mouse and Xerox *Fastmouse*. Figure illustrates a variety of 1st order (dashed lines) and 2nd order (solid lines) C-D gains.

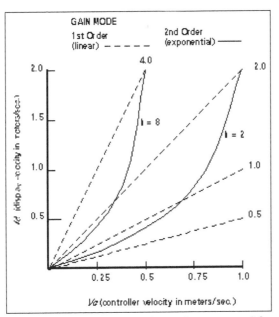

Linear vs. exponential mappings for C-D gain. Under exponential mapping, cursor velocity increases non-linearly by k times the square of the controller velocity.

The 2nd order gains are of the form,

$$V_d = k * V_c^2$$

where V_d is the display (cursor) velocity and V_c is the controller velocity. Note that the 2nd order function crosses several 1st order points as the controller velocity increases. A variation of this, which is easier to implement in software, uses discrete thresholds to increment k as the controller velocity increases. This relationship is,

$$V_d = k * V_c$$

where k increases by steps as V_c crosses pre-determined thresholds. Second order C-D gains have been explored as a means to boost user performance; however there is no evidence that performance is improved beyond the subjective preference of users. Jellinek and Card found no performance improvement using several 2nd order C-D gain relationships with a mouse, and suggested the only benefit is the smaller desktop footprint afforded by a 2nd order C-D gain.

Interaction

Today's software products invariably boast "user friendly" interfaces. This rather empty phrase would lead us to believe that human interface problems are of historical interest only. Not true. The problem of "interaction" persists. The 2D CAD tools of yesterday were precursors to today's 3D tools supporting an enhanced palette of commands and operations to control the workspace. The flat world of CRTs has stretched to its limit, and now 3D output (in numerous forms) is the challenge.

Input/Output Mappings

On the input side, challenges go beyond migrating from 2D devices (e.g., a mouse) to 3D devices.

Paradigms for interaction must evolve to meet and surpass the available functionality. It is apparent that *movement* is of increasing importance in the design of human-computer interfaces. Static considerations in the design of interfaces, such as command languages and menu layouts, give way to the dynamics of an interface--the human is a performer acting in concert with system resources.

One theme for 3D is developing interactions for mapping 2D devices into a 3D space. The mouse (for pointing), mouse buttons (for selecting or choosing), and keyboards (for specifying or valuating) are extensively used to capture and control 3D objects. Such interaction was demonstrated, for example, by Bier in manipulating polyhedrons using a technique called "snap dragging"; by Chen, Mountford, and Sellen in a three-axis rotation task using three simulated slider controls; by Houde for grasping and moving furniture in a 3D room; by Mackinlay, Card, and Robertson to specify the direction and extent of real-time navigation in 3-space; and by Phillips and Badler to manipulate limb positions and joint displacements of 3D animated human figures. These pseudo-3D interfaces do not employ gloves or other inherently 3D input technology, so the available devices--the mouse and keyboard--were exploited.

Perceptual Structure

Notwithstanding the success, low cost, and ease of implementation of the interaction styles noted above, a lingering problem is that an interaction technique must be learned. The interaction is not intuitive and, in general, there is no metaphoric link to everyday tasks. Such contrived mappings are criticized on theoretical grounds because they violate inherent structures of human perceptual processing for the input and output spaces. Besides force-fitting 2D devices into 3-space, there is the coincident problem of the different senses engaged by the devices vs. those stimulated by the task. Stated another way, input/output mappings of force-to-force, position-to-position, etc., are always superior to mappings such as force-to-position or force-to-motion.

Consider the joysticks mentioned earlier. The three degree-of-freedom displacement joystick senses pivotal motion about a base and twist about the y or vertical axis. A strong match to perceptual structures results when the task (output space) directly matches the properties sensed (input space). For example, a task demanding pivotal positioning of an object about a point combined with y-axis rotation would be ideal for this joystick: The input/output mapping is position-to-position. The four degree-of-freedom isometric joystick in Figure could perform the same task but with less fidelity, because of the force-to-position mapping.

There is some empirical support for the comparisons suggested above. Jagacinski, Repperger, Moran, Ward, and Glass and Jagacinski, Hartzell, Ward, and Bishop tested a displacement joystick in 2D target acquisition tasks. Position-to-position and position-to-velocity mappings were compared. Motor-sensory bandwidth was approximately 13 bits/s for the position-to-position system compared to only 5 bits/s for the position-to-velocity system. Kantowitz and Elvers used an isometric joystick in a 2D target acquisition task using both a force-to-position mapping (position control) and a force-to-motion mapping (velocity control). Since the application of force commonly evokes motion, a force-to-motion mapping seems closer to human perceptual processing than a force-to-position mapping. Indeed, performance was significantly better for the force-to-motion mapping compared to force-to-position mapping.

Additionally, motions or forces may be linear or rotary, suggesting that, within either the force or motion domain, linear-to-linear or rotary-to-rotary mappings will be stronger than mixed mappings. Thus, the use of a linear slider to control object rotation in the study by Chen et al. cited earlier is a weak mapping.

Jacob and Sibert focused on the "separability" of the degrees of freedom afforded by devices and required by tasks. The claim is that "non separable" degrees of freedom in a device, such as x, y, and z positioning in a 3D tracker, are a good match for a complex task with similar, non-separable degrees of freedom. Conversely, a device with "separable" degrees of freedom, such as the three degree-of-freedom joystick in Figure, will work well on complex tasks with multi-, yet separable, degrees of freedom. Any complex task with relatively independent sub-tasks, such as simultaneously changing the position and colour of an object, qualifies as separable.

Gestures

By far the most common interaction paradigm heralding a new age of human-machine interaction is that of *gesture*. There is nothing fancy or esoteric here--no definition required. Gestures are actions humans do all the time, and the intent is that intuitive gestures should map into cyberspace without sending users to menus, manuals, or help screens. Simple actions such as writing, scribbling, annotating, pointing, nodding, etc. are gestures that speak volumes for persons engaged in the act of communicating. The many forms of sign language (formal or otherwise), or even subtle aspects of sitting, walking or driving a bicycle contain gestures.

What is articulated less emphatically is that human-computer interfaces that exploit gestures are likely to spawn new paradigms of interaction, and in so doing re-define intuition. This is not a criticism. Today's intuition is the result of evolution and conscious design decisions in the past (e.g, pull-down menus). One of the most exciting aspects of interface design is imagining and experimenting with potential human-computer dialogues with gestural input.

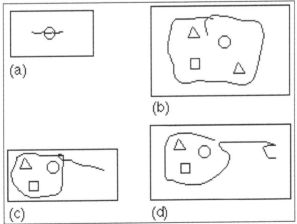

Gestures for graphic editing. (a) Delete an object by stroking through it. (b) Delete a group of objects by circling and finishing the stroke within the circle. (c) Move a group by circling and releasing outside the circle. (d) Copy by terminating with a "c".

Gestures are high-level. They map directly to "user intent" without forcing the user to learn and remember operational details of commands and options. They "chunk" together primitive actions into single directives. One application for gestural input is to recognize powerful yet simple commands for manipulating text, such as those proofreaders adopt when copy-editing a manuscript.

Can editing an electronic document be as direct? Numerous prototype systems have answered a resounding "yes". The gesture of circling an object to select it is simple to implement on a mouse- or stylus-based system and can yield fast and accurate performance, particularly when multiple objects are selected.

In an editor for 2D graphical objects, Kurtenbach and Buxton demonstrated a variety of gestures that simplify selecting, deleting, moving, or copying individual objects or groups of objects. As evident in figure above, the gestures are simple, intuitive, and easy to implement for a mouse or stylus. Recognition, as with speech input, remains a challenge. The open circle, for example, is easily recognized by humans as a slip, but may be misinterpreted by the recognizer. Other problems include defining and constraining the scope of commands and implementing an undo operation.

For the artist, gestural input can facilitate creative interaction. Buxton demonstrated a simple set of gestures for transcribing musical notation. As evident in figure below, the most common musical notes (shown across the top) map intuitively to simple strokes of a stylus.

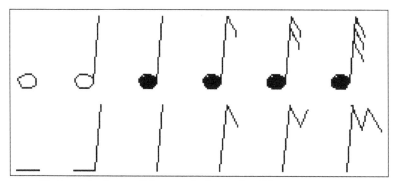

Gestures for transcribing musical notation. The most common
notes (top) are easily mapped to simple gestures.

Many touch technologies, such as the stylus or touch screen, sense pressure to 1 bit of resolution enough to implement the "select" operation. This is insufficient to capture the richness of an artist's brush stokes, however. In a stylus-based simulation of charcoal sketching by Bleser, Sibert, and McGee, pressure was sensed to 5 bits of resolution and x and y tilt to 7 bits. This permitted sketching with lines having thickness controlled by the applied pressure and texture controlled by tilt. The results were quite impressive.

The applications above are all 2D. Some of the most exciting new paradigms are those for direct, gestural interaction using an input glove in 3D virtual worlds. In fact, gesture recognition may be the easiest interaction task to cast with a glove. Pointing, delimiting a region of space, or rapid flicks of the wrist or arm are innate properties of hand and arm motion. Comparing gloves with mice and keyboards, the problems seem reversed. Selecting, specifying, choosing, etc. are easy with mice and keyboards, but defy the glove. This problem has been noted by Krueger, who calls input gloves, *gesture technology*. Sweeping motions with the hand, as though performing an action, are natural for gloves; selecting or initiating action is hard.

Typically, a glove is the input device, and a 3D graphical hand, or virtual hand, acts as a cursor. For example, Sturman, Zeltzer, and Pieper used a *DataGlove* to pick up and move 3D objects. When the virtual hand viewed on the CRT crossed a threshold region near an object, grasping with the hand locked the object to the graphical hand. The object moved with the graphical hand until the grasping posture was relaxed. An alternate technique is to use the index finger to point and thumb rotation to select.

Tactile and Force Feedback

That input gloves are inherently a gesture technology follows from a feedback void. Imagine the task of reaching behind a piece of virtual equipment to turn it on. Without the sense of force or touch, this task is formidable: The virtual hand passes through the equipment without any sense of the presence of the chassis or on/off switch.

It is naive to dig deep into "input" without recognizing the interdependency with output. The visual channel, as (computer) output, is primary; but the tactile and force senses are also important. A few examples of force and tactile feedback pertaining to the design of interface devices follow.

A simple use of tactile feedback is shape encoding of manual controls, such as those standardized in aircraft controls for landing flaps, landing gear, the throttle, etc. Shape encoding is particularly important if the operator's eyes cannot leave a primary focus point or when operators must work in the dark.

Not surprisingly, systems with tactile feedback, called *tactile displays*, have been developed as a sensory replacement channel for handicapped users. The most celebrated product is the *Octacon*, developed by Bliss and colleagues. This tactile reading aid, which is still in use, consists of 144 piezoelectric bimorph pins in a 24-by-6 matrix A single finger is positioned on the array (an output device) while the opposite hand maneuvers an optical pickup (an input device) across printed text. The input/output coupling is direct; that is, the tactile display delivers a one-for-one spatial reproduction of the printed characters. Reading speeds vary, but rates over 70 words/min. after 20 hr of practice have been reported.

A tactile display with over 7000 individually moveable pins was reported by Weber. Unlike the *Octacon*, both hands actively explore the display. With the addition of magnetic induction sensors worn on each index finger, user's actions are monitored. A complete, multi-modal, direct manipulation interface was developed supporting a repertoire of finger gestures. This amounts to a graphical user interface without a mouse or CRT true "touch-and-feel" interaction.

In another 2D application called *Sandpaper*, Minski, Ouh-Young, Steele, Brooks, and Behensky added mechanical actuators to a joystick and programmed them to behave as virtual springs. When the cursor was positioned over different grades of virtual sandpaper, the springs pulled the user's hand toward low regions and away from high regions. In an empirical test without visual feedback, users could reliably order different grades of sandpaper by granularity.

Akamatsu and Sato modified a mouse, inserting a solenoid-driven pin under the button for tactile feedback and an electromagnet near the base for force feedback. Tactile stimulus to the finger tip was provided by pulsing the solenoid as the cursor crossed the outline of screen objects. Force feedback to the hand was provided by passing current through the electromagnet to increase friction between the mouse and an iron mouse pad. Friction was high while the cursor was over dark regions of the screen and was low while over light regions (background). In an experiment using a target acquisition task, movement time and accuracy were improved with the addition of tactile and force feedback compared to the vision-only condition. A similar system was described by Haakma using a trackball with corrective force feedback to "guide" the user toward preferred cursor positions. One potential benefit in adding force and tactile feedback is that the processing demands of the visual channel are diminished, freeing up capacity for other purposes.

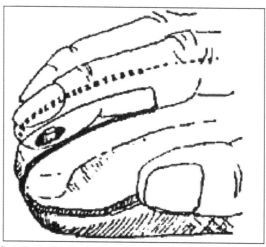

Tactile and force feedback. Tactile feedback is provided by a solenoid-driven pin in the mouse button.
Force feedback (friction) is provided by a magnetic field between an electromagnet
inside the housing (not shown) and an iron mouse pad.

Some of the most exciting work explores tactile feedback in 3D interfaces. Zimmerman et al. modified the *DataGlove* by mounting piezoceramic benders under each finger. When the virtual fingertips touched the surface of a virtual object, contact was cued by a "tingling" feeling created by transmitting a 20-40 Hz sine wave through the piezoceramic transducers. This is a potential solution to the blind touch problem cited above; however providing appropriate feedback when a virtual hand contacts a virtual hard surface is extremely difficulty. Brooks, Ouh-Young, Batter, and Kilpatrick confronted the same problem:

Even in a linear analog system, there is no force applied until the probe has overshot and penetrated the virtual surface. The system has inertia and velocity. Unless it is critically damped, there will be an unstable chatter instead of a solid virtual barrier.

They added a brake a variable damping system--and were able to provide reasonable but slightly "mushy" feedback for hard surface collision.

It is interesting to spectulate on the force equivalent of C-D gain. Indeed, such a mapping is essential if, for example, input controls with force feedback are implemented to remotely position heavy objects. The force sensed by the human operator cannot match that acting on the remote manipulator, however. Issues such as the appropriate mapping, thresholds for sensing very light objects, and learning times need further exploration.

Custom hand-operated input devices (not gloves) with force feedback are also described by Bejczy, Iwata, and Zhai (in press).

Multi-modal Input

The automobile is a perfect example of multi-modal interaction. Our hands, arms, feet, and legs contribute in parallel to the safe guidance of this vehicle. (A formidable challenge would be the design of a single-limb system for the same task.) With eyes, ears, and touch, we monitor the environment and our car's progress, and respond accordingly. In human-to-human communication, multi-modal interaction is the norm, as speech, gesture, and gaze merge in seamless streams of two-way intercourse. Equally rich modes of interaction have, to a limited extent, proven themselves in human-computer interaction.

Multi-modal interaction has exciting roots in entertainment. The movie industry made several leaps into 3D, usually by providing the audience with inexpensive glasses that filter the screen image and present separate views to each eye. Andy Warhol's *Frankenstein* is the most memorable example. "Smellorama" made a brief appearance in the B-movie *Polyester*, staring Devine. At critical points, a flashing number on the screen directed viewers to their scratch-and-sniff card to enjoy the full aromatic drama of the scene. A prototype arcade game from the 1960s called *Sensorama* exploited several channels of input and output. Players sat on a "motorcycle" and toured New York city in a multi-sensory environment. Binaural 3D sounds and viewing optics immersed the rider in a visual and auditory experience. The seat and handlebars vibrated with the terrain and driver's lean, and a chemical bank behind a fan added wind and smell at appropriate spots in the tour.

Back in the office, multi-modal input to computing systems occurs when more than one input channel participates simultaneously in coordinating a complex task. The input channels are typically the hands, feet, head, eyes, or voice. Two-handed input is the most obvious starting point. Experimental psychologists have shown that the brain can produce simultaneously optimal solutions to two-handed coordinated tasks, even when the tasks assigned to each hand are in a different physical space and of different difficulties. For human input to computing systems, Buxton and Myers offer empirical support in an experiment using a positioning/scaling task. Fourteen subjects manipulated a graphics puck with their right hand to move a square to a destination, and manipulated a slider with their left hand to re-size the square. Without prompting, subjects overwhelming adopted a multi-modal strategy. Averaged over all subjects, 41% of the time was spent in parallel activity.

Mouse input with word processors permits limited two-handed interaction. Selecting, deleting, moving, etc., are performed by point-click or point-drag operations with the mouse while the opposite hand prepares in parallel for the ensuing DELETE, COPY, or PASTE keystrokes. However, when corrections require new text, multi-modal input breaks down, the hand releases the mouse, adopts a two-handed touch-typing posture, and keys the new text. Approximately 360 ms is lost each way in "homing" between the mouse and keyboard.

One novel approach to reduce homing time, is to replace the mouse with a small isometric joystick embedded in the keyboard. Rutledge and Selker built such a keyboard with a "Pointing Stick" inserted between the G and H keys and a select button below the space bar. They conducted a simple experiment with six subjects selecting circular targets of random size and location using either the mouse or Pointing Stick. The task began and ended with a keystroke. Three measurements were taken, homing time to the pointing device, point-select time, and homing time to the keyboard. As shown in figure, performance was 22% faster overall with the Pointing Stick. Homing times for the Pointing Stick were less than for the mouse, particularly for the return trip to the keyboard (90 ms vs. 720 ms). Although the mouse was faster on the point-select portions of the task, the subjects were expert mouse users, so, further performance advantages can be expected as skill develops with the Pointing Stick. We should acknowledge however, that the mouse uses position-to-position mapping and the Pointing Stick, force-to-velocity mapping. There may be inherent advantages for the mouse that will hold through all skill levels.

The Pointing Stick. An isometric joystick is embedded between
the G and H keys and a select button is below the space bar.

Table: Task completion times for the mouse and Pointing Stick. The Pointing Stick has a 22% advantage overall.

Measurement	Task Completion Time (ms)[a]		Point Stick Advantage
	Mouse	Pointing Stick	
Homing Time to Pointing Device	640 (110)	390 (80)	39%
Point-Select Time	760 (190)	1180 (350)	-55%
Homing Time to Keyboard	720 (120)	90 (130)	875%
Total	2120 (260)	1660 (390)	22%
[a] standard deviation shown in parentheses			

Another technique for two-handed input in text editing tasks is to free-up one hand for point-select tasks and type with the other. This is possible using a one-handed technique known as Half-QWERTY. Intended for touch typists, the Half-QWERTY concept uses half a standard keyboard in conjunction with a "flip" operation implemented on the space bar through software. Using only the left (or right) hand, typists proceed as usual except the right-hand characters are entered by pressing and holding the space bar while pressing the mirror-image key with the left hand. The right hand is free to use the mouse or other input device. The claim is that learning time for the Half-QWERTY keyboard is substantially reduced with touch typists because of skill transfer. In an experiment with 10 touch typists, an average one-handed typing speed of 35 words/minute was achieved after 10 hr of practice. Each subject attained a one-handed typing speed between 43% and 76% of their two-hand typing speed. Prolonged testing with a limited subject pool indicates that speeds up to 88% of two-handed typing speeds may be attained with one hand. Besides applications for disabled users and portable computers, the Half-QWERTY keyboard allows the full point-select capabilities of the mouse in parallel with text editing *and entry*.

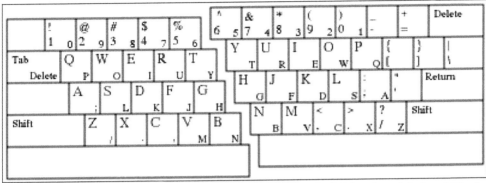

Table: The Half-QWERTY keyboard. Subjects type with either the left hand or right hand. The keys reflect in a mirror image from one side to the other. Using the left hand, a "y" is entered by pressing and holding the space bar while pressing "t".

Speech is a powerful channel for multi-modal input. The ability to combine speech input with pointing is particularly important with 3D input, since selecting is kinesthetically difficult. The potential for speech input has been shown in numerous successful implementations. In an experiment using speech and gesture input, Hauptmann asked 36 subjects to perform rotation, translation, and scaling tasks using hand gestures and speech commands of their own choosing. Subjects were told a computer was interpreting their verbal commands and gestures through video cameras and a microphone, however, an expert user in an adjoining room acted as an intermediary and entered low-level commands to realize the moves. Not only did a natural tendency to adopt a multi-modal strategy appear, the strategies across subjects were surprisingly uniform. As noted, "there are no expert users for gesture communications. It is a channel that is equally accessible to all computer users"

Early work in multi-modal input was done at the MIT Media Lab. In Bolt's *Put-that-there* demo, an object displayed on a large projection screen was selected by pointing at it and saying "put that". The system responded with "where". A new location was pointed to, and replying "there" completed the move. Recent extensions to this exploit the latest 3D technology, including input gloves and eye trackers. A 3D object is selected by spoken words, by pointing with the hand, or simply by looking at it. Scaling, rotating, twisting, relative positioning, etc., are all implemented using two hands, speech, and eye gaze. Speech specifies what to do and when to do it; hand positions, motions, or eye gaze specify objects, spatial coordinates, relative displacements, or rotations for the moves. This is illustrated schematically in Figure.

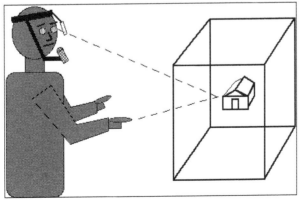

Multi-modal interaction. Speech, eye gaze, and pointing combine to control a virtual world.

Human-centered Computing

Human-centered computing (HCC) studies the design, development, and deployment of mixed-initiative human-computer systems. It is emerged from the convergence of multiple disciplines that are concerned both with understanding human beings and with the design of computational artifacts. Human-centered computing is closely related to human-computer interaction and information science. Human-centered computing is usually concerned with systems and practices of technology use while human-computer interaction is more focused on ergonomics and the usability of computing artifacts and information science is focused on practices surrounding the collection, manipulation, and use of information.

Human-centered computing researchers and practitioners usually come from one or more of disciplines such as computer science, human factors, sociology, psychology, cognitive science, anthropology, communication studies, graphic design and industrial design. Some researchers focus on understanding humans, both as individuals and in social groups, by focusing on the ways that human beings adopt and organize their lives around computational technologies. Others focus on designing and developing new computational artifacts.

HCC aims at bridging the existing gaps between the various disciplines involved with the design and implementation of computing systems that support human's activities. Meanwhile, it is a set of methodologies that apply to any field that uses computers in applications in which people directly interact with devices or systems that use computer technologies.

HCC facilitates the design of effective computer systems that take into account personal, social, and cultural aspects and addresses issues such as information design, human information interaction, human-computer interaction, human-human interaction, and the relationships between computing technology and art, social, and cultural issues.

The National Science Foundation (NSF) defines the trends of HCC research as "a three dimensional space comprising human, computer, and environment." According to the NSF, the human dimension ranges from research that supports individual needs, through teams as goal-oriented groups, to society as an unstructured collection of connected people. The computer dimension ranges from fixed computing devices, through mobile devices, to computational systems of visual/ audio devices that are embedded in the surrounding physical environment. The environment dimension ranges from discrete physical computational devices, through mixed reality systems, to immersive virtual environments. Some examples of topics in the field are listed below.

List of Topics in HCC Field

- Problem-solving in distributed environments, ranging across Internet-based information systems, grids, sensor-based information networks, and mobile and wearable information appliances.

- Multimedia and multi-modal interfaces in which combinations of speech, text, graphics, gesture, movement, touch, sound, etc. are used by people and machines to communicate with one another.

- Intelligent interfaces and user modeling, information visualization, and adaptation of content to accommodate different display capabilities, modalities, bandwidth and latency.

- Multi-agent systems that control and coordinate actions and solve complex problems in distributed environments in a wide variety of domains, such as disaster response teams, e-commerce, education, and successful aging.

- Models for effective computer-mediated human-human interaction under a variety of constraints, (e.g., video conferencing, collaboration across high vs. low bandwidth networks, etc.).

- Definition of semantic structures for multimedia information to support cross-modal input and output.

- Specific solutions to address the special needs of particular communities.

- Collaborative systems that enable knowledge-intensive and dynamic interactions for innovation and knowledge generation across organizational boundaries, national borders, and professional fields.

- Novel methods to support and enhance social interaction, including innovative ideas like social orthotics, affective computing, and experience capture.

- Studies of how social organizations, such as government agencies or corporations, respond to and shape the introduction of new information technologies, especially with the goal of improving scientific understanding and technical design.

- Knowledge-driven human-computer interaction that uses ontologies to address the semantic ambiguities between human and computer's understandings towards mutual behaviors.

- Human-centered semantic relatedness measure that employs human power to measure the semantic relatedness between two concepts.

Human-centered Systems

Human-centered systems (HCS) are systems designed for human-centered computing. This approach was developed by Mike Cooley in his book *Architect or Bee?* drawing on his experience working with the Lucas Plan. HCS focuses on the design of interactive systems as they relate to human activities. According to Kling et al., the Committee on Computing, Information, and Communication of the National Science and Technology Council, identified human-centered systems, or HCS, as one of five components for a High Performance Computing Program. Human-centered systems can be referred to in terms of human-centered automation. According to Kling et al., HCS refers to systems that are:

- Based on the analysis of the human tasks the system is aiding.

- Monitored for performance in terms of human benefits.

- Built to take account of human skills.

- Adaptable easily to changing human needs.

In addition, Kling et al. defines four dimensions of human-centeredness that should be taken into account when classifying a system: Systems that are human centered must analyze the complexity of the targeted social organization, and the varied social units that structure work and information; human centeredness is not an attribute of systems, but a process in which the stakeholder group of a particular system assists in evaluating the benefit of the system; the basic architecture of the system should reflect a realistic relationship between humans and machines; the purpose and audience the system is designed for should be an explicit part of the design, evaluation, and use of the system.

Human-centered Activities in Multimedia

Human-centered design visualization.

The human-centered activities in multimedia, or HCM, can be considered as follows according to: media production, annotation, organization, archival, retrieval, sharing, analysis, and communication, which can be clustered into three areas: production, analysis, and interaction.

Multimedia Production

Multimedia production is the human task of creating media. For instance, photographing, recording audio, remixing, etc. It is important that all aspects of media production concerned should directly involve humans in HCM. There are two main characteristics of multimedia production. The first is culture and social factors. HCM production systems should consider cultural differences and be designed according to the culture in which they will be deployed. The second is to consider human abilities. Participants involved in HCM production should be able to complete the activities during the production process.

Multimedia Analysis

Multimedia analysis can be considered as a type of HCM applications which is the automatic analysis of human activities and social behavior in general. There is a broad area of potential relevant uses from facilitating and enhancing human communications, to allowing for improved information access and retrieval in the professional, entertainment, and personal domains.

Multimedia Interaction

Multimedia interaction can be considered as the interaction activity area of HCM. It is paramount to understand both how humans interact with each other and why, so that we can build systems to facilitate such communication and so that people can interact with computers in natural ways. To achieve natural interaction, cultural differences and social context are primary factors to consider, due to the potential different cultural backgrounds. For instance, a couple of examples include: face-to-face communications where the interaction is physically located and real-time; live-computer mediated communications where the interaction is physically remote but remains real-time; and non-real time computer-mediated communications such as instant SMS, email, etc.

Mobile Interaction

Mobile Phone Device.

Mobile interaction is the study of interaction between mobile users and computers. Mobile interaction is an aspect of human–computer interaction that emerged when computers became small enough to enable mobile usage, around the 1990s.

Mobile devices are a pervasive part of people's everyday lives. People use mobile phones, PDAs, and portable media players almost everywhere. These devices are the first truly pervasive interaction devices that are currently used for a huge variety of services and applications. Mobile devices affect the way people interact, share, and communicate with others. They are growing in diversity and complexity, featuring new interaction paradigms, modalities, shapes, and purposes (e.g., e-readers, portable media players, handheld game consoles). The strong differentiating factors that characterize mobile devices from traditional personal computing (e.g., desktop computers), are their ubiquitous use, usual small size, and mixed interaction modalities.

The history of mobile interaction includes different design trends. The main six design trends are portability, miniaturization, connectivity, convergence, divergence, and application software (apps). The main reason behind those trends is to understand the requirements and needs of mobile users which is the main goal for mobile interaction. Mobile interaction is a multidisciplinary area with various academic subjects making contributions to it. The main disciplines involved in mobile interaction are psychology, computer science, sociology, design, and information systems. The processes in mobile interaction design includes three main activities: understanding users, developing prototype designs, and evaluation.

The history of mobile interaction can be divided into a number of eras, or waves, each characterized by a particular technological focus, interaction design trends, and by leading to fundamental changes in the design and use of mobile devices. Although not strictly sequential, they provide a good overview of the legacy on which current mobile computing research and design is built.

- Portability: One of the first work in the mobile interaction discipline was the concept of the Dynabook by Alan Kay in 1968. However, at that time the necessary hardware to build such system was not available. When the first laptops were built in the early 1980s they were seen as transportable desktop computers.

- Miniaturization: By the early 1990s, many types of handheld devices were introduced such as labelled palmtop computers, digital organizers, or personal digital assistants (PDAs).

- Connectivity: By 1973, Martin Cooper worked at Motorola developed a handheld mobile phone concept, which later on by 1983, led to the introduction of the first commercial mobile phone called the DynaTAC 8000X.

Apple iPhone.

- Convergence: During this era, different types of specialized mobile devices started to converge into new types of hybrid devices with primarily different form factors and interaction designs. On 1992, the first device of such technique, the "smartphones" was introduced. The first smart phone was the IBM Simon and it was used for making phone calls, calendars, addresses, notes, e-mail, fax and games.

- Divergence: During the 2000s, a trend toward a single function many devices started to spread. the basic idea behind divergence is that specialized tools facilitate optimization of functionality over time and enhancement of use. The most famous device of this era was the Apple iPod on 2001.

- Apps: During 2007, Apple Inc. introduced the first truly "smart" cellular phone; the iPhone. It was a converged mobile device with different features functionality. The most important thing is that it represents a significant rethinking of the design of mobile interactions and a series of notable interaction design choices. In less than a decade Apple Inc. would sell over one-billion iPhones.

Goals

With the evolution of both software and hardware on the mobile devices, the users are becoming more demanding of the user interface that provide both functionality and pleasant user experience. The goal of mobile interaction researches is to understand the requirements and needs of mobile users. Compared with stationary devices mobile devices have specific, often restricted, input and output requirements. A goal that is often named is to overcome the limitations of mobile devices. However, exploiting the special opportunities of mobile usage can also be seen as a central goal.

Disciplines Involved

Mobile interaction is a multidisciplinary area with various academic subjects making contributions. This is a reflection of the complicated nature of an individual's interaction with a computer system. This includes factors such as an understanding of the user and the task the user wants to perform with the system, understanding of the design tools, software packages that are needed to achieve this and an understanding of software engineering tools. The following are the main disciplines involved in mobile interaction:

Psychology

Many of the research methods and system evaluation techniques currently used in mobile human-computer interaction research are borrowed from psychology. As well as attitude measures, performance measures that are used in mobile human-computer interaction research studies come from the area of experimental psychology. Understanding users and their needs is a key aspect in the design of mobile systems, devices, and applications so that they will be easy and enjoyable to use. Individual user characteristics such as age, or personality physical disabilities such as blindness, all have an effect on users' performance when they are using mobile applications and systems, and these individual differences can also affect people's attitude towards the mobile service or device that they interact with.

Computer Science

Computer science (along with software engineering) is responsible for providing software tools to develop the interfaces that users need to interact with system. These include the software development tools.

Sociology

Sociologists working in this area are responsible for looking at socio-technical aspects of human-computer interaction. They bring methods and techniques from the social sciences (e.g., observational studies, ethnography) that can be used in the design and evaluation of mobile devices and applications.

Design

People working in this area are concerned with looking at the design layout of the interface (e.g., colors, positioning of text or graphics on a screen of a PDA). This is a crucial area of mobile human-computer interaction research due to the limited screen space available for most mobile devices. Therefore, it is crucial that services and applications reflect this limitation by reducing information complexity to fit the parameters of the mobile device, without losing any substantial content.

Information systems

People who work in information systems are interested in investigating how people interact with information and technologies in an organisational, managerial, and business context. In an organisational context, information system professionals and researchers are interested in looking at ways in which mobile technologies and mobile applications can be used to make an organisation more effective in conducting its business on a day-to-day business.

Mobile Interaction Design

Mobile interaction design is part of the interaction design which heavily focused on satisfying the needs and desires of the majority of people who will use the product. The processes in mobile interaction design are in the following main types of activity:

- Understanding users: having a sense of people's capabilities and limitations; gaining a rich picture of what makes up the detail of their lives, the things they do and use.

- Developing prototype designs: representing a proposed interaction design in such a way that it can be demonstrated, altered, and discussed.

- Evaluation: each prototype is a stepping stone to the next, better, refined design. Evaluation techniques identify the strengths and weaknesses of a design but can also lead the team to propose a completely different approach, discarding the current line of design thinking for a radical approach.

Mobile Computing

Mobile computing is human–computer interaction in which a computer is expected to be transported during normal usage, which allows for transmission of data, voice and video. Mobile computing involves mobile communication, mobile hardware, and mobile software. Communication issues include ad hoc networks and infrastructure networks as well as communication properties, protocols, data formats and concrete technologies. Hardware includes mobile devices or device components. Mobile software deals with the characteristics and requirements of mobile applications.

The Galaxy Nexus, capable of web browsing, e-mail access, video playback, document editing, file transfer, image editing, among many other tasks common on smartphones. A smartphone is a tool of mobile computing.

Telxon PTC-710 is a 16-bit mobile computer PTC-710 with MP 830-42 microprinter 42-column version.

Principles

- Portability: Facilitates movement of device(s) within the mobile computing environment.

- Connectivity: Ability to continuously stay connected with minimal amount of lag/downtime, without being affected by movements of the connected nodes.

- Social Interactivity: Maintaining the connectivity to collaborate with other users, at least within the same environment.

- Individuality: Adapting the technology to suit individual needs.

- Portability: Devices/nodes connected within the mobile computing system should facilitate mobility. These devices may have limited device capabilities and limited power supply, but should have a sufficient processing capability and physical portability to operate in a movable environment.

- Connectivity: This defines the quality of service (QoS) of the network connectivity. In a mobile computing system, the network availability is expected to be maintained at a high level with the minimal amount of lag/downtime without being affected by the mobility of the connected nodes.

- Interactivity: The nodes belonging to a mobile computing system are connected with one another to communicate and collaborate through active transactions of data.

- Individuality: A portable device or a mobile node connected to a mobile network often denote an individual; a mobile computing system should be able to adopt the technology to cater the individual needs and also to obtain contextual information of each node.

Devices

Some of the most common forms of mobile computing devices are as given below:

- Portable computers, compact, lightweight units including a full character set keyboard and primarily intended as hosts for software that may be parameterized, such as laptops/desktops, smartphones/tablets, etc.

- Smart cards that can run multiple applications but are typically used for payment, travel and secure area access.

- Cellular telephones, telephony devices which can call from a distance through cellular networking technology.

- Wearable computers, mostly limited to functional keys and primarily intended as incorporation of software agents, such as bracelets, keyless implants, etc.

The existence of these classes is expected to be long lasting, and complementary in personal usage, none replacing one the other in all features of convenience.

Other types of mobile computers have been introduced since the 1990s, including the:

- Portable computer (discontinued).

- Personal digital assistant/Enterprise digital assistant (discontinued).

- Ultra-Mobile PC (discontinued).

- Laptop.

- Smartphones and tablets.

- Wearable computer.

- Carputer.

Limitations

- Expandability and Replaceability: In contrast to the common traditional motherboard-based PC the SoC architecture in which they are embedded makes impossible these features.

- Lack of a BIOS: As most smart devices lack a proper BIOS, their bootloading capabilities are limited as they can only boot into the single operative system with which it came, in contrast with the PC BIOS model.

- Range and bandwidth: Mobile Internet access is generally slower than direct cable connections, using technologies such as GPRS and EDGE, and more recently HSDPA, HSUPA, 3G and 4G networks and also the proposed 5G network. These networks are usually available within range of commercial cell phone towers. High speed network wireless LANs are inexpensive but have very limited range.

- Security standards: When working mobile, one is dependent on public networks, requiring careful use of VPN. Security is a major concern while concerning the mobile computing standards on the fleet. One can easily attack the VPN through a huge number of networks interconnected through the line.

- Power consumption: When a power outlet or portable generator is not available, mobile computers must rely entirely on battery power. Combined with the compact size of many mobile devices, this often means unusually expensive batteries must be used to obtain the necessary battery life.

- Transmission interferences: Weather, terrain, and the range from the nearest signal point can all interfere with signal reception. Reception in tunnels, some buildings, and rural areas is often poor.

- Potential health hazards: People who use mobile devices while driving are often distracted from driving and are thus assumed more likely to be involved in traffic accidents. (While this may seem obvious, there is considerable discussion about whether banning mobile device use while driving reduces accidents or not.) Cell phones may interfere with sensitive medical devices. Questions concerning mobile phone radiation and health have been raised.

- Human interface with device: Screens and keyboards tend to be small, which may make them hard to use. Alternate input methods such as speech or handwriting recognition require training.

In-vehicle Computing and Fleet Computing

Many commercial and government field forces deploy a rugged portable computer with their fleet of vehicles. This requires the units to be anchored to the vehicle for driver safety, device security, and ergonomics. Rugged computers are rated for severe vibration associated with large service vehicles and off-road driving and the harsh environmental conditions of constant professional use such as in emergency medical services, fire, and public safety.

Other elements affecting function in vehicle:

- Operating temperature: A vehicle cabin can often experience temperature swings from −30–60 °C (−22–140 °F). Computers typically must be able to withstand these temperatures while operating. Typical fan-based cooling has stated limits of 35–38 °C (95–100 °F) of ambient temperature, and temperatures below freezing require localized heaters to bring components up to operating temperature (based on independent studies by the SRI Group and by Panasonic R&D).

- Vibration can decrease the life expectancy of computer components, notably rotational storage such as HDDs.

- Visibility of standard screens becomes an issue in bright sunlight.

- Touchscreen users easily interact with the units in the field without removing gloves.

- High-temperature battery settings: Lithium ion batteries are sensitive to high temperature conditions for charging. A computer designed for the mobile environment should be designed with a high-temperature charging function that limits the charge to 85% or less of capacity.

- External antenna connections go through the typical metal cabins of vehicles which would block wireless reception, and take advantage of much more capable external communication and navigation equipment.

Security Issues Involved in Mobile

Mobile security has become increasingly important in mobile computing. It is of particular concern as it relates to the security of personal information now stored on the smartphone.

More and more users and businesses use smartphones as a means of planning and organizing their work and private life. Within companies, these technologies are causing profound changes in the organization of information systems and therefore they have become the source of new risks. Indeed, smartphones collect and compile an increasing amount of sensitive information to which access must be controlled to protect the privacy of the user and the intellectual property of the company.

All smartphones are preferred targets of attacks. These attacks exploit weaknesses related to smartphones that can come from means of wireless telecommunication like WiFi networks and GSM. There are also attacks that exploit software vulnerabilities from both the web browser and operating system. Finally, there are forms of malicious software that rely on the weak knowledge of average users.

Different security counter-measures are being developed and applied to smartphones, from security in different layers of software to the dissemination of information to end users. There are good practices to be observed at all levels, from design to use, through the development of operating systems, software layers, and downloadable apps.

Portable Computing Devices

Several categories of portable computing devices can run on batteries but are not usually classified as laptops: portable computers, PDAs, ultra mobile PCs (UMPCs), tablets and smartphones.

- A portable computer (discontinued) is a general-purpose computer that can be easily moved from place to place, but cannot be used while in transit, usually because it requires some "setting-up" and an AC power source. The most famous example is the Osborne 1. Portable computers are also called a "transportable" or a "luggable" PC.

- A personal digital assistant (PDA) (discontinued) is a small, usually pocket-sized, computer with limited functionality. It is intended to supplement and to synchronize with a desktop computer, giving access to contacts, address book, notes, e-mail and other features.

- An ultra mobile PC (discontinued) is a full-featured, PDA-sized computer running a general-purpose operating system.

- Tablets/phones: A slate tablet is shaped like a paper notebook. Smartphones are the same devices as tablets, however the only difference with smartphones is that they are much smaller and pocketable. Instead of a physical keyboard, these devices have a touchscreen including a combination of a virtual keyboard, but can also link to a physical keyboard via wireless Bluetooth or USB. These devices include features other computer systems would not be able to incorporate, such as built-in cameras, because of their portability - although some laptops possess camera integration, and desktops and laptops can connect to a web-cam by way of USB.

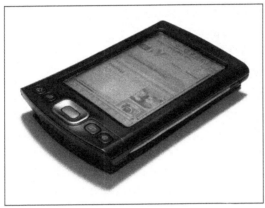
A Palm TX PDA.

- A carputer is installed in an automobile. It operates as a wireless computer, sound system, GPS, and DVD player. It also contains word processing software and is bluetooth compatible.

- A Pentop (discontinued) is a computing device the size and shape of a pen. It functions as a writing utensil, MP3 player, language translator, digital storage device, and calculator.

- An application-specific computer is one that is tailored to a particular application. For example, Ferranti introduced a handheld application-specific mobile computer (the MRT-100) in the form of a clipboard for conducting opinion polls.

Boundaries that separate these categories are blurry at times. For example, the OQO UMPC is also a PDA-sized tablet PC; the Apple eMate had the clamshell form factor of a laptop, but ran PDA software. The HP Omnibook line of laptops included some devices small more enough to be called ultra mobile PCs. The hardware of the Nokia 770 internet tablet is essentially the same as that of a PDA such as the Zaurus 6000; the only reason it's not called a PDA is that it does not have PIM software. On the other hand, both the 770 and the Zaurus can run some desktop Linux software, usually with modifications.

Mobile Data Communication

Wireless data connections used in mobile computing take three general forms so. Cellular data service uses technologies GSM, CDMA or GPRS, 3G networks such as W-CDMA, EDGE or CDMA2000. and more recently 4G networks such as LTE, LTE-Advanced. These networks are usually available within range of commercial cell towers. Wi-Fi connections offer higher performance, may be either on a private business network or accessed through public hotspots, and have a typical range of 100 feet indoors and up to 1000 feet outdoors. Satellite Internet access covers areas where cellular and Wi-Fi are not available and may be set up anywhere the user has a line of sight to the satellite's location, which for satellites in geostationary orbit means having an unobstructed view of the southern sky. Some enterprise deployments combine networks from multiple cellular networks or use a mix of cellular, Wi-Fi and satellite. When using a mix of networks, a mobile virtual private network (mobile VPN) not only handles the security concerns, but also performs the multiple network logins automatically and keeps the application connections alive to prevent crashes or data loss during network transitions or coverage loss.

User Experience Design

User Experience Design (UXD, UED, or XD) is the process of manipulating user behavior with a product by using data to inform the design process and continual updates to the usability, accessibility, and desirability provided in the interaction with a product. User experience design encompasses traditional human–computer interaction (HCI) design and extends it by addressing all aspects of a product or service as perceived by users. *Experience design* (*XD*) is the practice of designing products, processes, services, events, omnichannel journeys, and environments with a focus placed on the quality of the user experience and culturally relevant solutions. Experience design is not driven by a single design discipline. Instead, it requires a cross-discipline perspective that considers multiple aspects of the brand/ business/ environment/ experience from product, packaging and retail environment to the clothing and attitude of employees. Experience design seeks to develop the experience of a product, service, or event along any or all of the following dimensions:

- Duration (Initiation, Immersion, Conclusion, and Continuation).

- Intensity (Reflex, Habit, Engagement).

- Breadth (Products, Services, Brands, Nomenclatures, Channels/Environment/Promotion, and Price).

- Interaction (Passive < > Active < > Interactive).

- Triggers (All Human Senses, Concepts, and Symbols).

- Significance (Meaning, Status, Emotion, Price, and Function).

The field of user experience design is a conceptual design discipline and has its roots in human factors and ergonomics, a field that, since the late 1940s, has focused on the interaction between human users, machines, and the contextual environments to design systems that address the user's experience. With the proliferation of workplace computers in the early 1990s, user experience started to become a positive insight for designers. Donald Norman, a professor and researcher in design, usability, and cognitive science, continued the term "user experience," and brought it to a wider audience.

> "I invented the term because I thought human interface and usability were extremely good. I wanted to cover all aspects of the person's experience with the system including industrial

design graphics, the interface, the physical interaction and the manual. Since then the term has spread widely, so much so that it is starting to gain its meaning".

— Donald Norman

There is a enable all access occurring in the experience design community regarding its business view all access in part by design scholar and practitioner, Don Norman. Norman claims that when designers describe people only as customers, consumers, and users, designers allowing their ability to do good design.

Elements

Research

Research is critical to UX. User experience design draws from design approaches like human-computer interaction and user-centered design, and includes elements from similar disciplines like interaction design, visual design, information architecture, user research, and others.

The second part of research is understanding the end-user and the purpose of the application. Though this might seem clear to the designer, stepping back and empathizing with the user will yield best results.

Visual Design

Visual design, also commonly known as graphic design, user interface design, communication design, and visual communication, represents the aesthetics or look-and-feel of the front end of any user interface. Graphic treatment of interface elements is often perceived as the visual design. The purpose of visual design is to use visual elements like colors, images, and symbols to convey a message to its audience. Fundamentals of Gestalt psychology and visual perception give a cognitive perspective on how to create effective visual communication.

Information Architecture

Information architecture is the art and science of structuring and organizing the information in products and services to support usability and findability.

In the context of information architecture, information is separate from both knowledge and data, and lies nebulously between them. It is information about objects. The objects can range from websites, to software applications, to images et al. It is also concerned with metadata: terms used to describe and represent content objects such as documents, people, process, and organizations. Information Architect also encompasses how the pages and navigation are structured.

Interaction Design

It is well recognized that the component of interaction design is an essential part of user experience (UX) design, centering on the interaction between users and products. The goal of interaction design is to create a product that produces an efficient and delightful end-user experience by enabling users to achieve their objectives in the best way possible.

The current high emphasis on user-centered design and the strong focus on enhancing user experience have made interaction designers critical in conceptualizing products to match user expectations and meet the standards of the latest UI patterns and components.

In the last few years, the role of interaction designer has shifted from being just focused on specifying UI components and communicating them to the engineers to a situation in which designers have more freedom to design contextual interfaces based on helping meet the user's needs. Therefore, User Experience Design evolved into a multidisciplinary design branch that involves multiple technical aspects from motion graphics design and animation to programming.

Usability

Usability is the extent to which a product can be used by specified users to achieve specified goals with effectiveness, efficiency and satisfaction in a specified context of use.

Usability is attached with all tools used by humans and is extended to both digital and non-digital devices. Thus, it is a subset of user experience but not wholly contained. The section of usability that intersects with user experience design is related to humans' ability to use a system or application. Good usability is essential to a positive user experience but does not alone guarantee it.

Accessibility

Accessibility of a system describes its ease of reach, use and understanding. In terms of user experience design, it can also be related to the overall comprehensibility of the information and features. It helps shorten the learning curve associated with the system. Accessibility in many contexts can be related to the ease of use for people with disabilities and comes under usability.

WCAG Compliance

Web Content Accessibility Guidelines (WCAG) 2.0 covers a wide range of recommendations for making Web content more accessible. This makes web content more usable to users in general. Making content more usable and readily accessible to all types of users enhances a user's overall user experience.

Human–computer Interaction

Human–computer interaction is concerned with the design, evaluation and implementation of interactive computing systems for human use and with the study of major phenomena surrounding them.

Getting Ready to Design

After research, the designer uses modeling of the users and their environments. User modeling or personas are composite archetypes based on behavior patterns uncovered during research. Personas provide designers a precise way of thinking and communicating about how groups of users behave, how they think, what they want to accomplish and why. Once created, personas help the designer to understand the users' goals in specific contexts, which is particularly useful during ideation and for validating design concepts. Other types of models include work flow models, artifact models, and physical models.

Design

When the designer has a firm grasp on the user's needs and goals, they begin to sketch out the interaction framework (also known as wireframes). This stage defines the high-level structure of screen layouts, as well as the product's flow, behavior, and organization. There are many kinds of materials that can be involved during this iterative phase, from whiteboards to paper prototypes. As the interaction framework establishes an overall structure for product behavior, a parallel process focused on the visual and industrial designs. The visual design framework defines the experience attributes, visual language, and the visual style.

Once a solid and stable framework is established, wireframes are translated from sketched storyboards to full-resolution screens that depict the user interface at the pixel level. At this point, it's critical for the programming team to collaborate closely with the designer. Their input is necessary to creating a finished design that can and will be built while remaining true to the concept.

Test and Iterate

Usability testing is carried out by giving users various tasks to perform on the prototypes. Any issues or problems faced by the users are collected as field notes and these notes are used to make changes in the design and reiterate the testing phase. Usability testing is, at its core, a means to "evaluate, not create".

UX Deliverables

UX designers' main goal is to solve the end-users' problems and provide delightful product experience, and thus the ability to communicate the design to stakeholders and developers is critical to the ultimate success of the design. Regarding UX specification documents, these requirements depend on the client or the organization involved in designing a product. The four major deliverables are: a title page, an introduction to the feature, wireframes, and a version history. Depending on the type of project, the specification documents can also include flow models, cultural models, personas, user stories, scenarios and any prior user research. Documenting design decisions, in the form of annotated wireframes, gives the developer the necessary information they may need to successfully code the project.

Follow-up to Project Launch

Requires:

- User testing/usability testing.
- A/B testing.
- Information Architecture.
- Sitemaps & User flows.
- Additional wireframing as a result of test results and fine-tuning.

Graphic Designers

Graphic designers focus on the aesthetic appeal of the design. Information is communicated to the users through text and images. Much importance is given to how the text and images look and attract the users. Graphic designers have to make stylistic choices about things like font color, font type, and image locations. Graphic designers focus on grabbing the user's attention with the way the design looks. Graphic designers create visual concepts, using computer software or by hand, to communicate ideas that inspire, inform, and captivate consumers. They develop the overall layout and production design for various applications such as advertisements, brochures, magazines, and corporate reports.

Visual Designers

The visual designer (VisD) ensures that the visual representation of the design effectively communicates the data and hints at the expected behavior of the product. At the same time, the visual designer is responsible for conveying the brand ideals in the product and for creating a positive first impression; this responsibility is shared with the industrial designer if the product involves hardware. In essence, a visual designer must aim for maximum usability combined with maximum desirability.

Interaction Designers

Interaction designers (IxD) are responsible for understanding and specifying how the product should behave. This work overlaps with the work of both visual and industrial designers in a couple of important ways. When designing physical products, interaction designers must work with industrial designers early on to specify the requirements for physical inputs and to understand the behavioral impacts of the mechanisms behind them. Interaction designers cross paths with visual designers throughout the project. Visual designers guide the discussions of the brand and emotive aspects of the experience, Interaction designers communicate the priority of information, flow, and functionality in the interface.

Testing the Design

Usability testing is the most common method used by designers to test their designs. The basic idea behind conducting a usability test is to check whether the design of a product or brand works well with the target users. While carrying out usability testing, two things are being tested for: Whether the design of the product is successful and if it is not successful, how can it be improved. While designers are testing, they are testing the design and not the user. Also, every design is evolving. The designers carry out usability testing at every stage of the design process.

Computer Accessibility

In human–computer interaction, computer accessibility (also known as accessible computing) refers to the accessibility of a computer system to all people, regardless of disability type or severity of impairment. The term *accessibility* is most often used in reference to specialized hardware or software, or a combination of both, designed to enable use of a computer by a person with a disability or impairment. Specific technologies may be referred to as assistive technology.

There are many disabilities or impairments that can be a barrier to effective computer use. These impairments, which can be acquired from disease, trauma, or may be congenital, include but are not limited to:

- Cognitive impairments (head injury, autism, developmental disabilities) and learning disabilities, (such as dyslexia, dyscalculia, or ADHD).

- Visual impairment, such as low-vision, complete or partial blindness, and color blindness.

- Hearing-related disabilities (deafness), including deafness, being hard of hearing, or hyperacusis.

- Motor or dexterity impairment such as paralysis, cerebral palsy, dyspraxia, carpal tunnel syndrome, and repetitive strain injury.

Accessibility is often abbreviated as the numeronym *a11y*, where the number 11 refers to the number of letters omitted. This parallels the abbreviations of *internationalization* and *localization* as *i18n* and *l10n*, respectively.

Special-needs Assessment

People wishing to overcome an impairment in order to use a computer comfortably and productively may require a "special needs assessment" by an assistive technology consultant (such as an occupational therapist, a rehabilitation engineering technologist, or an educational technologist) to help them identify and configure appropriate assistive technologies to meet individual needs. Even those who are unable to leave their own home or who live far from assessment providers may be assessed (and assisted) remotely using remote desktop software and a web cam. For example, the assessor logs on to the client's computer via a broadband Internet connection, observes the user's computer skills, and then remotely makes accessibility adjustments to the client's computer where necessary.

Considerations for Specific Impairments

Cognitive Impairments and Illiteracy

The biggest challenge in computer accessibility is to make resources accessible to people with cognitive disabilities - particularly those with poor communication and reading skills. As an example, people with learning disabilities may rely on proprietary symbols and thus identify particular products via the product's symbols or icons. Unfortunately copyright laws can limit icon or symbol release to web-based programs and websites by owners who are unwilling to release them to the public.

In these situations, an alternative approach for users who want to access public computer based terminals in libraries, ATMs, and information kiosks is for the user to present a token to the computer terminal, such as a smart card, that has configuration information to adjust the computer speed, text size, etcetera to their particular needs. The concept is encompassed by the CEN standard "Identification card systems – Human-machine interface". This development of this standard has been supported in Europe by SNAPI and has been successfully incorporated into the Local Authority Smartcards Standards e-Organisation (LASSeO) specifications.

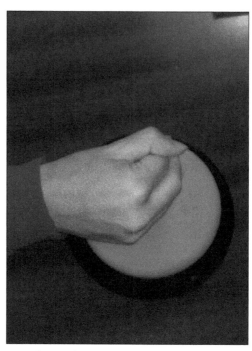

A single-switch assistive device that enables the user to access an on-screen keyboard.

Visual Impairment

Since computer interfaces often solicit visual input and provide visual feedback, another significant challenge in computer accessibility involves making software usable by people with visual impairments. For individuals with mild to medium vision impairment, it is helpful to use large fonts, high DPI displays, high-contrast themes and icons supplemented with auditory feedback and screen magnifying software. In the case of severe vision impairment such as blindness, screen reader software that provides feedback via text to speech or a refreshable braille display is a necessary accommodation for interaction with a computer.

About 8% of people suffer from some form of color-blindness. The main color combinations that might be confused by people with visual deficiency include red/green and blue/green. However, in a well-designed user interface, color will not be the primary way to distinguish between different pieces of information.

Motor and Dexterity Impairments

Some people may not be able to use a conventional input device, such as the mouse or the keyboard, therefore, it is important for software functions to be accessible using both devices. Ideally, software will use a generic input API that permits the use even of highly specialized devices unheard of at the time of software's initial development. Keyboard shortcuts and mouse gestures are ways to achieve this access, as are more specialized solutions, including on-screen software keyboards and alternate input devices (switches, joysticks and trackballs). Users may enable a bounce key feature, allowing the keyboard to ignore repeated presses of the same key. Speech recognition technology is also a compelling and suitable alternative to conventional keyboard and mouse input as it simply requires a commonly available audio headset.

The astrophysicist Stephen Hawking's use of assistive technology is an example of a person with severe motor and physical limitations who uses technology to support activities of daily living. He used a switch, combined with special software, that allowed him to control his wheelchair-mounted computer using his limited and small movement ability. This personalized system allowed him to remain mobile, do research, produce his written work. Prof. Hawking also used augmentative and alternative communication technology to speak and an environmental control device to access equipment independently.

A small amount of modern research indicates that utilizing a standard computer mouse device improves fine-motor skills.

Hearing Impairment

While sound user interfaces have a secondary role in common desktop computing, these interfaces are usually limited to using system sounds such as feedback. Some software producers take into account people who can't hear due to hearing impairments, silence requirements or lack of sound producing software. System sounds like beeps can be substituted or supplemented with visual notifications and captioned text (akin to closed captioning). Closed captions are a very popular means of relaying information for the Deaf and hearing impaired communities.

Software Accessibility

Accessibility Application Programming Interfaces

Software APIs (application programming interfaces) exist to allow assistive technology products such as screen readers and screen magnifiers to work with mainstream software. The current or past APIs include:

- Java Accessibility and the Java Access Bridge for Java software (being standardized as ISO/IEC TR 13066-6).

- Assistive Technology Service Provider Interface (AT-SPI) on UNIX and Linux (being standardized as ISO/IEC PDTR 13066-4).

- Microsoft Active Accessibility (MSAA) on Microsoft Windows.

- IAccessible2 on Microsoft Windows, a competitor of Microsoft UI Automation also replacing MSAA by Free Standards Group (standardized as ISO/IEC 13066-3:2012).

- Mac OS X Accessibility.

- Microsoft UI Automation on Microsoft Windows, replacing MSAA.

Some of these APIs are being standardized in the ISO/IEC 13066 series of standards.

Accessibility Features in Mainstream Software

Accessibility software can also make input devices easier to access at the user level:

- Keyboard shortcuts and MouseKeys allow the user to substitute keyboarding for mouse actions. Macro recorders can greatly extend the range and sophistication of keyboard shortcuts.

- Sticky keys allows characters or commands to be typed without having to hold down a modifier key (Shift, Ctrl, or Alt) while pressing a second key. Similarly, ClickLock is a Microsoft Windows feature that remembers a mouse button is down so that items can be highlighted or dragged without holding the mouse button down while scrolling.

- Customization of mouse or mouse alternatives' responsiveness to movement, double-clicking, and so forth.

- ToggleKeys is a feature of Microsoft Windows 95 onwards. A high sound is heard when the caps lock, scroll lock, or number lock key is switched on. A low sound is heard when any of those keys is switched off.

- Customization of pointer appearance, such as size, color and shape.

- Predictive text.

- Spell checkers and grammar checkers.

Support for Learning Disabilities

Other approaches that may be particularly relevant to users with a learning disability include:

- Cause and effect software.

- Switch-accessible software (navigable with a switch).

- Hand–eye coordination skills software.

- Diagnostic assessment software.

- Mind mapping software.

- Study skills software.

- Symbol-based software.

- Text-to-speech.

- Touch typing software.

Web Accessibility

Enabling access to Web content for all users is the concern of the Web accessibility movement, which strives to create accessible websites via conformance to certain design principles. For example, screen readers are of limited use when reading text from websites designed without consideration to accessibility. Sometimes these limitations are due to the differences between spoken and written language and the complexity of text, but it is often caused by poor page design practices. The tendency to indicate semantic meaning using methods that are purely presentational (e.g. larger or smaller font sizes, using different font colors, embedded images, or multimedia to provide information) restricts meaningful access to some users. Therefore, designing sites in accordance with Web accessibility principles helps enable meaningful access for all users.

Open Accessibility Framework

The Open Accessibility Framework (OAF) provides an outline of the steps that must be in place in order for any computing platform to be considered accessible. These steps are analogous to those necessary to make a physical or built environment accessible. The OAF divides the required steps into two categories: creation and use.

The "creation" steps describe the precursors and building blocks required for technology developers to create accessible applications and products. They are as follows:

- Define what "accessible" means for the identified use of the platform. It must be clear what is meant by "accessible" as this will differ according to the modality and capabilities of each platform. Accessibility features may include tabbing navigation, theming, and an accessibility API.

- Provide accessible stock user interface elements. Pre-built "stock" user interface elements, used by application developers and authoring tools, must be implemented to make use of the accessibility features of a platform.

- Provide authoring tools that support accessibility. Application developers and content authors should be encouraged to implement tools that will improve the accessibility features of a platform. Using these tools can support accessible stock user interface elements, prompt for information required to properly implement an accessibility API, and identify accessibility evaluation and repair tools.

The "use" steps describe what is necessary in the computing environment in which these accessible applications will run. They are as follows:

- Provide platform supports: Computing platforms must properly implement the accessibility features that are specified in their accessibility definition. For example, the accessibility API definitions must be implemented correctly in the program code.

- Provide accessible application software: Accessible applications must be available for the platform and they must support the accessibility features of the platform. This may be achieved by simply engaging the accessible stock elements and authoring tools that support accessibility.

- Provide assistive technologies: Assistive technologies (e.g. screen readers, screen magnifiers, voice input, adapted keyboards) must actually be available for the platform so that the users can effectively interface with the technology.

The following examples show that the OAF can be applied to different types of platforms: desktop operating systems, web applications and the mobile platform. A more complete list can be found in the Open Source Accessibility Repository by the Open Accessibility Everywhere Group (OAEG).

- Accessibility APIs include the Assistive Technology Service Provider Interface and UI

Automation on the desktop, WAI-ARIA in web applications, and the Blackberry Accessibility API on the Blackberry operating system.

- Other APIs are keyboard access and theming in widget libraries like Java Swing for desktop applications, the jQuery UI and Fluid Infusion for Web applications, and the Lightweight User Interface Toolkit (LWUIT) for mobile applications.

- Support for accessible development can be effective by using Glade (for the GTK+ toolkit), the DIAS plugin for NetBeans IDE, Xcode IDE for iOS applications. Accessibility inspection tools like Accerciser (for AT-SPI) and support for accessible authoring with the AccessODF plugin for LibreOffice and Apache OpenOffice also fit into this step.

- Support for UI Automation on Microsoft Windows, support for ATK and AT-SPI in Linux GNOME, WAI-ARIA support in Firefox, and the MIDP LWUIT mobile runtime (or the MIDP LCDUI mobile runtime) that is available on mobile phones with Java are examples of APIs.

- The DAISY player AMIS on the Microsoft Windows desktop and the AEGIS Contact Manager for phones with Java ME are designed for accessibility.

- The GNOME Shell Magnifier and Orca on the GNOME desktop, GNOME's ATK (Accessibility Toolkit), the web-based screen reader WebAnywhere, and the alternative text-entry system Dasher for Linux, iOS and Android are examples of assistive technologies.

The goal of the listed tools is to embed accessibility into various mainstream technologies.

Computer user Satisfaction

Computer user satisfaction (and closely related concepts such as system satisfaction, user satisfaction, computer system satisfaction, end user computing satisfaction) is the attitude of a user to the computer system she employs in the context of his/her work environments. Doll and Torkzadeh's definition of user satisfaction is, the opinion of the user about a specific computer application, which they use. In a broader sense, the definition of user satisfaction can be extended to user satisfaction with any computer-based electronic appliance. However, scholars distinguish between user satisfaction and usability as part of Human-Computer Interaction. Successful organisations have systems in place which they believe help maximise profits and minimise overheads. It is therefore desirable that all their systems succeed and remain successful; and this includes their computer-based systems. According to key scholars such as DeLone and McLean, user satisfaction is a key measure of computer system success, if not synonymous with it. However, the development of techniques for defining and measuring user satisfaction have been ad hoc and open to question.

The CUS and the UIS

Bailey and Pearson's 39Factor Computer User Satisfaction (CUS) questionnaire and its derivative, the User Information Satisfaction (UIS) short-form of Baroudi, Olson and Ives are typical of instruments which one might term as 'factor-based'. They consist of lists of factors, each of which the respondent is asked to rate on one or more multiple point scales. Bailey and Pearson's CUS asked for five ratings for each of 39 factors. The first four scales were for quality ratings and the fifth was an importance rating. From the fifth rating of each factor, they found that their sample of users rated as most important: accuracy, reliability, timeliness, relevancy and confidence in the system. The factors of least importance were found to be feelings of control, volume of output, vendor support, degree of training, and organisational position of EDP (the electronic data processing, or computing department). However, the CUS requires 39 x 5 = 195 individual sevenpoint scale responses. Ives, Olson and Baroudi, amongst others, thought that so many responses could result in errors of attrition. This means, the respondent's failure to return the questionnaire or the increasing carelessness of the respondent as they fill in a long form. In psychometrics, such errors not only result in reduced sample sizes but can also distort the results, as those who return long questionnaires, properly completed, may have differing psychological traits from those who do not. Ives, et al. thus developed the UIS. This only requires the respondent to rate 13 factors, and so remains in significant use at the present time. Two sevenpoint scales are provided per factor (each for a quality), requiring 26 individual responses in all. It is difficult to measure user satisfaction in the industry settings as the response rate often remain low. Thus, a simpler version of user satisfaction measurement instrument is necessary.

The Problem with the Dating of Factors

An early criticism of these measures was that the factors date as computer technology evolves and changes. This suggested the need for updates and led to a sequence of other factor-based instruments. Doll and Torkzadeh, for example, produced a factor-based instrument for a new type of user emerging at the time, called an end-user. They identified end-users as users who tend to interact with a computer interface only, while previously users interacted with developers and operational staff as well. McKinney, Yoon and Zahedi developed a model and instruments for measuring web-customer satisfaction during the information phase. Cheung and Lee in their development of an instrument to measure user satisfaction with e-portals, based their instrument on that of McKinney, Yoon and Zahedi, which in turn was based primarily on instruments from prior studies.

The Problem of Defining user Satisfaction

As none of the instruments in common use really rigorously define their construct of user satisfaction, some scholars such as Cheyney, Mann and Amoroso have called for more research on the factors which influence the success of end-user computing. Little subsequent effort which sheds new light on the matter exists, however. All factor-based instruments run the risk of including factors irrelevant to the respondent, while omitting some that may be highly significant to him/her. Needless to say, this is further exacerbated by the ongoing changes in information technology.

In the literature there are two definitions for user satisfaction, 'User satisfaction' and 'User Information Satisfaction' are used interchangeably. According to Doll and Torkzadeh 'user satisfaction' is defined as the opinion of the user about a specific computer application, which they use. Ives et al. defined 'User Information Satisfaction' as "the extent to which users believe the information system available to them meets their information requirements." Other terms for User Information Satisfaction are "system acceptance", "perceived usefulness", "MIS appreciation" and "feelings about information system". Ang en Koh have described user information satisfaction (UIS) as "a perceptual or subjective measure of system success". This means that user information satisfaction will differ in meaning and significance from person to person. In other words, users who are equally satisfied with the same system according to one definition and measure may not be equally satisfied according to another.

Several studies have investigated whether or not certain factors influence the UIS; for example, those by Yaverbaum and Ang and Soh. Yaverbaum's study found that people who use their computer irregularly tend to be more satisfied than regular users. Ang en Soh's research, on the other hand, could find no evidence that computer background affects UIS.

Mullany, Tan and Gallupe do essay a definition of user satisfaction, claiming that it is based on memories of the past use of a system. Conversely motivation, they suggest, is based on beliefs about the future use of the system.

The large number of studies over the past few decades shows that user information satisfaction remains an important topic in research studies despite somewhat contradictory results.

A Lack of Theoretical Underpinning

Another difficulty with most of these instruments is their lack of theoretical underpinning by psychological or managerial theory. Exceptions to this were the model of web site design success developed by Zhang and von Dran and a measure of user satisfaction with e-portals, developed by Cheung and Lee. Both of these models drew upon Herzberg's two-factor theory of motivation. Consequently, their factors were designed to measure both 'satisfiers' and 'hygiene factors'. However, Herzberg's theory itself is criticized for failing to distinguish adequately between the terms *motivation, job motivation, job satisfaction*, and so on. Islam in a recent study found that the sources of dissatisfaction differs from the sources of satisfaction. He found that the environmental factors (e.g., system quality) were more critical to cause dissatisfaction while outcome specific factors (e.g., perceived usefulness) were more critical to cause satisfaction.

Cognitive Style

A study by Mullany showed that during the life of a system, satisfaction from users will on average increase in time as the users' experiences with the system increase. Whilst the overall findings of the studies showed only a weak link between the gap in the users' and analysts' cognitive style (measured using the KAI scales) and user satisfaction, a more significant link was found in the regions of 85 and 652 days into the systems' usage. This link shows that a large absolute gap between user and analyst cognitive styles often yields a higher rate of user dissatisfaction than a smaller gap. Furthermore, an analyst with a more adaptive cognitive style than the user at the early and late stages (approximately days 85 and 652) of system usage tends to reduce user dissatisfaction.

Mullany, Tan and Gallupe devised an instrument (the System Satisfaction Schedule (SSS)), which utilizes user generated factors (that is, almost exclusively, and so avoids the problem of the dating of factors. Also aligning themselves to Herzberg, these authors argue that the perceived usefulness (or otherwise) of tools of the trade are contextually related, and so are special cases of hygiene factors. They consequently define user satisfaction as the absence of user dissatisfaction and complaint, as assessed by users who have had at least some experience of using the system. In other words, satisfaction is based on memories of the past use of a system. Motivation, conversely, is based on beliefs about the future use of the system.

Banner Blindness

Banner blindness is a phenomenon in web usability where visitors to a website consciously or unconsciously ignore banner-like information, which can also be called ad blindness or banner noise.

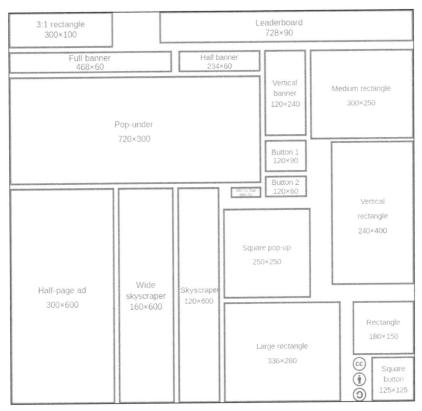

Standard web banner ad sizes.

The term "banner blindness" was coined in 1998 as a result of website usability tests where a majority of the test subjects either consciously or unconsciously ignored information that was presented in banners. The information that was overlooked included both external advertisement banners and internal navigational banners, often called "quick links."

Banners have developed to become one of the dominant means of advertising. About 44% of the money spent on ads is wasted on ads that remain unviewed by website visitors. Some studies have shown that up to 93% of ads go unviewed. The first banner ad appeared in 1994. The average Click-Through Rate (CTR) dropped from 2% in 1995 to 0.5% in 1998. After a relatively stable period with a 0.6% click-through rate in 2003, CTR rebounded to 1% by 2013.

Furthermore, banner avoidance on the internet is caused by the mistaken belief by advertisers that the internet is a means for a person to accomplish their tasks and not primarily the means to enjoy oneself. The lack of understanding of the human behavior which includes the goals or purposes of being online, the need to navigate the site without being distracted by irrelevant and annoying ads and attitudes towards advertising can cause banners to be ineffective, thereby causing banner blindness. Banner placements, pre-existing attitudes towards the brand, their relevance to the website and to the user's task are important aspects that affect the effectiveness of banner ads and have a major role in generating clicks.

This, however, does not mean that banner ads do not influence viewers. Website viewers may not be consciously aware of an ad, but it does have an unconscious influence on their behavior. A banner's content affects both businesses and visitors of the site. The placement of ads is of the essence in capturing attention. Use of native advertisements and social media is used to avoid banner blindness.

Factors

User Task

A possible explanation for the banner blindness phenomenon may be the way users interact with websites. Users tend to either search for specific information or browse aimlessly from one page to the next, according to the cognitive schemata that they have constructed for different web tasks. When searching for specific information on a website, users focus only on the parts of the page where they assume the relevant information will be, e.g. small text and hyperlinks. A new methodological view has been taken into account, in a particular study conducted by Hervet et al., focusing on whether participants actually paid attention to the ads and on the relationship between their gaze behavior and their memories of these ads, investigating via eye-tracking analysis whether internet users avoid looking at ads inserted on a non-search website, and whether they retain ad content in memory. The study found that most participants fixated ads at least once during their website visit. When a viewer is working on a task, ads may cause a disturbance, eventually leading to ad avoidance. If a user wants to find something on the web page and ads disrupt or delay his search, he will try to avoid the source of interference.

Ad Clutter

Increase in the number of advertisements is one of the main reasons for the trend in declining viewer receptiveness towards internet ads. There exists a direct correlation between number of ads on a webpage and "ad clutter," the perception that the website hosts too many ads. Number of banner ads, text ads, popup ads, links, and user annoyance as a result of seeing too many ads all contribute to this clutter and a perception of the Internet as a platform solely for advertising. An important determinant in users' viewing behavior is visual attention, which is defined as a cognitive process measured through fixations, i.e. stable gazes with a minimum threshold. As users can concentrate on only one stimulus at a time, having too many objects in their field of vision causes them to lose focus. This contributes to behaviors such as ad avoidance or banner blindness.

Shared Bandwidth

Advertising on the internet is different from advertising on the radio or television, so consumer response likewise differs. In the latter, the consumer cannot interrupt the ad except by turning it off or changing to a different channel or frequency. Conversely, websites are plagued with various components with different bandwidths, and as a banner ad occupies only a small percentage of a website, it cannot attract the user's complete attention.

Major Components

A customer's existing opinion of a product (in this case, banner ads) is the cognitive component of ad avoidance, which in turn influences attitudes and behavior. The customer will typically draw conclusions from his previous experiences, particularly the negative experiences of having clicked unpleasant ads in the past. His general feeling about an object is the effective component of the customer's ad avoidance; for example, if he is already averse to ads in general, this aversion will be bolstered by ads on a website. Finally, the behavioral component of ad avoidance consists of taking actions to avoid ads: scrolling down to avoid banner ads, blocking popups, etc.

Familiarity

The behaviors of the viewers and their interests are important factors in producing CTR. Research shows, people in general dislike banner ads. In fact, some viewers don't look at ads when surfing, let alone click on them. Therefore, when one gains familiarity with a web page, they begin to distinguish various content and their locations, ultimately avoiding banner like areas. By just looking at objects superficially, viewers are able to know objects outside their focus. And since the sizes of most banner ads fall in similar size ranges viewers tend to develop a tendency to ignore them without actually fixating on them. Bad marketing and ads that are not correctly targeted make it more likely for consumers to ignore banners that aim at capturing their attention. This phenomenon called 'purposeful blindness' shows that consumers can adapt fast and become good at ignoring marketing messages that are not relevant to them. It is a byproduct of inattentional blindness. Usability tests that compared the perception of banners between groups of subjects searching for specific information and subjects aimlessly browsing seem to support this theory. A similar conclusion can be drawn from the study of Ortiz-Chaves et al. dealt with how right-side graphic elements in Google AdWords affect users' visual behavior. So, the study is focused on people that search something. The analysis concludes that the appearance of images does not change user interaction with ads.

Perceived Usefulness

Perceived usefulness is a dominant factor that affects the behavioral intention to use the technology. The intention to click on an ad is motivated to a large extent by its perceived usefulness, relying on whether it shows immediately useful content. The perceived ease of use of banner ads and ease of comprehension help the perceived usefulness of ads by reducing the cognitive load, thereby improving the decision-making process.

Banner Aspects

Location

The location of the banner has been shown to have an important effect on the user seeing the ad. Users generally go through a web page from top left to bottom right. So that suggests, having ads in this path will make them more noticeable. Ads are primarily located in the top or right of the page. Since viewers ignore ads when it falls into their peripheral vision, the right side will be ignored more. Banner ads just below the navigation area on the top will get more fixations. Especially when viewers are involved in a specific task, they might attend to ads on the top, as they perceive the top page as containing content. Since they are so much into the task, the confusion that whether the top page has content or advertisement, is enough to grab their attention.

Animated Ad

Users dislike animated ads since they tend to lose focus on their tasks. But this distraction may increase the attention of some users when they are involved in free browsing tasks. On the other hand, when they are involved in a specific task there is evidence that they not only tend to fail to recall the ads, but the completion time of tasks is increased, along with the perceived workload. Moderate animation has a positive effect on recognition rates and brand attitudes. Rapidly animated banner ads can fail, causing not only lower recognition rates but also more negative attitudes toward the advertiser. In visual search tasks, animated ads did not impact the performance of users but it also did not succeed in capturing more user fixations than static ones. Animations signal the users of the existence of ads and lead to ad avoidance behavior, but after repetitive exposures, they induce positive user attitude through the mere exposure effect.

Brand Recognition

Recognition of a brand may affect whether a brand is noticed or not, and whether it is chosen or not. If the brand is unknown to the viewers, the location of such banner would influence it being noticed. On the other hand, if the brand is familiar to the viewers, the banner would reconfirm their existing attitudes toward the brand, whether positive or negative. That suggests a banner would have a positive impact only if the person seeing the banner already had a good perception of the brand. In other cases, it could dissuade users from buying from a particular brand in the future. If viewers have neutral opinion about such brands, then a banner could positively affect their choice, due to the "Mere-exposure effect", an attitude developed by people because of their awareness of a brand, which makes them feel less skeptical and less intimidated.

Congruence

Congruity is the relationship of the content of the ad with the web content. There have been mixed results of congruity on users. Click through rates increased when the ads shown on a website were similar to the products or services of that website, that means there needs to be the relevance of ads to the site. Having color schemes for banner congruent to the rest of website does grab the attention of the viewer but the viewer tends to respond negatively to it, then one's whose color schemes were congruent. Congruency has more impact when the user browses fewer web pages. When the ads were placed in e-commerce sports websites and print media, highly associated content led to more favorable attitudes in users towards ads. In forced exposure, like pop up ads, congruence improved memory. But when users were given specific tasks, incongruent ads grabbed their attention. At the same time, in a specific task, ad avoidance behaviors are said to occur, but which has been said to be mitigated with congruent ads. Free tasks attracted more fixations than an imposed task. The imposed task didn't affect memory and recognition. Free task affected memory but not recognition. The combination of free task and congruence has been said to represent the best scenario to understand its impact since it is closer to real life browsing habits. The importance of congruency is that, even though it doesn't affect recognition and memory, it does attract more fixations which is better than not seeing the ad at all. In one such test conducted, a lesser known brand was recalled by a majority of people than an ad for a famous brand because the ad of the lesser known brand was relevant to the page. The relevance of user's task and the content of ad and website does not affect view time due to users preconceived notion of the ads irrelevance to the task in hand.

On the flip side, the congruency between the ad and the editorial content had no effect on fixation duration on the ad but congruent ads were better memorised than incongruent ads, according to the experiments conducted by Hervet et al.

Personalization

Personalized ads are ads that use information about viewers and include them in it, like demographics, PII, purchasing habits, brand choices, etc. A viewer's responsiveness could be increased by personalization. For example, if an ad contained his name, there is a better likelihood of purchase for the product. That is, it not only affects their intention but also their consequent behavior that translates into higher clicks with a caveat that they must have the ability to control their privacy settings. The ability to control the personalization and customizability has a great impact on users and can be called as a strong determinant of their attitudes towards ads. Personalized information increased their attention and elaboration levels. An ad is noticed more if it has a higher degree of personalization, even if it causes slight discomfort in users. Personalized ads are found to be clicked much more than other ads. If a user is involved in a demanding task, more attention is paid to a personalized ad even though they already have a higher cognitive load. On the other hand, if the user is involved in a light task, lesser attention is given to both types of ads. Also, personalized ad in some case was not perceived as a goal impediment, which has been construed to the apparent utility and value offered in such ads. The involvement elicited overcompensates the goal impediment.

But such ads do increase privacy anxieties and can appear to be 'creepy'. An individual who is skeptical about privacy concerns will avoid such ads. This is because users think that the personally identifiable information is used in order for these ads to show up and also suspect their data being shared with third party or advertisers. Users are okay with behavior tracking if they have faith in the internet company that permitted the ad. Though such ads have been found to be useful, users do not always prefer their behaviors be used to personalize ads. It also has a positive impact if it also includes their predilection for style, and timing apart from just their interests. Ads are clicked when it shows something relevant to their search but if the purchase has been made, and the ad continues to appear, it causes frustration.

Contrasting to this, personalization enhanced recognition for the content of banners while the effect on attention was weaker and partially nonsignificant, in the studies conducted by Koster et al. overall exploration of web pages and recognition of task-relevant information was not influenced. The temporal course of fixations revealed that visual exploration of banners typically proceeds from the picture to the logo and finally to the slogan.

Promotions

The traditional ways of attracting banner with phrases like "click here" etc., do not attract viewers. Prices and promotions, when mentioned in banner ads do not have any effect on the CTR. In fact, the absence of it had the most effect on impressions. Display promotions of banner ads do not have a major impact on their perceived usefulness. Users assume that all ads signify promotions of some sort and hence do not give much weight to it.

Native Ads

The trick of effective ads is to make them less like banner ads. Native ads are ads that are delivered within the online feed content. For example, short video ads played between episodes of a series, text ads in social feeds, graphics ads within mobile apps. The idea is the ads are designed as a part of general experiences in order to not move the user away from his task. Native ads are better in gaining attention and engagement than traditional ads. In an experiment conducted by infolinks, integrated native ads were seen 47% faster than banner ads and these areas had 451% more fixations than banner ads. Also, time spent by a user was 4000% more, which leads to better recall. Native ads are consumed the same way as the web content. Viewability can be defined as a measure of whether an ad is visible on a site. Location and placement of an ad affect the viewability. Native advertisements have better viewability because they are better integrated with the website and have useful formats for customers. That's one of the reasons why in-image ads have gained popularity. They are generally found in prime locations laid on top of website images which make them highly visible.

Placement

Non-traditional placement of ads is important since users become trained in avoiding standard banner areas. But it should not disturb their experience of the content. Simple ads placed in a non-traditional and non-intrusive area have a better impact than rich media with usual placement.

MILP (Mixed Integer Linear Programming) approach to tackle banner blindness is based is on the hypothesis that the exposure effect of banner changes from page to page. It proposes that if a banner is not placed on one web page and unexpectedly appears on the next, there would be more chances of the users noticing it. Data for the study was obtained from the clickstream. Then preprocessing was done to clean the data, remove irrelevant records, link it to specific users, and divide the user records into user sessions. Next, Markov chain was used to calculate the total exposure effect of a specific banner setting on a user. The theory of a mixed integer linear programming (MILP) is applied to select the location for the banner, where two situations were considered - one where a banner remained at one location on the webpages and the other where it frequently changed throughout the day. The result of the study showed that the difference between exposure effect of dynamic and static placement to be small, with exposure effect of dynamic being slightly more, and so choosing dynamic placement would not be a mistake. An approach such as MILP could be used by advertisers to find the most efficient location of banners.

Relevance

If a website serves ads unrelated to its viewers' interests, about ¾ of viewers, experience frustration with the website. Advertising efforts must focus on the user's current intention and interest and not just previous searches. Publishing fewer, but more relative, ads is more effective. This can be done with the use of data analytics and campaign management tools to properly separate the viewers and present them ads with relevant content. Information about customers goals and aspirations could be gained through gamification tools which could reward them for providing valuable information that helps segment users according to their interests and helps effective targeting. Interactive ads could be used to make the customers aware of their products. Such tools could be quizzes, calculators, chats', questionnaires. This will further help in understanding the plans of potential customers. Ads should be presented as tips or expert advice, rather than just plain ads.

Social Media

All forms of advertising scored low in the trust factor study by the Nielsen Report on Global Trust in Advertising and Brand Messages from April 2012. But Facebook's "recommendations from people I know" scored highest on the trust factor, with 92 percent of consumers having no problem believing this source. Also, brand websites scored higher than paid advertising but lower than social recommendations. The promotion of product or services through known people piqued interests of users as well as the views of ads much more effective than banner ads. This way advertisers are able to elicit and transfer feelings of safety and trust from friends to the ads shown, thereby validating the ads. The social pressure by the peer group has the ability to not make the users view ads but also encourage them to change attitudes, and consequent behavior in order to adapt to group customs.

Businesses could interact with customers on social media, because not only they spend more time there, but also listen to recommendations from friends and family more than advertisers. Companies could reward customers for recommending products. Digital applications could include features that will allow them to share reviews or feedbacks on social media etc.

Human Action Cycle

The human action cycle is a psychological model which describes the steps humans take when they interact with computer systems. The model was proposed by Donald A. Norman, a scholar in the discipline of human–computer interaction. The model can be used to help evaluate the efficiency of a user interface (UI). Understanding the cycle requires an understanding of the user interface design principles of affordance, feedback, visibility and tolerance.

The human action cycle describes how humans may form goals and then develop a series of steps required to achieve that goal, using the computer system. The user then executes the steps, thus the model includes both cognitive activities and physical activities.

The three Stages of the Human Action Cycle

The model is divided into three stages of seven steps in total, and is (approximately) as follows:

Goal Formation Stage

- Goal formation.

Execution Stage

- Translation of goals into a set of unordered tasks required to achieve goals.

- Sequencing the tasks to create the action sequence.

- Executing the action sequence.

Evaluation Stage

- Perceiving the results after having executed the action sequence.

- Interpreting the actual outcomes based on the expected outcomes.

- Comparing what happened with what the user wished to happen.

Use in Evaluation of user Interfaces

Typically, an evaluator of the user interface will pose a series of questions for each of the cycle's steps, an evaluation of the answer provides useful information about where the user interface may be inadequate or unsuitable. These questions might be:

- Step 1 - Forming a goal:

    ◦ Do the users have sufficient domain and task knowledge and sufficient understanding of their work to form goals?

    ◦ Does the UI help the users form these goals?

- Step 2 - Translating the goal into a task or a set of tasks:

    ◦ Do the users have sufficient domain and task knowledge and sufficient understanding of their work to formulate the tasks?

    ◦ Does the UI help the users formulate these tasks?

- Step 3 - Planning an action sequence:

    ◦ Do the users have sufficient domain and task knowledge and sufficient understanding of their work to formulate the action sequence?

    ◦ Does the UI help the users formulate the action sequence?

- Step 4 - Executing the action sequence:

    ◦ Can typical users easily learn and use the UI?

    ◦ Do the actions provided by the system match those required by the users?

    ◦ Are the affordance and visibility of the actions good?

    ◦ Do the users have an accurate mental model of the system?

    ◦ Does the system support the development of an accurate mental model?

- Step 5 - Perceiving what happened:

  ◦ Can the users perceive the system's state?

  ◦ Does the UI provide the users with sufficient feedback about the effects of their actions?

- Step 6 - Interpreting the outcome according to the users' expectations:

  ◦ Are the users able to make sense of the feedback?

  ◦ Does the UI provide enough feedback for this interpretation?

- Step 7 - Evaluating what happened against what was intended:

  ◦ Can the users compare what happened with what they were hoping to achieve?

Gulfs of Evaluation and Execution

The term 'Gulfs of Evaluation and Execution' were introduced in Norman (1986) and popularised by his book, The Design of Everyday Things (Norman 1988), originally published as The *Psychology* of Everyday Things.

The Gulf of Execution

The gulf of execution is the degree to which the interaction possibilities of an artifact, a computer system or likewise correspond to the intentions of the person and what that person *perceives* is possible to do with the artifact/application/etc. In other words, the gulf of execution is the difference between the intentions of the users and what the system allows them to do or how well the system supports those actions. For example, if a person only wants to record a movie currently being shown with her VCR, she imagines that it requires hitting a 'record' button. But if the necessary action sequence involves specifying the time of recording and selection of a channel there is a gulf of execution: A gap between the psychological language (or mental model) of the user's goals and the very physical action-object language of the controls of the VCR via which it is operated. In the language of the user, the goal of recording the current movie can be achieved by the action sequence "Hit the record button," but in the language of the VCR the correct action sequence is:

- Hit the record button.

- Specify time of recording via the controls X, Y, and Z.

- Select channel via the channel-up-down control.

- Press the OK button.

Thus, to measure or determine the gulf of execution, we may ask how well the action possibilities of the system/artifact match the intended actions of the user.

In the rhetoric of the GOMS model, bridging the gulf of execution means that the user must form intentions, specify action sequences, execute actions, and select the right interface mechanisms (GOMS stands for Goals, Operators, Methods and Selection Rules).

The Gulf of Evaluation

The gulf of evaluation is the degree to which the system/artifact provide representations that can be directly perceived and interpreted in terms of the expectations and intentions of the user. Or put differently, the gulf of evaluation is the difficulty of assessing the state of the system and how well the artifact supports the discovery and interpretation of that state. "The gulf is small when the system provides information about its state in a form that is easy to get, is easy to interpret, and matches the way the person thinks of the system".

Thus, if the system does not "present itself" in a way that lets the user derive which sequence of actions will lead to the intended goal or system state, or derive whether previous actions have moved the user closer to her goal, there is a large gulf of evaluation. In this case, the person must exert a considerable amount of effort and expend significant attentional ressources to interpret the state of the system and derive how well her expectations have been met. In the VCR example from above, the design of the controls of the VCR should thus 'suggest' how to be used and be easily interpretable (e.g. when recording, the 'record' control should signal that is is activated or a display should).

The gulfs of evaluation and of execution refer to the mismatch between our internal goals on the one side, and, on the other side, the expectations and the availability of information specifying the state of the world (or an artifact) and how me may change it.

References

- Jaimes, A. (2006). "Human-centered multimedia: culture, deployment, and access". IEEE Multimedia., 13 (1): 12–19. Doi:10.1109/MMUL.2006.8

- Barfield, mack: yorku.ca, Retrieved 22 February, 2019

- Zimmermann, Andreas; Henze, Niels; Righetti, Xavier; Rukzio, Enrico (2009). Mobile Interaction with the Real World. Mobilehci'09, Article No. 106. Citeseerx 10.1.1.177.2166. Doi:10.1145/1613858.1613980. ISBN 978-1-60558-281-8

- Kullman, Joe (23 August 2011). "Note-Taker device promises to help students overcome visual impairments". ASU Now. Retrieved 28 December 2018

- Gulf-of-evaluation-and-gulf-of-execution, the-glossary-of-human-computer-interaction, book, literature: interaction-design.org, Retrieved 23 March, 2019

- Curedale, Robert (2018). Mapping Methods 2: Step-by-step guide Experience Maps Journey Maps Service Blueprints Affinity Diagrams Empathy Maps Business Model Canvas (2nd ed.). ISBN 978-1940805375

3

User Interface: Types of Elements

In human-computer interaction, the space where the interactions between humans and machines occur is referred to as user interface. The two main types of user interface are natural user interface and graphical user interface. The topics elaborated in this chapter will help in gaining a better understanding about these types of user interface as well as the user interface tools.

The user interface (UI) is the point of human-computer interaction and communication in a device. This can include display screens, keyboards, a mouse and the appearance of a desktop. It is also the way through which a user interacts with an application or a website. The growing dependence of many businesses on web applications and mobile applications has led many companies to place increased priority on UI in an effort to improve the user's overall experience.

Types of User Interfaces

- Graphical user interface (GUI).

- Command line interface (CLI).

- Menu-driven user interface.

- Touch user interface.

- Voice user interface (VUI).

- Form-based user interface.

- Natural language user interface.

Examples of User Interfaces

- Computer mouse.

- Remote control.

- Virtual reality.

- ATMs.

- Speedometer.

- The old iPod click wheel.

Websites such as Airbnb, Dropbox and Virgin America display strong user interface design. Sites like these have created pleasant, easily operable, user-centered designs (UCD) that focus on the user and their needs.

UI and UX

The UI is often talked about in conjunction with user experience (UX), which may include the aesthetic appearance of the device, response time and the content that is presented to the user within the context of the user interface. Both terms fall under the concept of human-computer interaction (HCI), which is the field of study focusing on the creation of computer technology and the interaction between humans and all forms of IT design. Specifically, HCI studies areas such as UCD, UI design and UX design.

An increasing focus on creating an optimized user experience has led some to carve out careers as UI and UX experts. Certain languages, such as HTML and CSS, have been geared toward making it easier to create a strong user interface and experience.

UI

In early computers, there was very little user interface except for a few buttons at an operator's console. Many of these early computers used punched cards, prepared using keypunch machines, as the primary method of input for computer programs and data. While punched cards have been essentially obsolete in computing since 2012, some voting machines still use a punched card system.

The user interface evolved with the introduction of the command line interface, which first appeared as a nearly blank display screen with a line for user input. Users relied on a keyboard and a set of commands to navigate exchanges of information with the computer. This command line interface led to one in which menus predominated.

Finally, the GUI arrived, originating mainly in Xerox's Palo Alto Research Center (PARC), adopted and enhanced by Apple and effectively standardized by Microsoft in its Windows operating systems. Elements of a GUI include such things as windows, pull-down menus, buttons, scroll bars and icons. With the increasing use of multimedia as part of the GUI, sound, voice, motion video and virtual reality are increasingly becoming the GUI for many applications.

The emerging popularity of mobile applications has also affected UI, leading to something called mobile UI. Mobile UI is specifically concerned with creating usable, interactive interfaces on the smaller screens of smartphones and tablets and improving special features, like touch controls.

Mode

In user interface design, a mode is a distinct setting within a computer program or any physical machine interface, in which the same user input will produce perceived results different from those that it would in other settings. The best-known modal interface components are probably the Caps lock and Insert keys on the standard computer keyboard, both of which put the user's typing into a different mode after being pressed, then return it to the regular mode after being re-pressed.

An interface that uses no modes is known as a modeless interface. Modeless interfaces avoid mode errors by making it impossible for the user to commit them.

Examples:

Several examples of well-known software have been described as *modal* and/or using interface modes:

- Text editors: Typically are in insert mode by default but can be toggled in and out of over-type mode by pressing the Insert key.

- vi: Has one mode for inserting text, and a separate mode for entering commands. There is also an "ex" mode for issuing more complex commands (e.g. search and replace). Under normal circumstances, the editor automatically returns to the previous mode after a command has been issued; however, it is possible to permanently move into this mode using *Shift-Q*.

- Emacs: Has the concept of "prefix keys", which trigger a modal state by pressing the control key plus a letter key. Emacs then waits for additional keypresses that complete a keybinding. This differs from *vi* in that the mode always ends as soon as the command is called (when the sequence of key presses that activates it is completed). Emacs also has many "major and minor" modes that change the available commands, and may be automatically invoked based on file type to more easily edit files of that type. Emacs modes are not restricted to editing text files; modes exist for file browsing, web browsing, IRC and email and their interaction patterns are equivalent to application software within the Emacs environment. Modes are written in Emacs Lisp, and all modes may not be included with all versions.

- Cisco IOS: Certain commands are executed in a "command mode".

- Tools chosen from a palette in photo-editing and drawing applications are examples of a modal interface. Some advanced image editors have a feature where the same tools can be accessed nonmodally by a keypress, and remain active as long as the key is held down. Releasing the key returns the interface to the modal tool activated by the palette.

- Video games can use game modes as a mechanic to enhance gameplay.

- Modal windows block all workflow in the top-level program until the modal window is closed.

Mode Errors

Modes are often frowned upon in interface design because they are likely to produce mode errors when the user forgets what state the interface is in, performs an action that is appropriate to a different mode, and gets an unexpected and undesired response. A mode error can be quite startling and disorienting as the user copes with the sudden violation of his or her user expectations.

Problems occur if a change in the system state happens unnoticed (initiated by the system, or by another person, such as the user who was previously using the machine), or if after some time the user forgets about the state change. Another typical problem is a sudden change of state that interrupts a user's activity, such as focus stealing. In such a situation it can easily happen that the user does some operations with the old state in mind, while the brain has not yet fully processed the signals indicating the state change.

A very frustrating type of modality is created by a mode where the user does not find a way out, in other words, where they cannot find how to restore the previous system state.

Examples of Mode Errors

- The most common source of mode errors may be the Caps Lock key. Other common modes available in PC keyboards are Insert and the other lock keys, Num lock and Scroll lock. Dead keys for diacritics also create a short-term mode, at least if they don't provide visual feedback that the next typed character will be modified.

- PC users whose language is not based on the Latin alphabet commonly have to interact using two different keyboard layouts: a local one and QWERTY. This gives rise to mode errors linked to the current keyboard layout: quite often, the synchronization of "current layout" mode between the human and the interface is lost, and text is typed in a layout which is not the intended one, producing meaningless text and confusion. Keyboard keys in UI elements like "(y/n)" can have opposite effect if a program is translated.

- A frequent example is the sudden appearance of a modal error dialog in an application while the user is typing, known as focus stealing; the user expects the typed text to be introduced into a text field, but the unexpected dialog may discard all the input, or may interpret some keystrokes (like "Y" for "yes" and "N" for "no") in a way that the user did not intend.

- The Unix text editor vi can be notoriously difficult for beginners precisely because it uses modes, and because earlier versions configured mode indication to be turned off by default.

- In many computer video games, the keyboard is used both for controlling the game and typing messages. A user may forget they are in "typing mode" as they attempt to react to something sudden in the game and find the controls unresponsive (and instead their text bar full of the command keys pressed).

In Transportation Accidents

- According to the NTSB, one of the factors contributing to Asiana Airlines Flight 214 crash was "the complexities of the autothrottle and autopilot flight director systems which increased the likelihood of mode error".

- Mode confusion was part of the events that led to the loss of Air France Flight 447 in 2009, and the loss of life of 228 people. The pilots reacted to a loss of altitude by pulling on the stick, which would have been an appropriate reaction with the autopilot fully enabled, which would then have put the aircraft in a climbing configuration. However, the airplane's systems had entered a mode of lesser automation ("direct law" in Airbus terms) due to a blocked airspeed sensor, allowing the pilots to put the plane in a nose-high stall configuration, from which they did not recover.

- On January 17, 2015, the offshore supply vessel "Red7 Alliance" collided with a lock gate of the Kiel Canal in Germany, damaging it severely. An investigation concluded that the levers controlling the ship's Azimuth thrusters were not used in a way appropriate to the mode they were set to, resulting in the ship accelerating instead of coming to a stop in the lock.

- On August 21, 2017, the US Navy destroyer USS John S. McCain collided with a commercial tanker in the Strait of Malacca, resulting in the loss of life of ten crew members. An investigation conducted by the US military concluded that immediately prior to the collision, helm and propulsion controls had been redistributed between bridge stations, and the bridge crew was not fully aware of that redistribution.

- On April 10, 2018, the 5000 ton supply vessel *VOS Stone* unberthed from a wind platform under construction in the Baltic Sea. The vessel's master decided to put the steering in an alternative mode to perform a test of the system. Insufficient communication with the officer of the watch led to a temporary loss of control, collision with the platform, injury to three crew members, and significant damage.

Assessment

Modes are intended to grab the user's full attention and to cause them to acknowledge the content present in them, in particular when critical confirmation from the user is required. This later use is criticised as ineffective for its intended use (protection against errors in destructive actions) due to habituation. Actually making the action reversible (providing an "undo" option) is recommended instead. Though modes can be successful in particular usages to restrict dangerous or undesired operations, especially when the mode is actively maintained by a user as a *quasimode*.

Modes are sometimes used to represent information pertinent to the task that doesn't fit well into the main visual flow. Modes can also work as well-understood conventions, such as painting tools.

Modal proponents may argue that many common activities are modal and users adapt to them. An example of modal interaction is that of driving motor vehicles. A driver may be surprised when pressing the acceleration pedal does not accelerate the vehicle in the forward direction, most likely because the vehicle has been placed in an operating mode like park, neutral, or reverse. Modal interfaces require training and experience to avoid mode errors like these.

Interface expert Jef Raskin came out strongly against modes, writing, "Modes are a significant source of errors, confusion, unnecessary restrictions, and complexity in interfaces." Later he notes, "'It is no accident that swearing is denoted by #&%!#$&,' writes my colleague, Dr. James Winter; it is 'what a typewriter used to do when you typed numbers when the Caps Lock was engaged'." Raskin dedicated his book The Humane Interface to describe the principles of a modeless interface for computers. Those principles were implemented in the Canon Cat and Archy systems.

Some interface designers have recently taken steps to make modal windows more obvious and user friendly by darkening the background behind the window or allowing any mouse click outside of the modal window to force the window to close – a design called a Lightbox – thus alleviating the risk of modal errors. Jakob Nielsen states as an advantage of modal dialogs that it improves user awareness. "When something does need fixing, it's better to make sure that the user knows about it." For this goal, the Lightbox design provides strong visual contrast of the dialog over the rest of the visuals. However, while such a method may reduce the risk of inadvertent wrong interactions, it does not solve the problem that the modal window blocks use of the application's normal features and so prevents the user from taking any action to fix the difficulty, or even from scrolling the screen to bring into view information which they need to correctly choose from the options the modal window presents, and it does nothing to alleviate the user's frustration at having blundered into a dead end from which they cannot escape without some more or less destructive consequence.

Larry Tesler, of Xerox PARC and Apple Computer, disliked modes sufficiently to get a personalized license plate for his car that reads: "NO MODES". He has used this plate from the early 1980s to the present, on various cars. Along with others, he has also been using the phrase "Don't Mode Me In" for years as a rally cry to eliminate or reduce modes.

Bruce Wyman, the designer of a multi-touch table for a Denver Art Museum art exhibition argues that interfaces for several simultaneous users must be modeless, in order to avoid bringing any single user into focus.

Design Recommendations

Avoid when Possible

Small signs make explicit the mappings from signal to roads.

Alternatives to modes such as the undo command and the recycle bin are recommended when possible. HCI researcher Donald Norman argues that the best way to avoid mode errors, in addition to clear indications of state, is helping the users to construct an accurate mental model of the system which will allow them to predict the mode accurately.

This is demonstrated, for example, by some stop signs at road intersections. A driver may be conditioned by a four-way stop sign near his or her home to assume that similar intersections will also be four way stops. If it happens to be only two way, the driver could proceed through if he or she sees no other cars. Especially if there is an obstructed view, a car could come though and hit the first car broadside. An improved design alleviates the problem by including a small diagram showing which of the directions have a stop sign and which don't, thus improving the situational awareness of drivers.

Proper Placement

Modal controls are best placed where the focus is in the task flow. For example, a modal window can be placed next to the graphical control element that triggers its activation. Modal controls can be disruptive, so efforts should be made to reduce their capacity to block user work. After completing the task for which the mode was activated, or after a cancel action such as the Escape key, returning to the previous state when a mode is dismissed will reduce the negative impact.

Quasimodes

In the book *The Humane Interface*, Jef Raskin championed what he termed *quasimodes*, which are modes that are kept in place only through some constant action on the part of the user; such modes are also called *spring-loaded modes*.

Modifier keys on the keyboard, such as the Shift key, the Alt key and the Control key, are all examples of a quasimodal interface.

The application enters into that mode as long as the user is performing a conscious action, like pressing a key and keeping it pressed while invoking a command. If the sustaining action is stopped without executing a command, the application returns to a neutral status.

The purported benefit of this technique is that the user doesn't have to remember the current state of the application when invoking a command: the same action will always produce the same perceived result. An interface that uses quasimodes only and has no full modes is still modeless according to Raskin's definition.

The StickyKeys feature turns a quasimode into a mode by serializing keystrokes of modifier keys with normal keys, so that they don't have to be pressed simultaneously. In this case the increased possibility of a mode error is largely compensated for by the improved accessibility for users with physical disabilities.

User Interface Design

User interface design (UI) or user interface engineering is the design of user interfaces for machines and software, such as computers, home appliances, mobile devices, and other electronic devices, with the focus on maximizing usability and the user experience. The goal of user interface design is to make the user's interaction as simple and efficient as possible, in terms of accomplishing user goals (user-centered design).

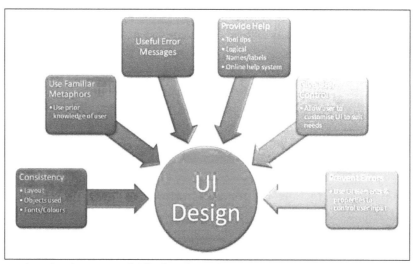

The graphical user interface is presented (displayed) on the computer screen. It is the result of processed user input and usually the primary interface for human-machine interaction. The touch user interfaces popular on small mobile devices are an overlay of the visual output to the visual input.

Good user interface design facilitates finishing the task at hand without drawing unnecessary attention to itself. Graphic design and typography are utilized to support its usability, influencing how the user performs certain interactions and improving the aesthetic appeal of the design; design aesthetics may enhance or detract from the ability of users to use the functions of the interface. The design process must balance technical functionality and visual elements (e.g., mental model) to create a system that is not only operational but also usable and adaptable to changing user needs.

Interface design is involved in a wide range of projects from computer systems, to cars, to commercial planes; all of these projects involve much of the same basic human interactions yet also require some unique skills and knowledge. As a result, designers tend to specialize in certain types of projects and have skills centered on their expertise, whether it is a software design, user research, web design, or industrial design.

Processes

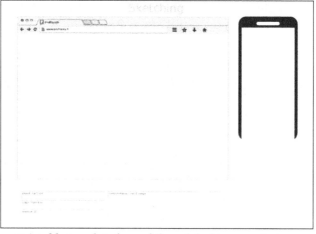

Printable template for mobile and desktop app design.

User interface design requires a good understanding of user needs. There are several phases and processes in the user interface design, some of which are more demanded upon than others, depending on the project, the word system is used to denote any project whether it is a website, application, or device.)

- Functionality requirements gathering: Assembling a list of the functionality required by the system to accomplish the goals of the project and the potential needs of the users.

- User and task analysis: A form of field research, it's the analysis of the potential users of the system by studying how they perform the tasks that the design must support, and conducting interviews to elucidate their goals. Typical questions involve:

  ◦ What would the user want the system to do?

  ◦ How would the system fit in with the user's normal workflow or daily activities?

  ◦ How technically savvy is the user and what similar systems does the user already use?

  ◦ What interface look & feel styles appeal to the user?

- Information architecture: Development of the process and/or information flow of the system (i.e. for phone tree systems, this would be an option tree flowchart and for web sites this would be a site flow that shows the hierarchy of the pages).

- Prototyping: Development of wire-frames, either in the form of paper prototypes or simple interactive screens. These prototypes are stripped of all look & feel elements and most content in order to concentrate on the interface.

- Usability inspection: Letting an evaluator inspect a user interface. This is generally considered to be cheaper to implement than usability testing, and can be used early on in the development process since it can be used to evaluate prototypes or specifications for the system, which usually cannot be tested on users. Some common usability inspection methods include cognitive walkthrough, which focuses the simplicity to accomplish tasks with the system for new users, heuristic evaluation, in which a set of heuristics are used to identify usability problems in the UI design, and pluralistic walkthrough, in which a selected group of people step through a task scenario and discuss usability issues.

- Usability testing: Testing of the prototypes on an actual user—often using a technique called think aloud protocol where you ask the user to talk about their thoughts during the experience. User interface design testing allows the designer to understand the reception of the design from the viewer's standpoint, and thus facilitates creating successful applications.

- Graphical user interface design: Actual look and feel design of the final graphical user interface (GUI). These are design's control panels and faces; voice-controlled interfaces involve oral-auditory interaction, while gesture-based interfaces witness users engaging with 3D design spaces via bodily motions. It may be based on the findings developed during the user research, and refined to fix any usability problems found through the results of testing.

Depending on the type of interface being created, this process typically involves some computer programming in order to validate forms, establish links or perform a desired action.

- Software Maintenance: After the deployment of a new interface, occasional maintenance may be required to fix software bugs, change features, or completely upgrade the system. Once a decision is made to upgrade the interface, the legacy system will undergo another version of the design process, and will begin to repeat the stages of the interface life cycle.

Requirements

The dynamic characteristics of a system are described in terms of the dialogue requirements contained in seven principles of part 10 of the ergonomics standard, the ISO 9241. This standard establishes a framework of ergonomic "principles" for the dialogue techniques with high-level definitions and illustrative applications and examples of the principles. The principles of the dialogue represent the dynamic aspects of the interface and can be mostly regarded as the "feel" of the interface. The seven dialogue principles are:

- Suitability for the task: The dialogue is suitable for a task when it supports the user in the effective and efficient completion of the task.

- Self-descriptiveness: The dialogue is self-descriptive when each dialogue step is immediately comprehensible through feedback from the system or is explained to the user on request.

- Controllability: The dialogue is controllable when the user is able to initiate and control the direction and pace of the interaction until the point at which the goal has been met.

- Conformity with user expectations: The dialogue conforms with user expectations when it is consistent and corresponds to the user characteristics, such as task knowledge, education, experience, and to commonly accepted conventions.

- Error tolerance: The dialogue is error tolerant if despite evident errors in input, the intended result may be achieved with either no or minimal action by the user.

- Suitability for individualization: The dialogue is capable of individualization when the interface software can be modified to suit the task needs, individual preferences, and skills of the user.

- Suitability for learning: The dialogue is suitable for learning when it supports and guides the user in learning to use the system.

The concept of usability is defined of the ISO 9241 standard by effectiveness, efficiency, and satisfaction of the user. Part 11 gives the following definition of usability:

- Usability is measured by the extent to which the intended goals of use of the overall system are achieved (effectiveness).

- The resources that have to be expended to achieve the intended goals (efficiency).

- The extent to which the user finds the overall system acceptable (satisfaction).

Effectiveness, efficiency, and satisfaction can be seen as quality factors of usability. To evaluate these factors, they need to be decomposed into sub-factors, and finally, into usability measures.

The information presentation is described in Part 12 of the ISO 9241 standard for the organization of information (arrangement, alignment, grouping, labels, location), for the display of graphical objects, and for the coding of information (abbreviation, color, size, shape, visual cues) by seven attributes. The "attributes of presented information" represent the static aspects of the interface and can be generally regarded as the "look" of the interface. The attributes are detailed in the recommendations given in the standard. Each of the recommendations supports one or more of the seven attributes. The seven presentation attributes are:

- Clarity: The information content is conveyed quickly and accurately.

- Discriminability: The displayed information can be distinguished accurately.

- Conciseness: Users are not overloaded with extraneous information.

- Consistency: A unique design, conformity with user's expectation.

- Detectability: The user's attention is directed towards information required.

- Legibility: Information is easy to read.

- Comprehensibility: The meaning is clearly understandable, unambiguous, interpretable, and recognizable.

The user guidance in Part 13 of the ISO 9241 standard describes that the user guidance information should be readily distinguishable from other displayed information and should be specific for the current context of use. User guidance can be given by the following five means:

- Prompts indicating explicitly (specific prompts) or implicitly (generic prompts) that the system is available for input.

- Feedback informing about the user's input timely, perceptible, and non-intrusive.

- Status information indicating the continuing state of the application, the system's hardware and software components, and the user's activities.

- Error management including error prevention, error correction, user support for error management, and error messages.

- On-line help for system-initiated and user initiated requests with specific information for the current context of use.

Command Line Interface

A command line interface (CLI) is a text-based user interface (UI) used to view and manage computer files. Command line interfaces are also called command-line user interfaces, console user interfaces and character user interfaces.

Before the mouse, users interacted with an operating system (OS) or application with a keyboard. Users typed commands in the command line interface to run tasks on a computer.

Typically, the command line interface features a black box with white text. The user responds to a prompt in the command line interface by typing a command. The output or response from the system can include a message, table, list, or some other confirmation of a system or application action.

Today, most users prefer the graphical user interface (GUI) offered by operating systems such as Windows, Linux and macOS. Most current Unix-based systems offer both a command line interface and a graphical user interface.

The MS-DOS operating system and the command shell in the Windows operating system are examples of command line interfaces. In addition, programming languages can support command line interfaces, such as Python.

An Explanation of a Shell

The software that handles the command line interface is the shell, also commonly referred to as a command language interpreter. Two well-known shells are Windows shell and Bash for Linux and macOS.

Shells are the outermost layer of the OS and are often separated from the underlying OS kernel. A shell operates like an application and can be replaced. Because the shell is only one layer above the OS, users can perform operations that are not available in other interface types, such as moving files within system folders and deleting locked files.

Shells require users to know the syntax of a scripting language. Most command line shells save sequences of commands for reuse in a script, which is the foundation of basic systems management automation.

Prompts and Commands

There are hundreds of different commands available in a command line. The set of commands may vary dramatically between operating systems or applications.

The following is a list of commands in the Microsoft task configuration and automation framework PowerShell:

- Get-Date: Retrieves the current time and date.

- cd: Used to change directories.

- Stop-Process: Terminates one or more system processes.

Although some commands operate alone, others require the use of arguments. The argument follows the command and provides additional details or specifics. For example, the cd command tells the OS to change to a different directory, but the command line must include the name of the desired directory path, as well.

For example, a full command with an argument appears as:

```
cd \documents\user
```

The arguments used with commands can also be extremely complex and granular. For example, the following command line string shows the PowerShell syntax to retrieve detailed network configuration information from a Windows machine:

```
Get-NetIPAddress | Sort InterfaceIndex | FT InterfaceIndex, InterfaceAlias, AddressFamily, IPAddress, PrefixLength -Autosize
```

CLI versus GUI

The graphical user interface is the most popular user interface today. A GUI uses windows, menus and icons to execute commands. A mouse is the most common way to navigate through a GUI, although many GUIs allow navigation and execution via a keyboard.

One example of a GUI-based application is Microsoft Word. A user can change options for page layouts and styles by selecting the corresponding icon with a mouse or keyboard.

An example of output from the PowerShell command line.

The advantage of a GUI is the interface visually displays the available functions. However, because of its simplicity and ease of use, a GUI does not have the same level of functionality and granular control as a command line interface. For example, it may take numerous clicks and movement through several dialog boxes in a GUI to accomplish the same result as a single command line.

In addition, GUIs do not readily support scripting or automation. For common tasks, a user must repeat each click or navigate each dialog within the GUI manually.

Administrators who manage thousands of systems or user configurations will find a GUI far less efficient than a CLI. But a simple CLI command can easily adjust configurations for a large group of systems at once.

Commands and arguments can also be combined and saved, then executed as a script each time that specific action or comprehensive set of actions is required. The CLI is the preferred tool for many enterprise-wide systems management tasks.

CLI Advantages and Disadvantages

The advantages of a command line interface are:

- Granular control of an OS or application.

- Faster management of a large number of operating systems.

- Ability to store scripts to automate regular tasks.

- Basic command line interface knowledge to help with troubleshooting, such as network connection issues.

The disadvantages of a command line interface are:

- GUI is more user-friendly.

- Steeper learning curve associated with memorizing commands and complex syntax/arguments.

- Different commands used in different shells.

User Interface Tools

User interface tools have been called various names over the years, with the most popular being User Interface Management Systems (UIMS). However, many people feel that the term UIMS should be used only for tools that handle the sequencing of operations (what happens after each event from the user), so other terms like Toolkits, User Interface Development Environments, Interface Builders, Interface Development Tools, and Application Frameworks have been used. This paper will try to define these terms more specifically, and use the general term "user interface tool" for all software aimed to help create user interfaces. Note that the word "tool" is being used to include what are called "toolkits," as well as higher-level tools, such as Interface Builders, that are not toolkits.

Four different classes of people are involved with user interface software, and it is important to have different names for them to avoid confusion. The first is the person using the resulting program, who is called the end user or just user. The next person creates the user interface of the program, and is called the user interface designer or just designer. Working with the user interface designer will be the person who writes the software for the rest of the application. This person is called the application programmer. The designer may use special user interface tools which are provided to help create user interfaces. These tools are created by the tool creator. Note that the designer will be a user of the software created by the tool creator, but we still do not use the term "user" here to avoid confusion with the end user. Although this classification discusses each role as a different person, in fact, there may be many people in each role or one person may perform multiple roles. The general term programmer is used for anyone who writes code, and may be a designer, application programmer, or tool creator.

Importance of User Interface Tools

There are many advantages to using user interface software tools. These can be classified into two main groups:

- The quality of the interfaces will be higher. This is because:

  ◦ Designs can be rapidly prototyped and implemented, possibly even before the application code is written.

  ◦ It is easier to incorporate changes discovered through user testing.

  ◦ There can be multiple user interfaces for the same application.

  ◦ More effort can be expended on the tool than may be practical on any single user interface since the tool will be used with many different applications.

  ◦ Different applications are more likely to have consistent user interfaces if they are created using the same user interface tool.

  ◦ It will be easier for a variety of specialists to be involved in designing the user interface, rather than having the user interface created entirely by programmers. Graphic artists, cognitive psychologists, and human factors specialists may all be involved. In particular, professional user interface designers, who may not be programmers, can be in charge of the overall design.

- The user interface code will be easier and more economical to create and maintain. This is because:

  ◦ Interface specifications can be represented, validated, and evaluated more easily.

  ◦ There will be less code to write, because much is supplied by the tools.

  ◦ There will be better modularization due to the separation of the user interface component from the application. This should allow the user interface to change without affecting the application, and a large class of changes to the application (such as changing the internal algorithms) should be possible without affecting the user interface.

  ◦ The level of programming expertise of the interface designers and implementors can be lower, because the tools hide much of the complexities of the underlying system.

  ◦ The reliability of the user interface will be higher, since the code for the user interface is created automatically from a higher level specification.

  ◦ It will be easier to port an application to different hardware and software environments since the device dependencies are isolated in the user interface tool.

Based on these goals for user interface software tools, we can list a number of important functions that should be provided. This list can be used to evaluate the various tools to see how much they cover. Naturally, no tool will help with everything, and different user interface designers may put different emphasis on the different features.

In general, the tools might:

- Help design the interface given a specification of the end users' tasks.

- Help implement the interface given a specification of the design.

- Help evaluate the interface after it is designed and propose improvements, or at least provide information to allow the designer to evaluate the interface.

- Create easy-to-use interfaces.

- Allow the designer to rapidly investigate different designs.

- Allow non-programmers to design and implement user interfaces.

- Allow the end user to customize the interface.

- Provide portability.

- Be easy to use themselves.

This might be achieved by having the tools:

- Automatically choose which user interface styles, input devices, widgets, etc. should be used.

- Help with screen layout and graphic design.

- Validate user inputs.

- Handle user errors.

- Handle aborting and undoing of operations.

- Provide appropriate feedback to show that inputs have been received.

- Provide help and prompts.

- Update the screen display when application data changes.

- Notify the application when the user updates application data.

- Deal with field scrolling and editing.

- Help with the sequencing of operations.

- Insulate the application from all device dependencies and the underlying software and hardware systems.

- Provide customization facilities to end users.

- Evaluate the graphic design and layout, usability, and learnability of the interface.

User Interface Software Tools

Since, user interface software is so difficult to create, it is not surprising that people have been working for a long time to create tools to help with it. Today, many of these tools and ideas have progressed from research into commercial systems, and their effectiveness has been amply demonstrated. Research systems also continue to evolve quickly, and the models that were popular five years ago have been made obsolete by more effective tools, changes in the computer market (e.g., the demise of OpenLook will take with it a number of tools), and the emergence of new styles of user interfaces such as pen-based computing and multi-media.

Components of User Interface Software

As shown in table below, user interface software may be divided into various layers: the windowing system, the toolkit and higher-level tools. Of course, many practical systems span multiple layers.

Table: The components of user interface software.

Application
Higher-level Tools
Toolkit
Windowing System
Operating System

The windowing system supports the separation of the screen into different (usually rectangular) regions, called windows. The X system divides the window functionality into two layers: the window system, which is the functional or programming interface, and the window manager which is the user interface. Thus the "window system" provides procedures that allow the application to draw pictures on the screen and get input from the user, and the "window manager" allows the end user to move windows around, and is responsible for displaying the title lines, borders and icons around the windows. However, many people and systems use the name "window manager" to refer to both layers, since systems such as the Macintosh and Microsoft Windows do not separate them. This article will use the X terminology, and use the term "windowing system" when referring to both layers.

On top of the windowing system is the toolkit, which contains many commonly used widgets such as menus, buttons, scroll bars, and text input fields. On top of the toolkit might be higher-level tools, which help the designer use the toolkit widgets.

Natural User Interface

In computing, a natural user interface, or NUI, or natural interface is a user interface that is effectively invisible, and remains invisible as the user continuously learns increasingly complex interactions. The word natural is used because most computer interfaces use artificial control devices whose operation has to be learned.

An NUI relies on a user being able to quickly transition from novice to expert. While the interface requires learning, that learning is eased through design which gives the user the feeling that they are instantly and continuously successful. Thus, "natural" refers to a goal in the user experience – that the interaction comes naturally, while interacting with the technology, rather than that the interface itself is natural. This is contrasted with the idea of an intuitive interface, referring to one that can be used without previous learning.

Several design strategies have been proposed which have met this goal to varying degrees of success. One strategy is the use of a "reality user interface" ("RUI"), also known as "reality-based interfaces" (RBI) methods. One example of an RUI strategy is to use a wearable computer to render real-world objects "clickable", i.e. so that the wearer can click on any everyday object so as to make it function as a hyperlink, thus merging cyberspace and the real world. Because the term "natural" is evocative of the "natural world", RBI are often confused for NUI, when in fact they are merely one means of achieving it.

One example of a strategy for designing a NUI not based in RBI is the strict limiting of functionality and customization, so that users have very little to learn in the operation of a device. Provided that the default capabilities match the user's goals, the interface is effortless to use. This is an overarching design strategy in Apple's iOS. Because this design is coincident with a direct-touch display, non-designers commonly misattribute the effortlessness of interacting with the device to that multi-touch display, and not to the design of the software where it actually resides.

Evolution of user interfaces.

In the 1990s, Steve Mann developed a number of user-interface strategies using natural interaction with the real world as an alternative to a command-line interface (CLI) or graphical user interface (GUI). Mann referred to this work as "natural user interfaces", "Direct User Interfaces", and "metaphor-free computing". Mann's EyeTap technology typically embodies an example of a natural user interface. Mann's use of the word "Natural" refers to both action that comes naturally to human users, as well as the use of nature itself, i.e. physics (*Natural Philosophy*), and the natural environment. A good example of an NUI in both these senses is the hydraulophone, especially when it is used as an input device, in which touching a natural element (water) becomes a way of inputting data.

In 2006, Christian Moore established an open research community with the goal to expand discussion and development related to NUI technologies. In a 2008, conference presentation "Predicting the Past," August de los Reyes, a Principal User Experience Director of Surface Computing at Microsoft described the NUI as the next evolutionary phase following the shift from the CLI to the GUI. Of course, this too is an over-simplification, since NUIs necessarily include visual elements – and thus, graphical user interfaces. A more accurate description of this concept would be to describe it as a transition from WIMP to NUI.

In the CLI, users had to learn an artificial means of input, the keyboard, and a series of codified inputs, that had a limited range of responses, where the syntax of those commands was strict.

Then, when the mouse enabled the GUI, users could more easily learn the mouse movements and actions, and were able to explore the interface much more. The GUI relied on metaphors for interacting with on-screen content or objects. The 'desktop' and 'drag' for example, being metaphors for a visual interface that ultimately was translated back into the strict codified language of the computer.

An example of the misunderstanding of the term NUI was demonstrated at the Consumer Electronics Show in 2010. "Now a new wave of products is poised to bring natural user interfaces, as these methods of controlling electronics devices are called, to an even broader audience."

In 2010, Microsoft's Bill Buxton reiterated the importance of the NUI within Microsoft Corporation with a video discussing technologies which could be used in creating a NUI, and its future potential.

In 2010, Daniel Wigdor and Dennis Wixon provided an operationalization of building natural user interfaces in their book. In it, they carefully distinguish between natural user interfaces, the technologies used to achieve them, and reality-based UI.

Examples of Interfaces Commonly Referred to as NUI

Perceptive Pixel

One example is the work done by Jefferson Han on multi-touch interfaces. In a demonstration at TED in 2006, he showed a variety of means of interacting with on-screen content using both direct manipulations and gestures. For example, to shape an on-screen glutinous mass, Jeff literally 'pinches' and prods and pokes it with his fingers. In a GUI interface for a design application for example, a user would use the metaphor of 'tools' to do this, for example, selecting a prod tool, or selecting two parts of the mass that they then wanted to apply a 'pinch' action to. Han showed that user interaction could be much more intuitive by doing away with the interaction devices that we are used to and replacing them with a screen that was capable of detecting a much wider range of human actions and gestures. Of course, this allows only for a very limited set of interactions which map neatly onto physical manipulation (RBI). Extending the capabilities of the software beyond physical actions requires significantly more design work.

Microsoft PixelSense

Microsoft PixelSense takes similar ideas on how users interact with content, but adds in the ability for the device to optically recognize objects placed on top of it. In this way, users can trigger actions on the computer through the same gestures and motions as Jeff Han's touchscreen allowed, but also objects become a part of the control mechanisms. So for example, when you place a wine glass on the table, the computer recognizes it as such and displays content associated with that wine glass. Placing a wine glass on a table maps well onto actions taken with wine glasses and other tables, and thus maps well onto reality-based interfaces. Thus, it could be seen as an entrée to a NUI experience.

3D Immersive Touch

"3D Immersive Touch" is defined as the direct manipulation of 3D virtual environment objects using single or multi-touch surface hardware in multi-user 3D virtual environments. Coined first in 2007 to describe and define the 3D natural user interface learning principles associated with Edusim. Immersive Touch natural user interface now appears to be taking on a broader focus and meaning with the broader adaption of surface and touch driven hardware such as the iPhone, iPod touch, iPad, and a growing list of other hardware. Apple also seems to be taking a keen interest in "Immersive Touch" 3D natural user interfaces over the past few years. This work builds atop the broad academic base which has studied 3D manipulation in virtual reality environments.

Xbox Kinect

Kinect is a motion sensing input device by Microsoft for the Xbox 360 video game console and Windows PCs that uses spatial gestures for interaction instead of a game controller. Kinect is designed for "a revolutionary new way to play: no controller required.". Again, because Kinect allows the sensing of the physical world, it shows potential for RBI designs, and thus potentially also for NUI.

Natural-language User Interface

Natural-language user interface (LUI or NLUI) is a type of computer human interface where linguistic phenomena such as verbs, phrases and clauses act as UI controls for creating, selecting and modifying data in software applications.

In interface design, natural-language interfaces are sought after for their speed and ease of use, but most suffer the challenges to understanding wide varieties of ambiguous input. Natural-language interfaces are an active area of study in the field of natural-language processing and computational linguistics. An intuitive general natural-language interface is one of the active goals of the Semantic Web.

Text interfaces are "natural" to varying degrees. Many formal (un-natural) programming languages incorporate idioms of natural human language. Likewise, a traditional keyword search engine could be described as a "shallow" natural-language user interface.

A natural-language search engine would in theory find targeted answers to user questions (as opposed to keyword search). For example, when confronted with a question of the form 'which U.S. state has the highest income tax?', conventional search engines ignore the question and instead search on the keywords 'state', 'income' and 'tax'. Natural-language search, on the other hand, attempts to use natural-language processing to understand the nature of the question and then to search and return a subset of the web that contains the answer to the question. If it works, results would have a higher relevance than results from a keyword search engine.

Challenges

Natural-language interfaces have in the past led users to anthropomorphize the computer, or at least to attribute more intelligence to machines than is warranted. On the part of the user, this has led to unrealistic expectations of the capabilities of the system. Such expectations will make it difficult to learn the restrictions of the system if users attribute too much capability to it, and will ultimately lead to disappointment when the system fails to perform as expected as was the case in the AI winter of the 1970s and 80s.

A 1995 paper titled 'Natural Language Interfaces to Databases – An Introduction', describes some challenges:

Modifier Attachment

The request "List all employees in the company with a driving licence" is ambiguous unless you know that companies can't have driving licences.

Conjunction and Disjunction

"List all applicants who live in California and Arizona" is ambiguous unless you know that a person can't live in two places at once.

Anaphora Resolution

Resolve what a user means by 'he', 'she' or 'it', in a self-referential query.

Other goals to consider more generally are the speed and efficiency of the interface, in all algorithms these two points are the main point that will determine if some methods are better than others and therefore have greater success in the market. In addition, localisation across multiple language sites requires extra consideration - this is based on differing sentence structure and language syntax variations between most languages.

Finally, regarding the methods used, the main problem to be solved is creating a general algorithm that can recognize the entire spectrum of different voices, while disregarding nationality, gender or age. The significant differences between the extracted features - even from speakers who says the same word or phrase - must be successfully overcome.

Uses and Applications

The natural-language interface gives rise to technology used for many different applications.

Some of the main uses are:

- Dictation: Is the most common use for automated speech recognition (ASR) systems today. This includes medical transcriptions, legal and business dictation, and general word processing. In some cases special vocabularies are used to increase the accuracy of the system.

- Command and control: ASR systems that are designed to perform functions and actions on the system are defined as command and control systems. Utterances like "Open Netscape" and "Start a new xterm" will do just that.

- Telephony: Some PBX/Voice Mail systems allow callers to speak commands instead of pressing buttons to send specific tones.

- Wearables: Because inputs are limited for wearable devices, speaking is a natural possibility.

- Medical, disabilities: Many people have difficulty typing due to physical limitations such as repetitive strain injuries (RSI), muscular dystrophy, and many others. For example, people with difficulty hearing could use a system connected to their telephone to convert a caller's speech to text.

- Embedded applications: Some new cellular phones include C&C speech recognition that allow utterances such as "call home". This may be a major factor in the future of automatic speech recognition and Linux.

- Software development: An integrated development environment can embed natural-language interfaces to help developers.

Below are named and defined some of the applications that use natural-language recognition, and so have integrated utilities listed above.

Ubiquity

Ubiquity, an add-on for Mozilla Firefox, is a collection of quick and easy natural-language-derived commands that act as mashups of web services, thus allowing users to get information and relate it to current and other webpages.

Wolfram Alpha

Wolfram Alpha is an online service that answers factual queries directly by computing the answer from structured data, rather than providing a list of documents or web pages that might contain the answer as a search engine would. It was announced in March 2009 by Stephen Wolfram, and was released to the public on May 15, 2009.

Siri

Siri is an intelligent personal assistant application integrated with operating system iOS. The application uses natural language processing to answer questions and make recommendations.

Siri's marketing claims include that it adapts to a user's individual preferences over time and personalizes results, and performs tasks such as making dinner reservations while trying to catch a cab.

Others

- Ask.com: The original idea behind Ask Jeeves (Ask.com) was traditional keyword searching with an ability to get answers to questions posed in everyday, natural language. The current Ask.com still supports this, with added support for math, dictionary, and conversion questions.

- Braina: Braina is a natural language interface for Windows OS that allows to type or speak English language sentences to perform a certain action or find information.

Screenshot of GNOME DO classic interface.

- GNOME Do: Allows for quick finding miscellaneous artifacts of GNOME environment (applications, Evolution and Pidgin contacts, Firefox bookmarks, Rhythmbox artists and albums, and so on) and execute the basic actions on them (launch, open, email, chat, play, etc.).

- Hakia: Hakia was an Internet search engine. The company invented an alternative new infrastructure to indexing that used SemanticRank algorithm, a solution mix from the disciplines of ontological semantics, fuzzy logic, computational linguistics, and mathematics. hakia closed in 2014.

- Lexxe: Lexxe was an Internet search engine that used natural-language processing for queries (semantic search). Searches could be made with keywords, phrases, and questions, such as "How old is india?" Lexxe closed its search engine services in 2015.

- Pikimal: Pikimal used natural-language tied to user preference to make search recommendations by template. Pikimal closed in 2015.

- Powerset: On May 11, 2008, the company unveiled a tool for searching a fixed subset of data using conversational phrases rather than keywords. On July 1, 2008, it was purchased by Microsoft.

- Q-go: The Q-go technology provides relevant answers to users in response to queries on a company's internet website or corporate intranet, formulated in natural sentences or keyword input alike. Q-go was acquired by RightNow Technologies in 2011.

- Yebol: Yebol is a vertical "decision" search engine that had developed a knowledge-based, semantic search platform. Yebol's artificial intelligence human intelligence-infused algorithms automatically cluster and categorize search results, web sites, pages and content that it presents in a visually indexed format that is more aligned with initial human intent. Yebol uses association, ranking and clustering algorithms to analyze related keywords or web pages. Yebol integrates natural-language processing, metasynthetic-engineered open complex systems, and machine algorithms with human knowledge for each query to establish a web directory that actually 'learns', using correlation, clustering and classification algorithms to automatically generate the knowledge query, which is retained and regenerated forward.

Graphical User Interface

The graphical user interface is a form of user interface that allows users to interact with electronic devices through graphical icons and visual indicators such as secondary notation, instead of text-based user interfaces, typed command labels or text navigation. GUIs were introduced in reaction to the perceived steep learning curve of command-line interfaces (CLIs), which require commands to be typed on a computer keyboard.

The actions in a GUI are usually performed through direct manipulation of the graphical elements. Beyond computers, GUIs are used in many handheld mobile devices such as MP3 players, portable media players, gaming devices, smartphones and smaller household, office and industrial controls. The term *GUI* tends not to be applied to other lower-display resolution types of interfaces, such as video games (where *head-up display* (HUD) is preferred), or not including flat screens, like volumetric displays because the term is restricted to the scope of two-dimensional display screens able to describe generic information, in the tradition of the computer science research at the Xerox Palo Alto Research Center.

User Interface and Interaction Design

Graphical User Interface.

Designing the visual composition and temporal behavior of a GUI is an important part of software application programming in the area of human–computer interaction. Its goal is to enhance the efficiency and ease of use for the underlying logical design of a stored program, a design discipline named *usability*. Methods of user-centered design are used to ensure that the visual language introduced in the design is well-tailored to the tasks.

The visible graphical interface features of an application are sometimes referred to as *chrome* or *GUI*. Typically, users interact with information by manipulating visual widgets that allow for interactions appropriate to the kind of data they hold. The widgets of a well-designed interface are selected to support the actions necessary to achieve the goals of users. A model–view–controller allows flexible structures in which the interface is independent from and indirectly linked to application functions, so the GUI can be customized easily. This allows users to select or design a different *skin* at will, and eases the designer's work to change the interface as user needs evolve. Good user interface design relates to users more, and to system architecture less. Large widgets, such as windows, usually provide a frame or container for the main presentation content such as a web page, email message or drawing. Smaller ones usually act as a user-input tool.

A GUI may be designed for the requirements of a vertical market as application-specific graphical user interfaces. Examples include automated teller machines (ATM), point of sale (POS) touchscreens at restaurants, self-service checkouts used in a retail store, airline self-ticketing and check-in, information kiosks in a public space, like a train station or a museum, and monitors or control screens in an embedded industrial application which employ a real-time operating system (RTOS).

By the 1980s, cell phones and handheld game systems also employed application specific touchscreen GUIs. Newer automobiles use GUIs in their navigation systems and multimedia centers, or navigation multimedia center combinations.

Examples: Sample graphical desktop environments.

GNOME Shell.

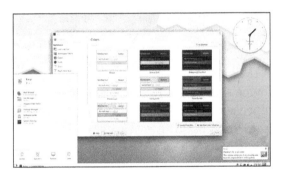
KDE Plasma 5.

MATE.

Windows on example Wayland compositor.

Components

A GUI uses a combination of technologies and devices to provide a platform that users can interact with, for the tasks of gathering and producing information.

A series of elements conforming a visual language have evolved to represent information stored in computers. This makes it easier for people with few computer skills to work with and use computer software. The most common combination of such elements in GUIs is the *windows, icons, menus, pointer* (WIMP) paradigm, especially in personal computers.

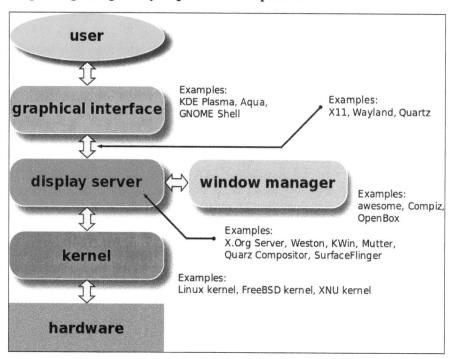

Layers of a GUI based on a windowing system.

The WIMP style of interaction uses a virtual input device to represent the position of a pointing device's interface, most often a mouse, and presents information organized in windows and represented with icons. Available commands are compiled together in menus, and actions are performed making gestures with the pointing device. A window manager facilitates the interactions between windows, applications, and the windowing system. The windowing system handles hardware devices such as pointing devices, graphics hardware, and positioning of the pointer.

In personal computers, all these elements are modeled through a desktop metaphor to produce a simulation called a desktop environment in which the display represents a desktop, on which documents and folders of documents can be placed. Window managers and other software combine to simulate the desktop environment with varying degrees of realism.

Post-WIMP Interface

Smaller mobile devices such as personal digital assistants (PDAs) and smartphones typically use the WIMP elements with different unifying metaphors, due to constraints in space and available input devices. Applications for which WIMP is not well suited may use newer interaction techniques, collectively termed *post-WIMP* user interfaces.

As of 2011, some touchscreen-based operating systems such as Apple's iOS (iPhone) and Android use the class of GUIs named post-WIMP. These support styles of interaction using more than one finger in contact with a display, which allows actions such as pinching and rotating, which are un-supported by one pointer and mouse.

Interaction

Human interface devices, for the efficient interaction with a GUI include a computer keyboard, especially used together with keyboard shortcuts, pointing devices for the cursor (or rather pointer) control: mouse, pointing stick, touchpad, trackball, joystick, virtual keyboards, and head-up displays (translucent information devices at the eye level).

There are also actions performed by programs that affect the GUI. For example, there are components like inotify or D-Bus to facilitate communication between computer programs.

Comparison to other Interfaces

Command-line Interfaces

A modern CLI.

Since the commands available in command line interfaces can be many, complex operations can be performed using a short sequence of words and symbols. This allows greater efficiency and productivity once many commands are learned, but reaching this level takes some time because the command words may not be easily discoverable or mnemonic. Also, using the command line can become slow and error-prone when users must enter long commands comprising many parameters or several different filenames at once. However, *windows, icons, menus, pointer* (WIMP) interfaces present users with many widgets that represent and can trigger some of the system's available commands.

GUIs can be made quite hard when dialogs are buried deep in a system, or moved about to different places during redesigns. Also, icons and dialog boxes are usually harder for users to script.

WIMPs extensively use modes, as the meaning of all keys and clicks on specific positions on the screen are redefined all the time. Command line interfaces use modes only in limited forms, such as for current directory and environment variables.

Most modern operating systems provide both a GUI and some level of a CLI, although the GUIs usually receive more attention. The GUI is usually WIMP-based, although occasionally other metaphors surface, such as those used in Microsoft Bob, 3dwm, or File System Visualizer.

GUI Wrappers

Graphical user interface (GUI) wrappers find a way around the command-line interface versions (CLI) of (typically) Linux and Unix-like software applications and their text-based user interfaces or typed command labels. While command-line or text-based application allow users to run a program non-interactively, GUI wrappers atop them avoid the steep learning curve of the command-line, which requires commands to be typed on the keyboard. By starting a GUI wrapper, users can intuitively interact with, start, stop, and change its working parameters, through graphical icons and visual indicators of a desktop environment, for example. Applications may also provide both interfaces, and when they do the GUI is usually a WIMP wrapper around the command-line version. This is especially common with applications designed for Unix-like operating systems. The latter used to be implemented first because it allowed the developers to focus exclusively on their product's functionality without bothering about interface details such as designing icons and placing buttons. Designing programs this way also allows users to run the program in a shell script.

Three-dimensional user Interfaces

For typical computer displays, *three-dimensional* is a misnomer—their displays are two-dimensional. Semantically, however, most graphical user interfaces use three dimensions. With height and width, they offer a third dimension of layering or stacking screen elements over one another. This may be represented visually on screen through an illusionary transparent effect, which offers the advantage that information in background windows may still be read, if not interacted with. Or the environment may simply hide the background information, possibly making the distinction apparent by drawing a drop shadow effect over it.

Some environments use the methods of 3D graphics to project virtual three dimensional user interface objects onto the screen. These are often shown in use in science fiction films. As the processing power of computer graphics hardware increases, this becomes less of an obstacle to a smooth user experience.

Three-dimensional graphics are currently mostly used in computer games, art, and computer-aided design (CAD). A three-dimensional computing environment can also be useful in other uses, like molecular graphics, aircraft design and Phase Equilibrium Calculations/Design of unit operations and chemical processes.

Several attempts have been made to create a multi-user three-dimensional environment, including the Croquet Project and Sun's Project Looking Glass.

Technologies

The use of three-dimensional graphics has become increasingly common in mainstream operating systems, from creating attractive interfaces, termed eye candy, to functional purposes only possible using three dimensions. For example, user switching is represented by rotating a cube which faces are each user's workspace, and window management is represented via a Rolodex-style flipping mechanism in Windows Vista. In both cases, the operating system transforms windows on-the-fly while continuing to update the content of those windows.

Interfaces for the X Window System have also implemented advanced three-dimensional user interfaces through compositing window managers such as Beryl, Compiz and KWin using the AIGLX or XGL architectures, allowing use of OpenGL to animate user interactions with the desktop.

Another branch in the three-dimensional desktop environment is the three-dimensional GUIs that take the desktop metaphor a step further, like the BumpTop, where users can manipulate documents and windows as if they were physical documents, with realistic movement and physics.

The Zooming User Interface (ZUI) is a related technology that promises to deliver the representation benefits of 3D environments without their usability drawbacks of orientation problems and hidden objects. It is a logical advance on the GUI, blending some three-dimensional movement with two-dimensional or *2.5D* vector objects. In 2006, Hillcrest Labs introduced the first zooming user interface for television,

Cut, Copy and Paste

Cut, copy and paste icons in ERP5.

In human–computer interaction and user interface design, cut, copy and paste are related commands that offer an interprocess communication technique for transferring data through a computer's user interface. The cut command removes the selected data from its original position, while the copy command creates a duplicate; in both cases the selected data is kept in temporary storage (the clipboard). The data from the clipboard is later inserted wherever a paste command is issued. The data remains available to any application supporting the feature, thus allowing easy data transfer between applications.

The command names are an interface metaphor based on the physical procedure used in manuscript editing to create a page layout.

This interaction technique has close associations with related techniques in graphical user interfaces (GUIs) that use pointing devices such as a computer mouse (by drag and drop, for example). Typically, clipboard support is provided by an operating system as part of its GUI and widget toolkit.

The capability to replicate information with ease, changing it between contexts and applications, involves privacy concerns because of the risks of disclosure when handling sensitive information.

Terms like cloning, copy forward, carry forward, or re-use refer to the dissemination of such information through documents, and may be subject to regulation by administrative bodies.

Inspired by early line and character editors that broke a move or copy operation into two steps between which the user could invoke a preparatory action such as navigation—Lawrence G. Tesler (Larry Tesler) proposed the names "cut" and "copy" for the first step and "paste" for the second step. Beginning in 1974, he and colleagues at Xerox Corporation Palo Alto Research Center (PARC) implemented several text editors that used cut/copy-and-paste commands to move/copy text.

Apple Computer widely popularized the computer-based cut/copy-and-paste paradigm through the Lisa and Macintosh operating systems and applications. Apple mapped the functionalities to key combinations consisting of the Command key (a special modifier key) held down while typing the letters X (for cut), C (for copy), and V (for paste), choosing a handful of keyboard shortcuts to control basic editing operations. The keys involved all cluster together at the left end of the bottom row of the standard QWERTY keyboard, and each key is combined with a special modifier key to perform the desired operation:

- Z to undo

- X to cut

- C to copy

- V to paste

The IBM Common User Access (CUA) standard also uses combinations of the Insert, Del, Shift and Control keys. Early versions of Windows used the IBM standard. Microsoft later also adopted the Apple key combinations with the introduction of Windows, using the control key as modifier key. For users migrating to Windows from MS-DOS this was a big change as MS-DOS users used the "copy" and "move" commands.

Similar patterns of key combinations, later borrowed by others, remain widely available today in most GUI text editors, word processors, and file system browsers.

Cut and Paste

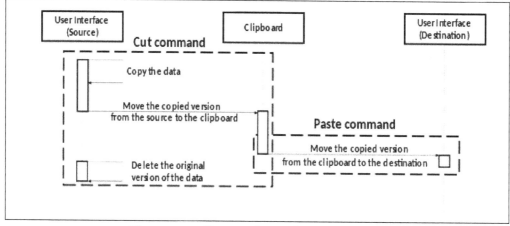

The sequence diagram of cut and paste operation.

Computer-based editing can involve very frequent use of cut-and-paste operations. Most software-suppliers provide several methods for performing such tasks, and this can involve (for example) key combinations, pulldown menus, pop-up menus, or toolbar buttons.

- The user selects or "highlights" the text or file for moving by some method, typically by dragging over the text or file name with the pointing-device or holding down the Shift key while using the arrow keys to move the text cursor.

- The user performs a "cut" operation via key combination Ctrl+x (⌘+x for Macintosh users), menu, or other means.

- Visibly, "cut" text immediately disappears from its location. "Cut" files typically change color to indicate that they will be moved.

- Conceptually, the text has now moved to a location often called the clipboard. The clipboard typically remains invisible. On most systems only one clipboard location exists, hence another cut or copy operation overwrites the previously stored information. Many UNIX text-editors provide multiple clipboard entries, as do some Macintosh programs such as Clipboard Master, and Windows clipboard-manager programs such as the one in Microsoft Office.

- The user selects a location for insertion by some method, typically by clicking at the desired insertion point.

- A *paste* operation takes place which visibly inserts the clipboard text at the insertion point. (The paste operation does not typically destroy the clipboard text: it remains available in the clipboard and the user can insert additional copies at other points).

Whereas cut-and-paste often takes place with a mouse-equivalent in Windows-like GUI environments, it may also occur entirely from the keyboard, especially in UNIX text editors, such as Pico or vi. Cutting and pasting without a mouse can involve a selection (for which Ctrl+x is pressed in most graphical systems) or the entire current line, but it may also involve text after the cursor until the end of the line and other more sophisticated operations.

When a software environment provides *cut* and *paste* functionality, a nondestructive operation called *copy* usually accompanies them; *copy* places a copy of the selected text in the clipboard without removing it from its original location.

The clipboard usually stays invisible, because the operations of cutting and pasting, while actually independent, usually take place in quick succession, and the user (usually) needs no assistance in understanding the operation or maintaining mental context. Some application programs provide a means of viewing, or sometimes even editing, the data on the clipboard.

Copy and Paste

The term "copy-and-paste" refers to the popular, simple method of reproducing text or other data from a source to a destination. It differs from cut and paste in that the original source text or data does not get deleted or removed. The popularity of this method stems from its simplicity and the ease with which users can move data between various applications visually – without resorting to permanent storage.

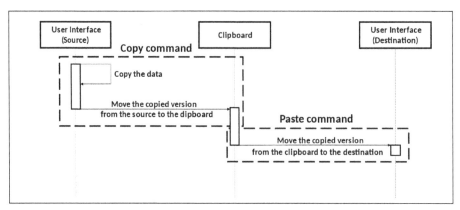

Sequence diagram of the copy-paste operation.

Once one has copied data into the clipboard, one may paste the contents of the clipboard into a destination document.

The X Window System maintains an additional clipboard containing the most recently selected text; middle-clicking pastes the content of this "selection" clipboard into whatever the pointer is on at that time.

Most terminal emulators and some other applications support the key combinations Ctrl-Insert to copy and Shift-Insert to paste. This is in accordance with the IBM Common User Access (CUA) standard.

Find and Go

The NeXTStep operating system extended the concept of having a single copy buffer by adding a second system-wide Find buffer used for searching. The Find buffer is also available in macOS.

Text can be placed in the Find buffer by either using the Find panel or by selecting text and hitting ⌘+E.

The text can then be searched with Find Next ⌘+G and Find Previous ⌘+D.

The functionality comes in handy when for example editing source code. To find the occurrence of a variable or function name elsewhere in the file, simply select the name by double clicking, hit ⌘+E and then jump to the next or previous occurrence with ⌘+G / ⌘+D.

Note that this does *not* destroy your copy buffer as with other UIs like Windows or the X Window System.

Together with copy and paste this can be used for quick and easy replacement of repeated text:

- Select the text that you want to replace (i.e. by double clicking).

- Put the text in the Find buffer with ⌘+E.

- Overwrite the selected text with your replacement text.

- Select the replacement text (try ⌥+⇧+← to avoid lifting your hands from the keyboard).

- Copy the replacement text ⌘+C.

- Find the next or previous occurrence ⌘+G / ⌘+D.

- Paste the replacement text ⌘+V.

- Repeat the last two steps as often as needed.

or in short:

- Select ⌘+ E, replstr, ⌐+⇧+←, ⌘+C, ⌘+G, ⌘+V, ⌘+G, ⌘+V.

While this might sound a bit complicated at first, it is often *much* faster than using the find panel, especial when only a few occurrences shall be replaced or when only some of the occurrences shall be replaced. When a text shall not be replaced, simply hit ⌘+G again to skip to the next occurrence.

The find buffer is system wide. That is, if you enter a text in the find panel (or with ⌘+E) in one application and then switch to another application you can immediately start searching without having to enter the search text again.

Copy and Paste Automation

Copying data one by one from one application to another, such as from Excel to a web form, might involve a lot of manual work. Copy and paste can be automated with the help of a program that would iterate through the values list and paste them to the active application window. Such programs might come in the form of macros or dedicated programs which involve more or less scripting. Alternatively, applications supporting simultaneous editing may be used to copy or move collections of items.

Additional Differences between Moving and Copying

In a spreadsheet, moving (cut and paste) need not equate to copying (copy and paste) and then deleting the original: when moving, references to the moved cells may move accordingly.

Windows Explorer also differentiates moving from merely copy-and-delete: a "cut" file will not actually disappear until pasted elsewhere and cannot be pasted more than once. The icon fades to show the transient "cut" state until it is pasted somewhere. Cutting a second file while the first one is cut will release the first from the "cut" state and leave it unchanged. Shift+Delete cannot be used to cut files; instead it deletes them without using the Recycle bin.

Multiple Clipboards

Several editors allow copying text into or pasting text from specific clipboards, typically using a special keystroke-sequence to specify a particular clipboard-number.

Clipboard managers can be very convenient productivity-enhancers by providing many more features than system-native clipboards. Thousands of clips from the clip history are available for future pasting, and can be searched, edited, or deleted. Favorite clips that a user frequently pastes (for example, the current date, or the various fields of a user's contact info) can be kept standing ready to be pasted with a few clicks or keystrokes.

Similarly, a kill ring provides a LIFO stack used for cut-and-paste operations as a type of clipboard capable of storing multiple pieces of data. For example, the GNU Emacs text editor provides a kill ring. Each time a user performs a cut or copy operation, the system adds the affected text to the ring. The user can then access the contents of a specific (relatively numbered) buffer in the ring when performing a subsequent paste-operation. One can also give kill-buffers individual names, thus providing another form of multiple-clipboard functionality.

Pejorative use of Expression

An action can be described as "cut/copy-and-paste" in a pejorative, negative sense, to mean that a person creating some item, has in fact merely copied from a previously existing item. Examples may include film screenplays, books, and other creative endeavors that appear to "lift" their content substantially from existing sources, and papers submitted for examinations which are directly copied from other reference sources.

Use in Software Development

Copy and paste programming is an anti-pattern arising from the careless pasting of pre-existing code into another source code file. Shared interfaces ("abstract classes") with the same named methods should be exposed, and each module should subclass the interface to provide needed differences in functionality.

Elements of Graphical User Interfaces

Pointer

In computing, a pointer or mouse cursor (as part of a personal computer WIMP style of interaction) is a symbol or graphical image on the computer monitor or other display device that echoes movements of the pointing device, commonly a mouse, touchpad, or stylus pen. It signals the point where actions of the user take place. It can be used in text-based or graphical user interfaces to select and move other elements. It is distinct from the cursor, which responds to keyboard input. The cursor may also be repositioned using the pointer.

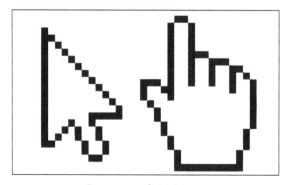

Common pointer types.

The pointer commonly appears as an angled arrow (angled because historically that improved appearance on low resolution screens), but it can vary within different programs or operating systems. The use of a pointer is employed when the input method, or pointing device, is a device that can move fluidly across a screen and select or highlight objects on the screen. In GUIs, where the input method relies on hard keys, such as the five-way key on many mobile phones, there is no pointer employed, and instead the GUI relies on a clear focus state.

Appearance

A wait cursor replaces the pointer with an hourglass.

The pointer "hotspot" is the active pixel of the pointer, used to target a click or drag. The hotspot is normally along the pointer edges or in its center, though it may reside at any location in the pointer.

In many GUIs, moving the pointer around the screen may reveal other screen hotspots as the pointer changes shape depending on the circumstances. For example:

- In text that the user can select or edit, the pointer changes to a vertical bar with little cross-bars (or curved serif-like extensions) at the top and bottom — sometimes called an "I-beam" since it resembles the cross-section of the construction detail of the same name.

- When displaying a document, the pointer can appear as a hand with all fingers extended allowing scrolling by "pushing" the displayed page around.

- Graphics-editing pointers such as brushes, pencils or paint buckets may display when the user edits an image.

- On an edge or corner of a window the pointer usually changes into a double arrow (horizontal, vertical, or diagonal) indicating that the user can drag the edge/corner in an indicated direction in order to adjust the size and shape of the window.

- The corners and edges of the whole screen may also act as hotspots. According to Fitts's law, which predicts the time it takes to reach a target area, moving mouse and stylus pointers to those spots is easy and fast. As the pointer usually stops when reaching a screen edge, the size of those spots can be considered of virtual infinite size, so the hot corners and edges can be reached quickly by throwing the pointer toward the edges.

- While a computer process is performing tasks and cannot accept user input, a wait pointer (an hourglass in Windows before Vista and many other systems, spinning ring in Windows Vista and later, watch in classic Mac OS, or spinning pinwheel in macOS) is displayed when the mouse pointer is in the corresponding window.

- When the pointer hovers over a hyperlink, a mouseover event changes the pointer into a hand with an outstretched index finger. Often some informative text about the link may pop up in a tooltip, which disappears when the user moves the pointer away. The tooltips revealed in the box depend on the implementation of the web browser; many web browsers will display the "title" of the element, the "alt" attribute, or the non-standard "tooltips" attribute. This pointer shape was first used for hyperlinks in Apple Computer's HyperCard.

- In Windows 7, when Windows Touch was introduced in the mainstream to make Windows more touch friendly, a touch pointer is displayed instead of the mouse pointer. The touch pointer can be switched off in Control Panel and resembles a small diamond shape. When the screen is touched a blue ripple appears around the touch pointer to provide visual touch feedback. When swiping to scroll etc., the touch pointer would follow the finger as it moves. If touch and hold to right click is enabled, touching and holding will show a thick white ring around the touch pointer. When this ring appears, releasing one's finger would perform a right click.

   ○ If a pen is used the left-click ripple is colourless instead of blue and the right-click ring is a thinner ring which appears closer to the pen tip making contact with the screen. A click (either left or right) will not show the touch pointer, but swiping would still show the pointer which would follow the pen tip.

   ○ Also, the touch pointer would only appear on the desktop once a user has signed in to Windows 7. On the sign in screen the mouse cursor would simply jump to the point which is touched and a left click would be sent on a tap, similarly to when touch input is used on operating systems prior to Windows 7.

- In Windows 8 and above, visual touch feedback displays a translucent circle where the finger makes contact with the screen, and a square when attempting to touch and hold to right-click. A swipe is shown by a translucent line of varying thickness. Feedback can be switched on and off in Pen and Touch settings of the Control Panel in Windows 8 and Windows 8.1 or in the Settings app on Windows 10, and feedback can also be made darker and larger where it needs to be emphasised, such as when presenting. However, the touch pointer is normally less commonly visible in touchscreen environments of Windows operating systems later than Windows 7.

- The mouse-over or hover gesture can also show a tooltip, which presents information about what the pointer is hovering over; the information is a description of what selecting an active element is for or what it will do. The tooltip appears only when stationary over content. A common use of viewing the information is when browsing the internet to know the destination of a link before selecting it, if the URL of the text is not recognisable.

   ○ When using touch or a pen with Windows, hovering when supported or performing a set gesture or flick may show the tooltip

Pointer Trails and Animation

Pointer trails can be used to enhance its visibility during movement. Pointer trails are a feature of

GUI operating systems to enhance the visibility of the pointer. Although disabled by default, pointer trails have been an option in every version of Microsoft Windows since Windows 3.1x.

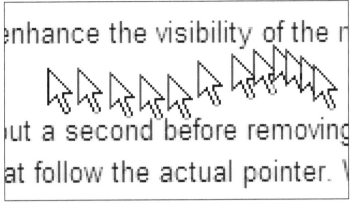

An example of mouse pointer trails.

When pointer trails are active and the mouse or stylus is moved, the system waits a moment before removing the pointer image from the old location on the screen. A copy of the pointer persists at every point that the pointer has visited in that moment, resulting in a snake-like trail of pointer icons that follow the actual pointer. When the user stops moving the mouse or removes the stylus from the screen, the trails disappear and the pointer returns to normal.

Pointer trails have been provided as a feature mainly for users with poor vision and for screens where low visibility may become an issue, such as LCD screens in bright sunlight.

In Windows, pointer trails may be enabled in the Control Panel, usually under the Mouse applet.

Introduced with Windows NT, an *animated pointer* was a small looping animation that was played at the location of the pointer. This is used, for example, to provide a visual cue that the computer is busy with a task. After their introduction, many animated pointers became available for download from third party suppliers. Unfortunately, animated pointers are not without their problems. In addition to imposing a small additional load on the CPU, the animated pointer routines did introduce a security vulnerability. A client-side exploit known as the *Windows Animated Cursor Remote Code Execution Vulnerability* used a buffer overflow vulnerability to load malicious code via the animated cursor load routine of Windows.

Editor

A pointer editor is software for creating and editing static or animated mouse pointers. Pointer editors usually support both static and animated mouse cursors, but there are exceptions. An animated cursor is a sequence of static cursors representing individual frames of an animation. A pointer editor should be able to:

- Modify pixels of a static cursor or of each individual frame in an animated cursor.

- Set the hot spot of a static cursor or of a frame of an animated cursor. The hot spot is a designated pixel that defines the clicking point.

- Add or remove frames in an animated cursor and set their animation speed.

Pointer editors are occasionally combined with icon editors, because computer icons and cursors share similar properties. Both contain small raster images and the file format used to store icons and static cursors in Microsoft Windows is similar.

Despite the similarities, pointer editors differ from icon editors in a number of ways. While icons contain multiple images with different sizes and color depths, static cursors (for Windows) only contain a single image. Pointer editors must provide means to set the hot spot. Animated pointer editors additionally must be able to handle animations.

Widget (Computing)

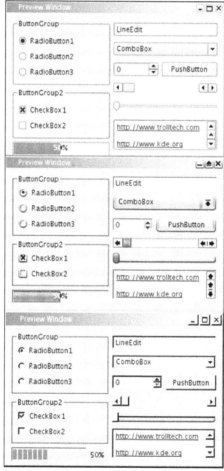

Qt widgets rendered according to three different skins (artistic design): Plastik, Keramik, and Windows.

A graphical widget (sometimes called a control or widget) in a graphical user interface is an element of interaction, such as a button or a scroll bar. Controls are software components that a computer user interacts with through direct manipulation to read or edit information about an application. User interface libraries such as Windows Presentation Foundation, GTK, and Cocoa, contain a collection of controls and the logic to render these.

Each widget facilitates a specific type of user-computer interaction, and appears as a visible part of the application's GUI as defined by the theme and rendered by the rendering engine. The theme makes all widgets adhere to a unified aesthetic design and creates a sense of overall cohesion.

Some widgets support interaction with the user, for example labels, buttons, and check boxes. Others act as containers that group the widgets added to them, for example windows, panels, and tabs.

Structuring a user interface with widget toolkits allows developers to reuse code for similar tasks, and provides users with a common language for interaction, maintaining consistency throughout the whole information system.

gtk3-demo, a program to demonstrate the widgets in GTK+ version 3.

Graphical user interface builders facilitate the authoring of GUIs in a WYSIWYG manner employing a user interface markup language. They automatically generate all the source code for a widget from general descriptions provided by the developer, usually through direct manipulation.

Any widget displays an information arrangement changeable by the user, such as a window or a text box. The defining characteristic of a widget is to provide a single interaction point for the direct manipulation of a given kind of data. In other words, widgets are basic visual building blocks which, combined in an application, hold all the data processed by the application and the available interactions on this data.

GUI widgets are graphical elements used to build the human-machine-interface of a program. GUI widgets are implemented like software components. Widget toolkits and software frameworks, like e.g. GTK+ or Qt, contain them in software libraries so that programmers can use them to build GUIs for their programs.

A family of common reusable widgets has evolved for holding general information based on the Palo Alto Research Center Inc. research for the Xerox Alto User Interface. Various implementations of these generic widgets are often packaged together in widget toolkits, which programmers use to build graphical user interfaces (GUIs). Most operating systems include a set of ready-to-tailor widgets that a programmer can incorporate in an application, specifying how it is to behave. Each type of widget generally is defined as a class by object-oriented programming (OOP). Therefore, many widgets are derived from class inheritance.

In the context of an application, a widget may be *enabled* or *disabled* at a given point in time. An enabled widget has the capacity to respond to events, such as keystrokes or mouse actions. A widget that cannot respond to such events is considered disabled. The appearance of a widget typically differs depending on whether it is enabled or disabled; when disabled, a widget may be drawn in a lighter color or be obscured visually in some way.

Widgets are sometimes qualified as *virtual* to distinguish them from their physical counterparts, e.g. *virtual* buttons that can be clicked with a pointer, vs. physical buttons that can be pressed with a finger.

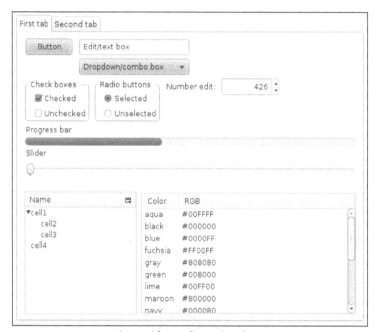

Various widgets shown in Ubuntu.

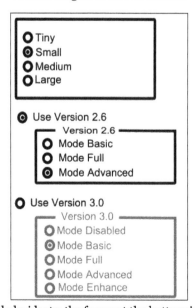

Example of enabled and disabled widgets; the frame at the bottom is disabled, they are grayed out.

A related (but different) concept is the desktop widget, a small specialized GUI application that provides some visual information and/or easy access to frequently used functions such as clocks, calendars, news aggregators, calculators and desktop notes. These kinds of widgets are hosted by a widget engine.

List of Common Generic Widgets

- Selection and display of collections:

  - Button: Control which can be clicked upon to perform an action. An equivalent to a push-button as found on mechanical or electronic instruments:

    - Radio button: Control which can be clicked upon to select one option from a selection of options, similar to selecting a radio station from a group of buttons dedicated to radio tuning. Radio buttons always appear in pairs or larger groups, and only one option in the group can be selected at a time; selecting a new item from the group's buttons also de-selects the previously selected button.

    - Check box: Control which can be clicked upon to enable or disable an option. Also called a tick box. The box indicates an "on" or "off" state via a check mark/tick ☑ or a cross ☒. Can be shown in an intermediate state (shaded or with a dash) to indicate that various objects in a multiple selection have different values for the property represented by the check box. Multiple check boxes in a group may be selected, in contrast with radio buttons.

    - Split button: Control combining a button (typically invoking some default action) and a drop-down list with related, secondary actions.

    - Cycle button: A button that cycles its content through two or more values, thus enabling selection of one from a group of items.

  - Slider: Control with a handle that can be moved up and down (vertical slider) or right and left (horizontal slider) on a bar to select a value (or a range if two handles are present). The bar allows users to make adjustments to a value or process throughout a range of allowed values.

  - List box: A graphical control element that allows the user to select one or more items from a list contained within a static, multiple line text box.

  - Spinner: Value input control which has small up and down buttons to step through a range of values.

  - Drop-down list: A list of items from which to select. The list normally only displays items when a special button or indicator is clicked.

  - Menu: Control with multiple actions which can be clicked upon to choose a selection to activate:

    - Context menu: A type of menu whose contents depend on the *context* or state in effect when the menu is invoked.

    - Pie menu: A circular context menu where selection depends on direction.

- ◦ Menu bar: A graphical control element which contains drop down menus.

- ◦ Toolbar: A graphical control element on which on-screen buttons, icons, menus, or other input or output elements are placed:

  - ▪ Ribbon: A hybrid of menu and toolbar, displaying a large collection of commands in a visual layout through a tabbed interface.

- ◦ Combo box (text box with attached menu or List box): A combination of a single-line text box and a drop-down list or list box, allowing the user to either type a value directly into the control or choose from the list of existing options.

- ◦ Icon: A quickly comprehensible symbol of a software tool, function, or a data file.

- ◦ Tree view: A graphical control element that presents a hierarchical view of information

- ◦ Grid view or datagrid: A spreadsheet-like tabular view of data that allows numbers or text to be entered in rows and columns.

- • Navigation:

  - ◦ Link: Text with some kind of indicator (usually underlining and/or color) that indicates that clicking it will take one to another screen or page.

  - ◦ Tab: A graphical control element that allows multiple documents or panels to be contained within a single window.

  - ◦ Scrollbar: a graphical control element by which continuous text, pictures, or any other content can be scrolled in a predetermined direction (up, down, left, or right).

- • Text/value input:

  - ◦ Text box - (Edit field): A graphical control element intended to enable the user to input text.

  - ◦ Combo box: A graphical control element combining a drop-down list or list box and a single-line editable textbox.

- • Output:

  - ◦ Label: Text used to describe another widget.

  - ◦ Tooltip: Informational window which appears when the mouse hovers over another control.

  - ◦ Balloon help.

  - ◦ Status bar: A graphical control element which poses an information area typically found at the window's bottom.

  - ◦ Progress bar: A graphical control element used to visualize the progression of an extended computer operation, such as a download, file transfer, or installation.

- Infobar: A graphical control element used by many programs to display non-critical information to a user.

- Container:

  - Window: A graphical control element consisting of a visual area containing some of the graphical user interface elements of the program it belongs to.

  - Collapsible panel: A panel that can compactly store content which is hidden or revealed by clicking the tab of the widget:

    - Drawer: Side sheets or surfaces containing supplementary content that may be anchored to, pulled out from, or pushed away beyond the left or right edge of the screen.

  - Accordion: A vertically stacked list of items, such as labels or thumbnails where each item can be "expanded" to reveal the associated content.

  - Modal window: A graphical control element subordinate to an application's main window which creates a mode where the main window can't be used.

  - Dialog box: A small window that communicates information to the user and prompts for a response.

  - Palette window: Also known as "Utility window" - a graphical control element which floats on top of all regular windows and offers ready access tools, commands or information for the current application:

    - Inspector window: A type of dialog window that shows a list of the current attributes of a selected object and allows these parameters to be changed on the fly.

  - Frame: A type of box within which a collection of graphical control elements can be grouped as a way to show relationships visually.

  - Canvas: Generic drawing element for representing graphical information.

  - Cover Flow: An animated, three-dimensional element to visually flipping through snapshots of documents, website bookmarks, album artwork, or photographs.

  - Bubble Flow: An animated, two-dimensional element that allows users to browse and interact the entire tree view of a discussion thread.

Multiple Document Interface

A multiple document interface (MDI) is a graphical user interface in which multiple windows reside under a single parent window. Such systems often allow child windows to embed other windows inside them as well, creating complex nested hierarchies. This contrasts with single document interfaces (SDI) where all windows are independent of each other.

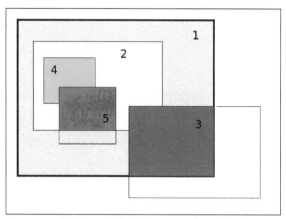

An example of a multiple document interface layout.

Comparison with Single Document Interface

In the usability community, there has been much debate about whether the multiple document or single document interface is preferable. Software companies have used both interfaces with mixed responses. For example, Microsoft changed its Office applications from SDI to MDI mode and then back to SDI, although the degree of implementation varies from one component to another. SDI can be more useful in cases where users switch more often between separate applications than among the windows of one application.

MDI can be confusing if it has a lack of information about the currently opened windows. In MDI applications, the application developer must provide a way to switch between documents or view a list of open windows, and the user might have to use an application-specific menu ("window list" or something similar) to switch between open documents. This is different from SDI applications where the window manager's task bar or task manager displays the currently opened windows. In recent years, it has become increasingly common for MDI applications to use "tabs" to display the currently opened windows. An interface in which tabs are used to manage open documents is referred to as a "tabbed document interface" (TDI). Another option is "tiled" panes or windows, which make it easier to prevent content from overlapping.

Some applications allow the user to switch between these modes at their choosing, depending on personal preference or the task at hand.

Nearly all graphical user interface toolkits to date provide at least one solution for designing MDIs. A notable exception was Apple's Cocoa API until the advent of tabbed window groups in MacOS High Sierra. The Java GUI toolkit, Swing, for instance, provides the class javax.swing.JDesktopPane which serves as a container for individual frames (class javax.swing.JInternalFrame). GTK lacks any standardized support for MDI.

Advantages

- With multiple document interfaces (and also tabbed document interfaces), a single menu bar and toolbar is shared between all child windows, reducing clutter and increasing efficient use of screen space. This argument is less relevant on an operating system which uses a common menu bar.

- An application's child windows can be hidden/shown/minimized/maximized as a whole.

- Features such as "Tile" and "Cascade" can be implemented for the child windows.

- Authors of cross-platform applications can provide their users with consistent application behaviour between platforms.

- If the windowing environment and OS lack good window management, the application author can implement it themselves.

- Modularity: An advanced window manager can be upgraded independently of the applications.

Disadvantages

- Without an MDI frame window, floating toolbars from one application can clutter the workspace of other applications, potentially confusing users with the jumble of interfaces.

- Can be tricky to implement on desktops using multiple monitors as the parent window may need to span two or more monitors, hiding sections.

- Virtual desktops cannot be spanned by children of the MDI. However, in some cases, this is solveable by initiating another parent window; this is the case in Opera and Chrome, for example, which allows tabs/child windows to be dragged outside of the parent window to start their own parent window. In other cases, each child window is also a parent window, forming a new, "virtual" MDI.

- MDI can make it more difficult to work with several applications at once, by restricting the ways in which windows from multiple applications can be arranged together without obscuring each other.

- The shared menu might change, which may cause confusion to some users.

- MDI child windows behave differently from those in single document interface applications, requiring users to learn two subtly different windowing concepts. Similarly, the MDI parent window behaves like the desktop in many respects, but has enough differences to confuse some users.

- Deeply nested, branching hierarchies of child windows can be confusing.

- Many window managers have built-in support for manipulating groups of separate windows, which is typically more flexible than MDI in that windows can be grouped and ungrouped arbitrarily. A typical policy is to group automatically windows that belong to the same application. This arguably makes MDI redundant by providing a solution to the same problem.

- Controls and hotkeys learned for the MDI application may not apply to others, whereas with an advanced Window Manager, more behavior and user preference settings are shared across client applications on the same system.

Application Examples

- Internet Explorer 6: A typical SDI application.

- Visual Studio 6 development environment: A typical modern MDI.

- Visual Studio .NET: MDI or TDI with "Window" menu, but not both.

- Opera: Combination of MDI and TDI (a true MDI interface with a tab bar for quick access).

- Chrome: Combination of MDI and TDI.

- Paint.NET: Thumbnail-based, TDI.

- Firefox: TDI by default, can be SDI.

- Kate: Text editor designed for the KDE Software Compilation, with advanced features and a sophisticated MDI.

- KWrite: Another text editor designed for the KDE Software Compilation, with a simplified SDI but sharing many of Kate's features via a mutual back end.

- GIMP: SDI with floating windows (MDI is available as an option called "Single-Window Mode" since version 2.8).

- GIMPshop: A fork of GIMP aiming to be more like Adobe Photoshop. The Windows version has limited MDI.

- AmiBroker: Is a multiple document interface (MDI) application (for technical analysis and financial market trading). In short, it means that it allows you to open and work with multiple windows at the same time.

- Adobe Photoshop: MDI under MS Windows. In newer versions, toolbars can move outside the frame window. Child windows can be outside the frame unless they are minimized or maximized.

- Adobe Acrobat: MDI until version 7.0 (Windows-only); SDI default in 8.0 (configurable to MDI); SDI only in 9.0; MDI (with a tabbed interface) in version 2015.

- Microsoft Excel 2003: SDI if you start new instances of the application, but MDI if you click the "File → New" menu (but child windows optionally appear on the OS taskbar). SDI only as of 2013.

- Microsoft Word 2003: MDI until Microsoft Office 97. After 2000, Word has a Multiple Top-Level Windows Interface, thus exposing to shell individual SDI instances, while the operating system recognizes it as a single instance of an MDI application. In Word 2000, this was the only interface available, but 2002 and later offer MDI as an option. Microsoft Foundation Classes (which Office is loosely based on) supports this metaphor since version 7.0, as a new feature in Visual Studio 2002. SDI only as of 2013.

- UltraEdit: Combination of MDI and TDI (a true MDI interface with a tab bar for quick access).

- VEDIT: Combination of MDI and TDI (a true MDI interface with a tab bar for quick access). Special "Full size" windows act like maximized windows, but allow smaller overlapping windows to be used at the same time. Multiple instances of Vedit can be started, which allows it to be used like an SDI application.

- Notepad++, Sublime Text, PSPad, TextMate and many other text editors: TDI.

- EmEditor: Options for either SDI or MDI.

- Macromedia Studio for Windows: a hybrid interface; TDI unless document windows are un-maximized. (They are maximized by default.)

- Corel Wordperfect: MDI a user can open multiple instances of WP with a single document in each, if they have multiple versions of WordPerfect installed on their computer. Recent versions maintain a list of open documents for a given window on the status bar at the bottom of the window, providing a variant of the TDI.

- Zeus for Windows: Combination of MDI and TDI (a true MDI interface with a tab bar for quick access).

- mIRC: MDI by default, can also work on SDI mode.

IDE-style Interface

Graphical computer applications with an IDE-style interface (IDE) are those whose child windows reside under a single parent window (usually with the exception of modal windows). An IDE-style interface is distinguishable from the Multiple Document Interface (MDI), because all child windows in an IDE-style interface are enhanced with added functionality not ordinarily available in MDI applications. Because of this, IDE-style applications can be considered a functional superset and descendant of MDI applications.

Examples of enhanced child-window functionality include:

- Dockable child windows.

- Collapsible child windows.

- Tabbed document interface for sub-panes.

- Independent sub-panes of the parent window.

- GUI splitters to resize sub-panes of the parent window.

- Persistence for window arrangements.

Collapsible Child Windows

A common convention for child windows in IDE-style applications is the ability to collapse child windows, either when inactive, or when specified by the user. Child windows that are collapsed will conform to one of the four outer boundaries of the parent window, with some kind of label or indicator that allows them to be expanded again.

Tabbed Document Interface for Sub-panes

In contrast to (MDI) applications, which ordinarily allow a single tabbed interface for the parent window, applications with an IDE-style interface allow tabs for organizing one or more subpanes of the parent window.

IDE-style Application Examples

- NetBeans
- dBASE
- Eclipse
- Visual Studio 6
- Visual Studio .NET
- RSS Bandit
- JEdit
- MATLAB
- Microsoft Excel when in MDI mode

Macintosh

Mac OS and its GUI are document-centric instead of window-centric or application-centric. Every document window is an object with which the user can work. The menu bar changes to reflect whatever application the front window belongs to. Application windows can be hidden and manipulated as a group, and the user may switch between applications (i.e., groups of windows) or between individual windows, automatically hiding palettes, and most programs will stay running even with no open windows. Indeed, prior to Mac OS X, it was purposely impossible to interleave windows from multiple applications.

In spite of this, some unusual applications breaking the human interface guidelines (most notably Photoshop) do exhibit different behavior.

Zooming User Interface

In computing, a zooming user interface or zoomable user interface is a graphical environment where users can change the scale of the viewed area in particular order through different documents. A ZUI is a type of graphical user interface (GUI). Information elements appear directly on an infinite virtual desktop (usually created using vector graphics), instead of in windows. Users can pan across the virtual surface in two dimensions and zoom into objects of interest. For example, as you zoom into a text object it may be represented as a small dot, then a thumbnail of a page of text, then a full-sized page and finally a magnified view of the page.

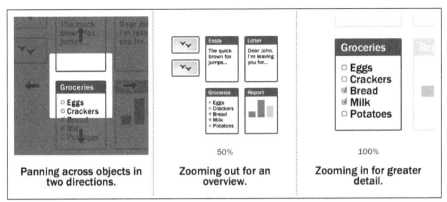

| Panning across objects in two directions. | Zooming out for an overview. | Zooming in for greater detail. |

Example of a ZUI.

ZUIs use zooming as the main metaphor for browsing through hyperlinked or multivariate information. Objects present inside a zoomed page can in turn be zoomed themselves to reveal further detail, allowing for recursive nesting and an arbitrary level of zoom.

When the level of detail present in the resized object is changed to fit the relevant information into the current size, instead of being a proportional view of the whole object, it's called semantic zooming.

Some consider the ZUI paradigm as a flexible and realistic successor to the traditional windowing GUI, being a Post-WIMP interface.

Ivan Sutherland presented the first program for zooming through and creating graphical structures with constraints and instancing, on a CRT in his Sketchpad program in 1962.

A more general interface was done by the Architecture Machine Group in the 1970s at MIT. Hand tracking, touchscreen, joystick and voice control was employed to control an infinite plane of projects, documents, contacts, video and interactive programs. One of the instances of this project was called Spatial Dataland.

Another GUI environment of the 70's which used the zooming idea was Smalltalk at Xerox Parc, which had infinite "desktops" (only later coined as such by Apple Computer), that could be zoomed in upon from a birds eye view after the user had recognized a miniature of the window setup for the project.

The longest running effort to create a ZUI has been the Pad++ project started by Ken Perlin, Jim Hollan, and Ben Bederson at New York University and continued at the University of New Mexico under Hollan's direction. After Pad++, Bederson developed Jazz, then Piccolo, and now Piccolo2D at the University of Maryland, College Park, which is maintained in Java and C#. More recent ZUI efforts include Archy by the late Jef Raskin, ZVTM developed at INRIA (which uses the Sigma lens technique), and the simple ZUI of the Squeak Smalltalk programming environment and language. The term ZUI itself was coined by Franklin Servan-Schreiber and Tom Grauman while they worked together at the Sony Research Laboratories. They were developing the first Zooming User Interface library based on Java 1.0, in partnership with Prof. Ben Bederson, University of New Mexico, and Prof. Ken Perlin, New York University.

GeoPhoenix, a Cambridge, MA, startup associated with the MIT Media Lab, founded by Julian

Orbanes, Adriana Guzman, Max Riesenhuber, released the first mass-marketed commercial Zoomspace in 2002-3 on the Sony CLIÉ PDA handheld, with Ken Miura of Sony

In 2006, Hillcrest Labs introduced the HoME television navigation system, the first graphical, zooming interface for television.

In 2007, Microsoft's Live Labs has released a zooming UI for web browsing called Microsoft Live Labs Deepfish for the Windows Mobile 5 platform.

Apple's iPhone (premiered June 2007) uses a stylized form of ZUI, in which panning and zooming are performed through a touch interface. A more fully realised ZUI is present in the iOS home screen (as of iOS 7), with zooming from the homescreen into folders and finally in to apps. The photo app zooms out from a single photo to moments, to collections, to years. And similarly in the calendar app with day, month and year views. It is not a full ZUI implementation since these operations are applied to bounded spaces (such as web pages or photos) and have a limited range of zooming and panning.

Franklin Servan-Schreiber founded Zoomorama, based on work he did at the Sony Research Laboratories in the mid-nineties. The Zooming Browser for Collage of High Resolution Images was released in Alpha in October 2007. Zoomorama's browser is all Flash based. Development of this project was stopped in 2010, but many examples are still available on the site.

In 2017, bigpictu.re offers an infinite notepad (infinite both in panning and zooming) as a web-application based on one of the first ZUI open-source libraries.

Also, Zircle UI offers an Open Source UI Library that uses zoomable navigation and circular shapes.

Crossing-based Interfaces

Crossing-based interfaces are graphical user interfaces that use crossing gestures instead of, or in complement to, pointing.

Goal-crossing Tasks

A pointing task involves moving a cursor inside a graphical object and pressing a button, whereas a goal-crossing task involves moving a cursor beyond a boundary of a targeted graphical object.

Goal crossing has been little investigated, despite sometimes being used on today's interfaces (e.g., mouse-over effects, hierarchical menus navigation, auto-retractable taskbars and hot corners). Still, several advantages of crossing over pointing have been identified:

- Elongated objects such as hyperlinks are faster to cross than to point.

- Several objects can be crossed at the same time within the same gesture.

- Crossing allows triggering actions when buttons are not available (e.g., while an object is being dragged).

- Crossing-based widgets can be designed to be more compact than pointing-based ones. This may be useful for small display devices.

- Goal crossing is particularly natural on stylus-based devices. On these devices, crossing an object back and forth is easier than double-clicking.

- Crossing can be a good alternative for users who have difficulties with clicking or double-clicking.

There are several other ways of triggering actions in user interfaces, either graphic (gestures) and non-graphic (keyboard shortcuts, speech commands).

Laws of Crossing

Variants of Fitts' law have been described for goal-crossing tasks. Fitts' law is seen as a *Law of pointing*, describing variability in the direction of the pointer's movement. The *Law of crossing* describes the allowed variability in the direction perpendicular to movement, and the steering law describes movement along a tunnel.

Drag-and-drop

In computer graphical user interfaces, drag and drop is a pointing device gesture in which the user selects a virtual object by "grabbing" it and dragging it to a different location or onto another virtual object. In general, it can be used to invoke many kinds of actions, or create various types of associations between two abstract objects.

As a feature, drag-and-drop support is not found in all software, though it is sometimes a fast and easy-to-learn technique. However, it is not always clear to users that an item can be dragged and dropped, or what is the command performed by the drag and drop, which can decrease usability.

Actions

The basic sequence involved in drag and drop is:

- Move the pointer to the object.

- Press, and hold down, the button on the mouse or other pointing device, to "grab" the object.

- "Drag" the object to the desired location by moving the pointer to this one.

- "Drop" the object by releasing the button.

Dragging requires more physical effort than moving the same pointing device without holding down any buttons. Because of this, a user cannot move as quickly and precisely while dragging. However, drag-and-drop operations have the advantage of thoughtfully chunking together two operands (the object to drag, and the drop location) into a single action. Extended dragging and dropping (as in graphic design) can stress the mousing hand.

A design problem appears when the same button selects and drags items. Imprecise movement can cause an attempt to select an object to register as a dragging motion.

Another problem is that the target of the dropping can be hidden under other objects. The user would have to stop the dragging, make both the source and the target visible and start again. In classic Mac OS the top-of-screen menu bar served as a universal "drag cancel" target. This issue has been dealt with in Mac OS X with the introduction of Exposé.

In Mac OS

Drag and drop, called click and drag at the time, was used in the original Macintosh to manipulate files (for example, copying them between disks or folders.). System 7 added the ability to open a document in an application by dropping the document icon onto the application's icon.

In System 7.5, drag and drop was extended to common clipboard operations like copying or moving textual content within a document. Content could also be dragged into the filesystem to create a "clipping file" which could then be stored and reused.

For most of its history Mac OS has used a single button mouse with the button covering a large portion of the top surface of the mouse. This may mitigate the ergonomic concerns of keeping the button pressed while dragging.

In OS/2

The Workplace Shell of OS/2 uses dragging and dropping extensively with the secondary mouse button, leaving the primary one for selection and clicking. Its use like that of other advanced Common User Access features distinguished native OS/2 applications from platform-independent ports.

In HTML

The HTML5 working draft specification includes support for drag and drop. HTML5 supports different kinds of dragging and dropping features including:

- Drag and Drop texts and HTML codes.

- Drag and Drop HTML elements.

- Drag and Drop files.

Based on needed action, one of the above types can be used. Note that when an HTML element is dragged for moving its current position, its ID is sent to the destination parent element; so it sends a text and can be considered as the first group.

Google's web-based e-mail application Gmail supports drag-and-drop of images and attachments in the latest Google Chrome browser and Apple's Safari (5.x). And Google Image search supports drag & drop.

On a Touch Screen

Touch screen interfaces also include drag and drop, or more precisely, long press, and then drag, e.g. on the iPhone or Android home screens.

iOS 11 implements a drag-and-drop feature which allows the user to touch items (and tap with other fingers to drag more) within an app or between apps on iPads. On iPhones, the functionality is only available within the same app that the user started the drag.

In End-user Programming

Drag and drop is considered an important program construction approach in many end-user development systems. In contrast to more traditional, text-based programming languages, many end-user programming languages are based on visual components such as tiles or icons that are manipulated by end users through drag-and-drop interfaces. AgentSheets, a programming environment for kids, introduced the modern notion of drag and drop blocks programming providing 4 core affordances: 1) Blocks that are end-user composable, 2) blocks are end-user editable, 3) blocks can be nested to represent tree structures, 4) blocks are arranged geometrically to define syntax. Drag and drop is also featured in many shader editing programs for graphics tools, such as Blender. Drag and drop also features in some video game engines, including Unreal Engine, GameMaker Studio, Construct 2 and, with expansion, Unity (game engine).

Examples:

A common example is dragging an icon on a virtual desktop to a special trashcan icon to delete a file.

Further examples include:

- Dragging a data file onto a program icon or window for viewing or processing. For instance, dropping an icon that represents a text file into a Microsoft Word window signifies "Open this document as a new document in Word".

- Moving or copying files to a new location/directory/folder.

- Adding objects to a list of objects to be processed.

- Rearranging widgets in a graphical user interface to customize their layout.

- Dragging an attribute onto an object to which the command is to be applied.

- e.g. dragging a color onto a graphical object to change its color.

- Dragging a tool to a canvas location to apply the tool at that location.

- Creating a hyperlink from one location or word to another location or document.

- Most word processors allow dragging selected text from one point to another.

- Dragging a series of code blocks such as in Blender for designing shaders and materials.

WIMP

Windows, icons, menus and pointing device (WIMP) denotes a style of computer-human interaction involving the aforementioned elements of the graphical user interface (GUI) which is the most common interaction method being used by desktop computers today. WIMP interaction was developed at Xerox PARC in 1973, and the term coined by Merzouga Wilberts in 1980, with the method popularized by Apple's Macintosh in 1984.

Windows, icons, menus and pointing device (WIMP) interaction is what the general public is used to in computing, because it is the most common interaction used in popular operating systems such as Windows, Apple' OS and even in modern Linux and UNIX-like operating systems. But in more development-oriented operating systems such as Linux and UNIX, there is an option to forgo the pointing device altogether and perform all interaction with the OS through the command prompt or shell, but the windows remain.

Characteristics of a WIMP system:

- A window isolates programs from each other, which allows a user to switch between running programs by giving focus to specific windows.

- Icons act as shortcuts to various programs, locations and actions possible in the OS.

- A menu which can be text-based, icon-based or a combination of both can be used as a selection system for various tasks.

- A pointer represents the location of a device movement, typically a mouse used to make selections in the GUI.

Because WIMP is so common, it has been erroneously used as a synonym for the GUI. This is false because even though all WIMP systems are a type of GUI, not all types of GUIs are WIMP, some do not use windows to isolate applications, and mobile operating systems like Android and iOS use icons, widgets and menus, but not windows or pointing devices.

References

- Vincent, James (7 June 2017). "The iphone is also getting drag and drop with ios 11". The Verge. Retrieved 23 June 2017

- Command-line-interface-CLI, definition: searchwindowsserver.techtarget.com, Retrieved 24 April, 2019

- "Moving Beyond Syntax: Lessons from 20 Years of Blocks Programing in agentsheets" (PDF). Journal of Visual Languages and Sentient Systems

- Staff (2007). Encyclopedia Of Information Technology. Atlantic Publishers & Distributors. P. 24. ISBN 978-81-269-0752-6

- Windows-icons-menus-and-pointing-device-wimp, definition: techopedia.com, Retrieved 25 May, 2019

- Laubach, Lori; Wakefield, Catherine (June 8, 2012). "Cloning and Other Compliance Risks in Electronic Medical Records" (PDF). Moss Adams LLP, multicare. Archived (PDF) from the original on August 20, 2014. Retrieved April 23, 2014

4
Interface Design Methods

The design of user interfaces for machines and software such as mobile devices and computers, with a focus on maximizing the user experience and usability, is known as user interface design. Common types of interface design methods are user-centered design and ecological interface design. This chapter discusses in detail these methods of interface design.

User-centered Design

The User-centered design (UCD) process outlines the phases throughout a design and development life-cycle all while focusing on gaining a deep understanding of who will be using the product. The international standard 13407 is the basis for many UCD methodologies. It's important to note that the UCD process does not specify exact methods for each phase.

User-centered Design Process

There are multiple principles that underlie user centered design. Design is based upon an explicit understanding of users, tasks, and environments; is driven and refined by user-centered evaluation; and addresses the whole user experience. The process involves users throughout the design and development process and it is iterative. And finally, the team includes multidisciplinary skills and perspectives.

The following are the general phases of the UCD process:

- Specify the context of use: Identify the people who will use the product, what they will use it for, and under what conditions they will use it.

- Specify requirements: Identify any business requirements or user goals that must be met for the product to be successful.

- Create design solutions: This part of the process may be done in stages, building from a rough concept to a complete design.

- Evaluate designs: Evaluation - ideally through usability testing with actual users - is as integral as quality testing is to good software development.

There are many variations of the UCD process. It can be incorporated into waterfall, agile, and other approaches. Depending on your needs, the user-centered design process is composed of several methods and tasks. What you are developing, your requirements, team, timeline, and the environment in which you are developing will all help determine the tasks you perform and the order in which you perform them.

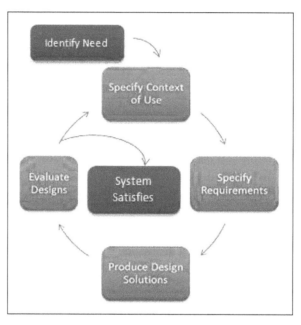

Contextual Design

Contextual design (CD) is a user-centered design process developed by Hugh Beyer and Karen Holtzblatt. It incorporates ethnographic methods for gathering data relevant to the product via field studies, rationalizing workflows, and designing human-computer interfaces. In practice, this means that researchers aggregate data from customers in the field where people are living and applying these findings into a final product. Contextual design can be seen as an alternative to engineering and feature driven models of creating new systems.

The contextual design process consists of the following top-level steps: contextual inquiry, interpretation, data consolidation, visioning, storyboarding, user environment design, and prototyping.

Collecting Data – Contextual Inquiry

Contextual inquiry is a field data collection technique used to capture detailed information about how users of a product interact with the product in their normal work environment. This information is captured by both observations of user behavior and conversations with the user while she or he works. A key aspect of the technique is to partner with the user, letting their work and the issues they encounter guide the interview. Key takeaways from the technique are to learn what users actually do, why they do it that way, latent needs, desires, and core values.

Interpretation

Data from each interview is analyzed and key issues and insights are captured. Detailed work models are also created in order to understand the different aspects of the work that matter for design.

Contextual design consists of five work models which are used to model the work tasks and details of the working environment. These work models are:

- Flow model: Represents the coordination, communication, interaction, roles, and responsibilities of the people in a certain work practice

- Sequence model: Represents the steps users go through to accomplish a certain activity, including breakdowns

- Cultural model: Represents the norms, influences, and pressures that are present in the work environment

- Artifact model: Represents the documents or other physical things that are created while working or are used to support the work. Artifacts often have a structure or styling that could represent the user's way of structuring the work

- Physical model: Represents the physical environment where the work tasks are accomplished; often, there are multiple physical models representing, e.g., office layout, network topology, or the layout of tools on a computer display.

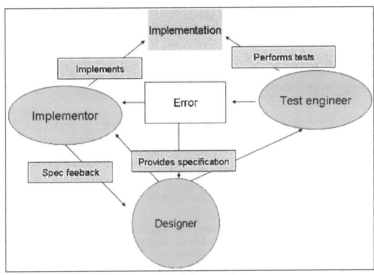

Simplified flow model.

Data Consolidation

Data from individual customer interviews are analyzed in order to reveal patterns and the structure across distinct interviews. Models of the same type can be consolidated together (but not generalized—detail must be maintained). Another method of processing the observations is making an affinity diagram ("wall"), as described by Beyer & Holtzblatt:

- A single observation is written on each piece of paper.

- Individual notes are grouped according to the similarity of their contents.

- These groups are labeled with colored Post-it notes, each color representing a distinct level in the hierarchy.

- Then the groups are combined with other groups to get the final construct of observations in a hierarchy of up to three levels.

Beyer & Holtzblatt propose the following color-coding convention for grouping the notes, from lowest to highest level in the hierarchy:

- White notes: Individual notes captured during interpretation, also known as "affinity notes".

- Blue notes: Summaries of groups of white notes that convey all the relevant details.

- Pink notes: Summaries of groups of blue notes that reveal key issues in the data.

- Green notes: Labels identifying an area of concern indicated by pink notes.

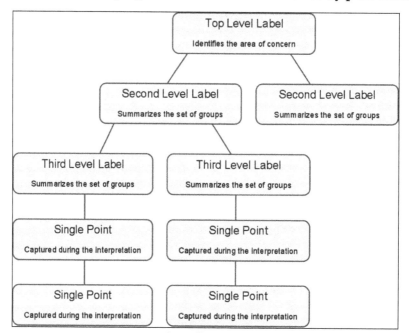

Part of an affinity diagram.

Beyer & Holtzblatt emphasize the importance of building the entire affinity diagram in one or two sessions rather than building smaller affinity diagrams over many sessions. This immersion in the data for an extended period of time helps teams see the broad scope of a problem quickly and encourages a paradigm shift of thought rather than assimilation of ideas.

The design ideas and relevant issues that arise during the process should be included in the affinity diagram. Any holes in the data and areas that need more information should also be labeled. After completing the wall, participants "walk" the affinity diagram to stimulate new ideas and identify any remaining issues or holes in data. The affinity diagram is a bottom-up method. Consolidated data may also be used to create a cause-and-effect diagram or a set of personas describing typical users of the proposed system.

Visioning

In visioning, a cross-functional team comes together to create stories of how new product concepts, services, and technology can better support the user work practice. The visioning team starts by reviewing the data to identify key issues and opportunities. The data walking session is followed by a group visioning session during which the visioning team generates a variety of new product concepts by telling stories of different usage scenarios based on the data collected. A vision includes the system, its delivery, and support structures to make the new work practice successful, but is told from the user's point of view.

Storyboarding

After visioning, the team develops the vision in storyboards, capturing scenarios of how people will work with the new system. Understanding the current way of working, its structure and the complete workflow helps the design team address the problems and design the new workflow. Storyboards work out the details of the vision, guided by the consolidated data, using pictures and text in a series of hand-drawn cells.

User Environment Design

The User Environment Design captures the floor plan of the new system. It shows each part of the system, how it supports the user's work, exactly what function is available in that part, and how the user gets to and from other parts of the system. Contextual design uses the User Environment Design (UED) diagram, which displays the focus areas, i.e., areas which are visible to the user or which are relevant to the user. Focus areas can be defined further as functions in a system that support a certain type or part of the work. The UED also presents how the focus areas relate to each other and shows the links between focus areas.

Prototyping

Testing the design ideas with paper prototypes or even with more sophisticated interactive prototypes before the implementation phase helps the designers communicate with users about the new system and develop the design further. Prototypes test the structure of a User Environment Design and initial user interface ideas, as well as the understanding of the work, before the implementation phase. Depending on the results of the prototype test, more iterations or alternative designs may be needed.

Uses and Adaptations

Contextual design has primarily been used for the design of computer information systems, including hardware, software. Parts of contextual design have been adapted for use as a usability evaluation method and for contextual application design. Contextual design has also been applied to the design of digital libraries and other learning technologies.

Contextual design has also been used as a means of teaching user-centered design/Human—computer interaction at the university level.

A more lightweight approach to contextual design has been developed by its originators to address an oft-heard criticism that the method is too labor-intensive or lengthy for some needs. Yet others find the designer/user engagement promoted by contextual design to be too brief.

Ecological Interface Design

Ecological interface design (EID) is an approach to interface design that was introduced specifically for complex sociotechnical, real-time, and dynamic systems. It has been applied in a variety of domains including process control (e.g. nuclear power plants, petrochemical plants), aviation, and medicine.

EID differs from some interface design methodologies like User-Centered Design (UCD) in that the focus of the analysis is on the work domain or environment, rather than on the end user or a specific task.

The goal of EID is to make constraints and complex relationships in the work environment perceptually evident (e.g. visible, audible) to the user. This allows more of users' cognitive resources to be devoted to higher cognitive processes such as problem solving and decision making. EID is based on two key concepts from cognitive engineering research: the Abstraction Hierarchy (AH) and the Skills, Rules, Knowledge (SRK) framework.

By reducing mental workload and supporting knowledge-based reasoning, EID aims to improve user performance and overall system reliability for both anticipated and unanticipated events in a complex system.

Ecological interface design was proposed as a framework for interface design by Kim Vicente and Jens Rasmussen in the late 80s and early 90s following extensive research into human-system reliability at the Risø National Laboratory in Denmark. The term ecological in EID originates from a school of psychology developed by James J. Gibson known as ecological psychology. This field of psychology focuses on human-environment relationships, in particular in relation to human perception in actual environments rather than in laboratory environments. EID borrows from ecological psychology in that the constraints and relationships of the work environment in a complex system are reflected perceptually (through an interface) in order to shape user behaviour. In order to develop ecological designs, analytical tools developed earlier by researchers at the Risø National Laboratory were adopted, including the Abstraction Hierarchy (AH) and the Skills, Rules, Knowledge (SRK) framework. The EID framework was first applied and evaluated in nuclear power plant systems. These tools are also used in Cognitive work analysis. To date, EID has been applied in a variety of complex systems including computer network management, anaesthesiology, military command and control, and aircraft.

Motivation

Rapid advances in technologies along with economic demands have led to a noticeable increase in the complexity of engineering systems. As a result, it is becoming more and more difficult for designers to anticipate events that may occur within such systems. Unanticipated events by definition cannot be specified in advance and thus cannot be prevented through training, procedures, or automation. A complex sociotechnical system designed based solely on known scenarios frequently loses the flexibility to support unforeseen events. System safety is often compromised by the operators' inability to adapt to new and unfamiliar situations. Ecological interface design attempts to provide the operators with the necessary tools and information to become active problem solvers as opposed to passive monitors, particularly during the development of unforeseen events. Interfaces designed following the EID framework aim to lessen mental workload when dealing with unfamiliar and unanticipated events, which are attributed to increased psychological pressure. In doing so, cognitive resources may be freed up to support efficient problem solving.

In addition to providing operators with the means to successfully manage unanticipated events, EID is also proposed for systems that require users to become experts. Through the use of the Abstraction Hierarchy (AH) and the Skills, Rules, Knowledge (SRK) framework, EID enables novice users to more easily acquire advanced mental models that generally take many years of experience and training to develop. Likewise, EID provides a basis for continuous learning and distributed, collaborative work. When faced with complex sociotechnical systems, it is not always possible for designers to ask operators what kinds of information they would like to see since each person understands the system at a different level (but rarely fully) and will provide very different answers. The EID framework allows designers to determine what kinds of information are required when it is not possible or feasible to ask users. It is not the intention of EID to replace existing design methodologies such as UCD and task analysis, but to complement them.

UCD and EID: Why use EID at All?

As we can see from today's windows based interfaces User-Centered Design (UCD) has done an excellent job of identifying user preferences and limitations and incorporating them into the interfaces. In the pre-UCD era, interface design was almost an afterthought to a program and was completely dependent on the programmers while totally neglecting the end user.

Benefits of UCD

UCD adds three key ideas:

- That Interface Design is a field on its own because it bridges between humans and the program/environment.

- That an understanding of human perception, cognition, and behavior is critical to designing interfaces.

- That much can be learned by getting feedback from the actual users of the interface, at the early design stages, and then testing through various points in the design.

But there are some problems in this approach as well.

How is EID Relevant?

The UCD approach commonly focuses on single user interactions between the user and the interface which is not enough to deal with today's increasingly complex systems where centralized control of information is needed and it is displayed on a variety of interfaces in varying detail. EID is a preferable addition to the complex systems' design process when even very experienced users do not have a complete understanding of how the entire complex system (power plant, nuclear plant, petrochemical refinery etc.) works. It is a known fact that users don't always understand or even feel the need to understand all the relationships behind the complex processes that they control via their interfaces.

Furthermore, the users are not always aware of the constraints that affect the system that they work with, and discovering these constraints can take some extra effort. EID incorporates this constraint based style in the design approach where it examines the constraints of the user domain before getting user input. EID focuses on understanding the complex system – its build, its architecture, and its original intent and then relaying this information to the end user thereby reducing their learning curve and helping them achieve higher level of expertise.

The constraint based style in interface design also facilitates the handling of unanticipated events because, regardless of the event, the constraint is broken and it can be seen by the user who in turn can proactively work with the interface to restore the constraint and fix the system.

This does not in any way take away the usefulness of UCD but stresses the fact that EID offers some unique insight into the design process and it could be used in conjunction with other cognitive engineering techniques to enhance the user interfaces and increase human reliability in human-machine interactions.

The Abstraction Hierarchy (AH)

The abstraction hierarchy (AH) is a 5-level functional decomposition used for modelling the work environment, or more commonly referred to as the work domain, for complex sociotechnical systems. In the EID framework, the AH is used to determine what kinds of information should be displayed on the system interface and how the information should be arranged. The AH describes a system at different levels of abstraction using how and why relationships. Moving down the model levels answers how certain elements in the system are achieved, whereas moving up reveals why certain elements exist. Elements at highest level of the model define the purposes and goals of the system. Elements at the lowest levels of the model indicate and describe the physical components (i.e. equipment) of the system. The how and why relationships are shown on the AH as means-ends links. An AH is typically developed following a systematic approach known as a Work Domain Analysis. It is not uncommon for a Work Domain Analysis to yield multiple AH models; each examining the system at a different level of physical detail defined using another model called the Part-Whole Hierarchy.

Each level in the AH is a complete but unique description of the work domain.

Functional Purpose

The functional purpose (FP) level describes the goals and purposes of the system. An AH typically includes more than one system goal such that the goals conflict or complement each other. The relationships between the goals indicate potential trade-offs and constraints within the work domain of the system. For example, the goals of a refrigerator might be to cool food to a certain temperature while using a minimal amount of electricity.

Abstract Function

The abstract function (AF) level describes the underlying laws and principles that govern the goals of the system. These may be empirical laws in a physical system, judicial laws in a social system, or even economic principles in a commercial system. In general, the laws and principles focus on things that need to be conserved or that flow through the system such as mass. The operation of the refrigerator (as a heat pump) is governed by the second law of thermodynamics.

Generalised Function

The generalised function (GF) level explains the processes involved in the laws and principles found at the AF level, i.e. how each abstract function is achieved. Causal relationships exist between the elements found at the GF level. The refrigeration cycle in a refrigerator involves pumping heat from an area of low temperature into an area of higher temperature (sink).

Physical Function

The physical function (PFn) level reveals the physical components or equipment associated with the processes identified at the GF level. The capabilities and limitations of the components such as maximum capacity are also usually noted in the AH. A refrigerator may consist of heat exchange pipes and a gas compressor that can exert a certain maximum pressure on the cooling medium.

Physical form

The physical form (PFo) level describes the condition, location, and physical appearance of the components shown at the PFn level. In the refrigerator example, the heat exchange pipes and the gas compressor are arranged in a specific manner, basically illustrating the location of the components. Physical characteristics may include things as colour, dimensions, and shape.

Causal Abstraction Hierarchy

The hierarchy described before is a *functional* Abstraction Hierarchy representation. A *functional* Abstraction Hierarchy emphasizes the "means-ends" or "how/why" links of the hierarchy. These connections are direct and illustrated across the five levels of the Abstraction Hierarchy.

As the systems get more and more complex, we need to follow the flow structure as well as to understand how the system works. This is when a *causal* Abstraction Hierarchy representation becomes necessary. As the flow patterns become increasingly complex and it becomes increasingly difficult to derive the flows directly from the system diagram, we add causal models to the functional models.

The causal models help to detail the flow structure and understand more complex flow patterns within a specified Abstraction Hierarchy level. A *causal* Abstraction Hierarchy representation has the same structure as a *functional* Abstraction Hierarchy representation but with causal links drawn. Causal links are also known as "within the level" links. These links show how the processes and flows are connected within each level.

The two representations are closely related but are usually developed separately because doing so results in a clearer model which captures most of the system constraints.

In very elaborate flow systems causal models can be used to simplify or abstract the flows. In such a scenario we may find it easier to identify the main feed and product lines at first, then control lines, emergency supply lines, or emergency shunting lines. Causal links are most useful at the Generalized Function and the Abstract Function levels which show flows of materials, processes, mass, or energy.

The Skills, Rules and Knowledge (SRK) Framework

The Skills, Rules, Knowledge (SRK) framework or SRK taxonomy defines three types of behaviour or psychological processes present in operator information processing. The SRK framework was developed by Rasmussen to help designers combine information requirements for a system and aspects of human cognition. In EID, the SRK framework is used to determine how information should be displayed to take advantage of human perception and psychomotor abilities. By supporting skill- and rule-based behaviours in familiar tasks, more cognitive resources may be devoted to knowledge-based behaviours, which are important for managing unanticipated events. The three categories essentially describe the possible ways in which information, for example, from a human-machine interface is extracted and understood:

Skill-based Level

A skill-based behaviour represents a type of behaviour that requires very little or no conscious control to perform or execute an action once an intention is formed; also known as a sensorimotor behaviour. Performance is smooth, automated, and consists of highly integrated patterns of behaviour in most skill-based control. For example, bicycle riding is considered a skill-based behaviour in which very little attention is required for control once the skill is acquired. This automaticity allows operators to free up cognitive resources, which can then be used for higher cognitive functions like problem solving. Errors in skills-based behaviour are routine errors.

Rule-based Level

A rule-based behaviour is characterised by the use of rules and procedures to select a course of action in a familiar work situation. The rules can be a set of instructions acquired by the operator through experience or given by supervisors and former operators.

Operators are not required to know the underlying principles of a system, to perform a rule-based control. For example, hospitals have highly-proceduralised instructions for fire emergencies. Therefore, when one sees a fire, one can follow the necessary steps to ensure the safety of the patients without any knowledge of fire behaviour. Errors in rule-based behaviour are due to insufficient technical knowledge.

Knowledge-based Level

A knowledge-based behaviour represents a more advanced level of reasoning. This type of control must be employed when the situation is novel and unexpected. Operators are required to know the fundamental principles and laws by which the system is governed. Since operators need to form explicit goals based on their current analysis of the system, cognitive workload is typically greater than when using skill- or rule-based behaviours.

Rapid Prototyping

Prototypes are experimental and incomplete designs which are cheaply and fast developed. Prototyping, which is the process of developing prototypes, is an integral part of iterative user-centered design because it enables designers to try out their ideas with users and to gather feedback.

The main purpose of prototyping is to involve the users in testing design ideas and get their feedback in the early stage of development, thus to reduce the time and cost. It provides an efficient and effective way to refine and optimize interfaces through discussion, exploration, testing and iterative revision. Early evaluation can be based on faster and cheaper prototypes before the start of a full-scale implementation. The prototypes can be changed many times until a better understanding of the user interface design has been achieved with the joint efforts of both the designers and the users.

Prototyping can be divided into low-fidelity prototyping, medium-fidelity prototyping and high-fidelity prototyping. In some literature, it is only simply classified as low-fidelity prototyping (also called Lo-Fi) and high-fidelity prototyping (also called Hi-Fi), where low-fidelity prototyping is mainly about paper-based mock-up, and high-fidelity is mainly about computer-based simulation. The determining factor in prototype fidelity is the degree to which the prototype accurately represents the appearance and interaction of the product, not the degree to which the code and other attributes invisible to the user are accurate. Other prototypes will be divided into low-fidelity and medium-fidelity prototypes.

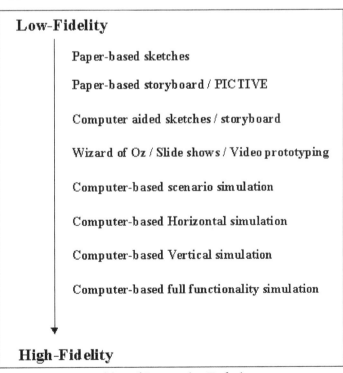

Transition of Prototyping Techniques.

Low-fidelity prototypes are quickly constructed to depict concepts, design alternatives, and screen layouts, rather than to model the user interaction with a system. Low-fidelity prototypes provide limited or no functionality. They are intended to demonstrate the general look and the feel of the interface, but not the detail how the application operates. They are created to communicate and exchange ideas with the users, but not to serve as a basis for coding and testing. A facilitator who knows the application thoroughly is generally needed to demonstrate the prototype to the users.

In contrast, high-fidelity prototypes are fully interactive, simulating much of the functionality in the final product. Users can operate on the prototype, or even perform some real tasks with it. High-fidelity prototypes are not as quick and easy to create as low-fidelity prototypes, but they faithfully represent the interface to be implemented in the product. Medium-fidelity prototypes partially simulate the system interaction and functionality.

Figure shows the transition of techniques from low-fidelity prototyping to high-fidelity prototyping. However, the fidelity degree of each technique may vary in diffirent practice.

Prototyping Techniques

Sketches

Sketching techniques, a kind of visual brainstorming, can be useful for exploring all kinds of design ideas. After producing initial sketches the best ideas can be further developed by constructing cardboard representations of the design, which can be evaluated with users. This can then be followed by developing scenarios, software or video prototypes.

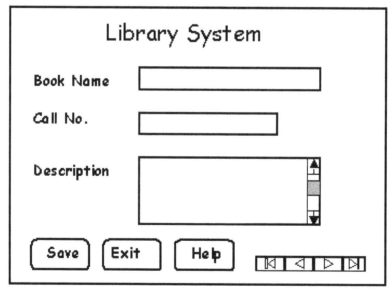

A Sketched Screen Design.

Freehand sketches are essential for crystallizing ideas in the early stages of design. Through the act of putting ideas down on paper and inspecting them, designers see new relations and features that suggest ways to refine and revise their ideas. Sketches make apparent to designers not only perceptual features but also inherently non-visual functional relations, allowing them to extract functions from perception in sketches.

The type of mock-up depends on how advanced the idea is. It may be quicker and cheaper to use paper-and-pencil forms at early stages, whereas computer-based prototypes may be important in later stages for exploring and demonstrating interaction and design consistency.

As one can imagine, the sketch technique is as simple as drawing the outward appearance of intended system on paper. However, creativeness is needed. There are some useful training exercises in to help designers get used to visual thinking. Figure is a sketch of a screen design.

Besides paper-and-pencil work, sketches can also be made with the aid of computer software, such as the Paint package in Windows[R] and SILK. SILK allows designers to quickly sketch an interface electronically and interactively. Figure is a sketch created by SILK.

Sketched Application Interface Created with SILK.

Storyboard

Storyboard origins from the film industry, where a series of panels roughly depicts snapshots from an intended film sequence in order to get the idea about the eventual scene.

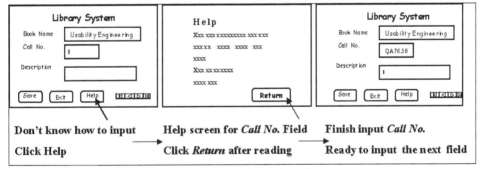

An Example of Storyboard.

Storyboard is a graphical depiction of the outward appearance of the intended system without accompanying system functionality. Storyboard provides snapshots of the interface at particular points in the interaction so that the users can determine quickly if the design is heading in the right direction.

Storyboards do not require much in terms of computing power to construct, in fact, they can be mocked up without the aid of computers. The materials needed are office stationery, such as pens or pencils of different colors, Post-It, stickers, and so on. However, modern graphical drawing packages make it possible to create storyboards with the aid of a computer instead of by hand. It is also possible to provide crude but effective animation by automated sequencing through a series of snapshots.

Pictive

PICTIVE stands for Plastic Interface for Collaborative Technology Initiatives through Video Exploration. It was developed at Bell Communications Research (Bellcore) in 1990 within the context of participatory design. The initial experiments of PICTIVE were conducted by Muller and his group in their projects. It is an experimental participatory design technique that is intended to enhance user participation in the design process.

The rationale behind PICTIVE is the methodology of participatory design. PICTIVE insures that users have early exposure to the target implementation technology. The PICTIVE technique provides a fine-grained, dynamic paper and pencil concretization mock-up of what the system will eventually look like and how it will behave. The components are literally made of colored plastic. Their relative durability and inexpensiveness encourage an atmosphere of exploration and invention. The PICTIVE mock-up is intended to be extensively modified in real-time by the users. PICTIVE is less as a means for the evaluation of an already-designed interface, but rather for the creation of the design of an interface.

PICTIVE was begun in reaction to software rapid prototyping environments, in which developers have a disproportionate design impact, but non-computer users are relatively disempowered by the complexity of current software prototyping environments. The PICTIVE techniques were designed to be used by people who were not necessarily programming professionals, so all participants have equal opportunity to contribute their ideas.

The apparatus for PICTIVE includes video camera and a collection of design objects. The design objects fall into two categories: The first category is simple office materials, including pens, high-lighters, papers, Post-It, stickers labels and paper clips all in a range of bright colors. The second category is materials prepared by the developer, such as menu bars, dialogue boxes, special icons for the project and so on.

The Procedures of Pictive are as Follows

First, both the users and the developers are asked to prepare a "homework". Typically, the users are asked to think about task scenarios, for instance, "what you would like the system to do for you and what steps are required to finish the job". The developers need to construct a preliminary set of system components for the users to manipulate based on prior discussions with the users. Figure shows some of such components made of plastic.

Second, during the PICTIVE session, both the users and developers manipulate the design objects on a design surface, where the designs are put together as multiple layers of sticky notes and overlays that can be changed by simple colored pens. Each participant brings her or his expertise. The resulting design is not driven by any single participant, but represents a synthesis of the different participants' different views. The users' work scenarios are explored in detail, leading to a discussion of how the developers' technology can be applied to meet the users' human needs. A coordinator may be needed to keep the group on track.

A video camera is focused on the design objects and to record the voices of the design team as they manipulate those objects. The video record of the design session will serve as a dynamic presentation of the design. Figure illustrates a scene in the PICTIVE session.

PICTIVE Plastic "Icons".

PICTIVE Setting.

PICTIVE is especially suited for prototyping activities carried out as part of a participatory design process since the low-tech nature of the materials make them equally accessible to both the users and the developers. In general, PICTIVE appears to be appropriate in circumstances similar to those of knowledge-based system development, i.e., when there are users available who understand what they need from the product or the project.

More studies on PICTIVE had been conducted and described in. In, an experimental object-oriented software prototype named TelePICTIVE was introduced. TelePICTIVE was designed to allow naive as well as expert users to work together in designing GUIs based on the PICTIVE paper participatory design methodology. Introduced how to practice design exercises derived from the PICTIVE method.

Sample Steps of Building a Low-fidelity Prototyping

Assemble a kit:

- White, unlined, heavy paper, size 11 by 17 inches is nice.

- Hundreds of 5-by-8-inch cards as construction material or notes cards.

- Various of adhesives: tape, glue sticks, Post-It, white correction tape.

- Various of markers: colored pens and pencils, highlighters.

- Lots of sticky note pads of various sizes and colors.

- Acetate sheets to make overhead presentations.

- Scissors, knives, straightedges, Band-Aids.

Set a Deadline

No matter how hard you think about it, you are not going to start getting it right until you put something in front of actual users and start refining your idea by their experience with your design.

Construct Models and not Illustrations

Make a working model, for example, make the menus dropping down, dialogs popping up, selection highlights and so forth. Photocopier can be useful.

Preparing for a Test

Select people who are the users or similar to the users to test your prototype.Write a set of scenarios, describing the product during use in a typical work situation.

Conduct several dry runs before tests with people outside. Check if there are missing components, confusing representation, etc. Make people in the team familiar with the prototype.

Conducting a Test

Team members are assigned different tasks. The greeter welcomes and tries to put users at ease. Facilitator takes the lead, giving user instructions, encouraging them to express their thoughts, making sure everything gets done on time. One team member acts as the "computer". He or she knows the application logic thoroughly, and sustains the illusion that paper prototype behaves similar to a real computer. The rest of the team are observers who take notes. It is recommended to use a video camera during the test.

Evaluating Results

Sort and prioritize the note cards. The team works through the piles of cards and agrees on suggested changes.

Table: Gives a brief comparison of the three low-fidelity prototyping techniques.

Techniques	Advantages	Disadvantages
Sketches	Very simple & cheap.	Must concentrate on high level concepts hard to envision the progression.
Storyboard	Simple & cheap users can evaluate the direction of the interface is heading.	Can only roughly display the system interaction HCI expertise needed.
PICTIVE	Simple & cheap fine-grained, dynamic paper represents the system interaction encourage users' modification.	Video needed HCI expertise needed.

Medium-fidelity Prototyping

Computer-based Simulation

Medium-fidelity prototypes simulate or animate some but not all features of the intended system. There are three approaches to limit prototype functionality.

Vertical Prototyping

Vertical prototyping cuts down on the number of features, so that the result is a narrow system that includes in-depth functionality, buy only for a few selected features.

Vertical prototypes allow users to perform and test some real tasks.

Horizontal Prototyping

Horizontal prototyping reduces the level of functionality so that the result is a surface layer that includes the entire user interface to a full-featured system without underlying functionality. Horizontal prototypes allow users to feel the entire interface, even though they can not perform any real tasks. The main advantages of horizontal prototypes are that they can be implemented fast with the use of prototyping and screen design tools, and they can be used to assess the interface as a whole.

Scenario

Scenario reduces both the number of features and the level of functionality. It can simulate the user interface as long as the user follows a previously planned path, i.e., a user can use a specific set of computer facilities to achieve a specific outcome under specified circumstances.

Scenarios can be easy and cheap to build, and to be used during early evaluation of a user interface design to get user feedback without the expense of constructing a running prototype. It can also be used for user testing if they are developed with slightly more detail than a pure narrative.

The concepts of vertical, horizontal and scenario prototyping are illustrated in figure.

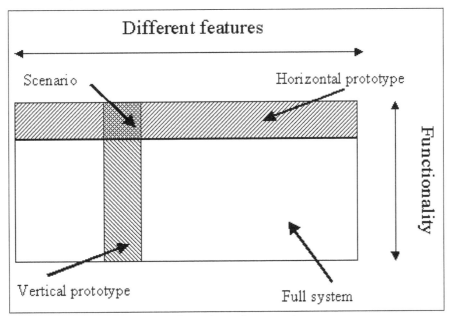

Two Dimensions of Prototyping.

Computer-based prototypes become easier to implement than before because there are more and more software prototyping tools, such as RAPID, HyperCard, CHIRP. Besides, there are many easy-to-learn and easy-to-use 4th generation languages, such as Smalltalk and Microsoft Visual Basic.

Wizard of Oz

It allows designers to test ideas without implementation a system.

The Wizard of Oz technique works as follows: The user interacts with a screen, but instead of a piece of software responding to the user's requests, a developer (the wizard) is sitting at another screen (generally in another room) simulating the system's intelligence and interacting with the user. The wizard may simulate all or part of the system function. When setting up a Wizard of Oz simulation, experience with previously implemented systems is helpful in order to place realistic bounds on the wizard's "abilities".

Early study of Wizard of Oz was the "listening typewriter" simulation of a speech recognition interface where the user's spoken input was typed into a word processor by a human typist located in another room. Wizard of Oz is usually used for the design of intelligent system, the experiment and development of natural-language recognition system, and the simulation of the system function which is difficult to implement in a prototype.

Wizard of Oz is ideal for the testing of preliminary prototypes and to gather users' expectations on the system. With this technique, the developers can develop a limited functionality prototype and enhance its functionality in evaluation by providing the missing functionality through human intervention without cost on programming. Extra understanding of the users can also be achieved through being involved so closely with the users.

Slide Shows and Video Prototyping

These techniques use the communication media to facilitate prototyping.

In slide shows, the storyboard prototype is encoded on a computer with software tools. The scene transition is activated by simple user input. The slides form a simple horizontal or vertical prototype.

Video prototyping eliminates software limitations. It requires no post-production editing or any special expertise in video production. The studies and experiments with video prototyping can be found in. It is more like Muller's PICTIVE work, where multi-disciplinary design teams use it in informal brainstorming sessions. Unlike PICTIVE, video prototyping does not simply record design ideas, but create an evocative simulation of the proposed interface.

Here is an example of how to make video prototype for a pull down menu. First, we draw a menu bar on paper and a mouse arrow on clear acetate. Second, turn on the camera and move the acetate so that it looks as if the mouse is moving over the menu bar. When the mouse is over the menu title, we make a clicking sound and pause the camera. In the third step, we draw the menu on a small piece of paper, put it under the menu title, and restart the camcorder. When viewing the tape, the menu appears to have been pulled down from the menu bar.

Both slide shows and video prototyping provide kind of simulation of the system. They appear to behave as a real system although they only show some scenes. The simulation is restricted by some tightly predefined tasks, and the user is hardly to interact with the system.

Table: Gives a brief comparison of the medium-fidelity proto typings.

Techniques	Advantages	Disadvantages
Vertical	Test in depth under realistic circumstances test with real user tasks.	Only test a limited part of the system.
Horizontal	Test the entire interface can be implemented fast.	Can not perform real tasks.
Scenario	Easy and cheap to build.	Only test a limited part of the system can not perform real tasks.
Wizard of Oz	Save time on programming extra understanding of users can be achieved by closely involved with them.	People need to be trained to act as computers less realistic.
Slide and video Simulation	Simple system simulation	Lack of flexibility users can not interact with the system.

When, Where and How to use the Prototyping Method?

When to use Prototyping Techniques?

Prototyping is part of the design and development process, especially in the early stage. Figure below shows when and what kind of prototyping techniques are applied in the design life cycle.

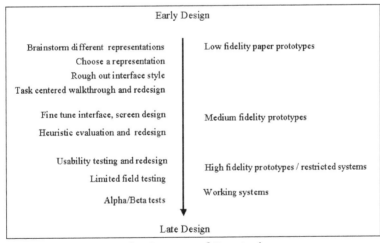

Design Process and Prototyping.

Comparison of Low-fidelity and Medium (High)-fidelity Prototyping

Table Comparison of Low-fidelity and Medium-fidelity Prototyping:

Type	Advantages	Disadvantages
Low-Fidelity	Less time & lower cost evaluate multiple design concepts useful communication device address screen layout issues.	Limited usefulness for usability tests navigational and flow limitations facilitator-driven poor detailed specification.

Medium(high)-Fidelity	Partial/complete functionality interactive user-driven clearly defines navigational scheme use for exploration and test marketing and sales tool.	Time-consuming to create inefficient for proof-of-concept designs blind users to major representaional flaws managements may think it is real.

Considerations when Choosing Prototyping Techniques

Although prototyping is recognized as an efficient way in interface design, the optimum methods of prototyping have not yet been agreed upon. There is a long time debate about which prototyping approach is better, low-fidelity or high-fidelity. The list below summarizes some of the key points to consider when deciding whether a low or medium(high)-fidelity prototyping approach would be most appropriate for your design and development needs.

- Cost and Schedule Constraints: If your budget and schedule are limited, you should first consider low-fidelity prototyping, especially paper mock-up, because they are very cheap and fast to develop. If there are experienced programmers and you have fast tools to build a computer-based prototype, medium-fidelity prototyping is also a consideration. High-fidelity prototyping is not recommended because it is expensive to build.

- Proof-of-concept: Low-fidelity prototyping is the most efficient way to test design ideas because it is concentrated on the concept evaluation of a design. Medium(high) prototyping will not help more, however, you spend more time and money on a Medium(high)-fidelity prototype than on a low-fidelity one.

- Navigation and Flow: Medium-fidelity prototyping is good to simulate the system's interaction. In low-fidelity prototyping, storyboard can show the system's direction.

- User Driven or Facilitator-driven: If you need a user-driven prototype, medium(high)-fidelity prototyping is recommended because users can directly interact with the prototype. Otherwise, if you need a facilitator-driven prototype, low-fidelity prototyping is the choice.

- Look-and-feel the Product: Medium(high)-fidelity prototyping can help users gain the feeling of how the product works. If using a low-fidelity prototype, you must be good at facilitating the prototyping process. You need to know clearly what the real system will work, and you need to show and explain to cycle to the users.

- Usability Test: Medium(high)-fidelity prototyping are good for usability tests because they provide a relatively realistic appearance and functionality which is close to the final product. The usefulness that low-fidelity prototyping provides is too limited to conduct an usability test.

- What is your Facilitation Skill/Programming Skill: If there are people who have the expertise in human-computer interaction and facilitation, low-fidelity could be the choice because running a low-fidelity prototyping needs such experience. However, if there are people who are experienced programmers, and you also have fast tools for interface generation, medium(high)-fidelity prototyping could be considered. Even though generally medium(high)-fidelity prototyping needs more time than low-fidelity prototyping, the expertise in programming and efficient tools could reduce the time and energy.

- What development stage you are: Figure shows the relationship of prototyping and product development. If you are in the very early stage of the design, low-fidelity prototyping will be efficient to help you work out the design concepts with the users. If you are in the medium stage, such as screen design and usability testing, medium-fidelity prototyping will be more useful.

Integrate Prototypes and Products

The relationship of prototypes and final products is as follows:

- Throw-away: Prototypes only serve to elicit users' reaction and to evaluate design ideas. Prototypes will be thrown away in the later development phases. Such prototypes must be created rapidly and cheaply. Otherwise it will be too expensive to do prototyping.

- Incremental: Product is built as separate modules. Each module is prototyped and tested, then added to the final system.

- Evolutionary: A prototype is built from low-fidelity to high-fidelity, incorporating design changes, Eventually the prototype becomes the final product.

The Performance of Prototyping on Some Attributes

- Is it quick and cheap to do? Low-fidelity prototyping is fast and cheap to do because it is paper-based and provides limited or no functionality. Medium(high)-fidelity prototyping is more expensive than low-fidelity because it is interactive and provides partial or full functionality. Coding and debugging is needed in a computer-based prototyping.

- Does it provide for controlled study? Low-fidelity prototyping is good for participatory design, but not for controlled study because of their inherent restrictions, i.e., they can not simulate the system interaction so that the users can not perform tasks without facilitator's instructions. Medium(high)-fidelity prototyping can simulate system interaction. However, the simulation is not very realistic, so that the controlled study based on prototypes will be less reliable.

- Is it suitable for qualitative analysis? Prototyping is suitable for qualitative analysis. Prototypes provide a way for users to react to the conceptual design of a system, or to interact with a simulation of a system. Qualitative methods such as introspection, direct observation, heuristic evaluation are commonly used in evaluation of the design. Comparing to the evaluation of a final product, qualitative results, such as users' feedback and discussion are important in evaluation of a prototype.

- Is it suitable for quantitative analysis? Low-fidelity prototyping is not suitable for quantitative analysis. Low-fidelity prototypes are too conceptual for a quantitative study. Medium(high)-fidelity prototypes, especially computer-based ones, can be used to get quantitative results, such as the users speed of performing a task and the errors they made. But the results will not be very realistic based on prototypes.

- Does it require special equipment? Low-fidelity prototyping does not require special equipment. Video camera may be needed, for example, in the video prototyping and PICTIVE prototyping. Prototyping software is needed for computer-based prototypes.

- Does it require special personnel? Paper prototyping generally requires a facilitator, who knows the application thoroughly, to demonstrate or to test the application. The user is dependent on the facilitator to respond to the user's commands to turn cards or advance screen to simulate the flow of the application. The expertise in application and human-computer interaction is required. Computer-based prototyping requires people with expertise in programming.

References

- Bennett, K. B. & Flach, J. M. (2011). Display and Interface Design - Subtle Science, Exact Art. CRC Press. ISBN 978-1-4200-6439-1

- User-centered-design, what-and-why: usability.gov, Retrieved 26 February, 2019

- Eyer, H. & Holtzblatt, K. (1998). Contextual Design: Defining Customer-Centered Systems. San Francisco: Morgan Kaufmann. ISBN 1-55860-411-1

- Holtzblatt, K: Contextual Design: Experience in Real Life. Mensch & Computer 2001. Archived from the original(PDF) on 2005-08-16. Retrieved 2007-01-11.)

- Vicente, K. J. (2001). Cognitive engineering research at Risø from 1962-1979. In E. Salas (Ed.), Advances in Human Performance and Cognitive Engineering Research, Volume 1 (pp. 1-57), New York: Elsevier. ISBN 0-7623-0748-X

5

Human-Computer Interaction: Models and Laws

The main models of human-computer interaction are Keystroke-level model and GOMS. Some of the various laws of human-computer interaction are Fitts' law, Steering law and Hick's Law. This chapter closely examines these models and laws of human-computer interaction to provide an extensive understanding of the subject.

Keystroke-level Model

Keystroke-level model, sometimes referred to as KLM or KLM-GOMS, is an approach to human–computer interaction, developed by David Kieras and based on CMN-GOMS. CMN-GOMS for its part was developed by Card, Moran, and Newell, The model is an 11-step method that can be used by individuals or companies seeking ways to estimate the time it takes to complete simple data input tasks using a computer and mouse. By using KLM-GOMS, individuals often find more efficient or better ways to complete a task simply by analyzing the steps required in the process and rearranging or eliminating unneeded steps. It is designed to be easier to use than other GOMS methods, such that companies who cannot afford human–computer interaction specialists can use it. KLM-GOMS is usually applied in situations that require minimal amounts of work and interaction with a computer interface or software design. The calculations and the number of steps required to accurately compute the overall task time increase quickly as the number of tasks involved increases. Thus, KLM-GOMS is best suited to evaluate time specific tasks that require, on average, less than 5 minutes to complete.

Estimation of Execution Times using Keystroke-level Model

The following is a step-by-step description of how to apply the KLM to estimate the execution time required by a specified interface design:

- Choose one or more representative task scenarios.

- Have the design specified to the point that keystroke-level actions can be listed for the specific task scenarios.

- For each task scenario, figure out the best way to do the task, or the way that you assume users will do it.

- List the keystroke-level actions and the corresponding physical operators involved in doing the task.

- If necessary, include operators for when the user must wait for the system to respond.

- Insert mental operators for when user has to stop and think.

- Look up the standard execution time to each operator.

- Add up the execution times for the operators.

- The total of the operator times is the estimated time to complete the task.

Activity Centred Design (ACD) is a model of design that focuses on how a system produces an outcome as a result of activity. The focus is on the *whole system* rather than just the user.

It's important to note that ACD is a model, not a process. ACD is just one of many perspectives you can employ when designing.

The ACD model is an X-Ray into the social and technical workings of an activity. It considers the broader system beyond a single user. For example, this perspective may allow us to see it's more appropriate to focus our design work on the *community* or *social rules* rather than the individual users *interface*.

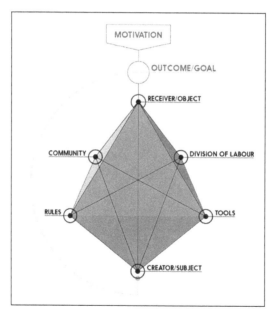

The model represents a whole activity. Some outcome backed by a motivation at the top provides context.

The specifics of each node are important. Adding, removing, altering and considering these node over time and how they impact the other nodes is key to developing insight.

It's possible for nodes to contradict each other and the overall design still function, just like in real life not everything is logical. In existing systems the history of nodes is often important to look at to gain proper context.

ACD has it's roots in Activity Theory and it's worth pointing out some of the words used such as "goals" and "tasks" have specific ordering and hierarchy.

The key ones, using the example of listening to the radio in the car:

- "Task" (Scan radio stations).

- "Actions" (Turn radio on, Select next station).

- "Operations" (Press On button, Turn dial to the right).

Benefits of Activity Centred Design

ACD can be ideal for new projects, new padagrims or encouraging innovative rethinks. The model can also be effective in creating very focused products as elements that do not support the desired activity are naturally removed.

The model encourages participants to take a broader perspective of the system by "telling the story" through the model. This quality makes it a good tool for generating better design outcomes in businesses that are either too siloed or too heavily geared towards one skill set e.g. technical teams that tend to see all problems as technical problems.

Disadvantages of Activity Centred Design

- Less suited to finer refinements.

- May not be useful if designers have narrow scope of latitude or are conducting low level design work.

GOMS

GOMS is a specialized human information processor model for human-computer interaction observation that describes a user's cognitive structure on four components. In the book The Psychology of Human-Computer Interaction. written in 1983 by Stuart K. Card, Thomas P. Moran and Allen Newell, the authors introduce: "a set of Goals, a set of Operators, a set of Methods for achieving the goals, and a set of Selections rules for choosing among competing methods for goals." GOMS is a widely used method by usability specialists for computer system designers because it produces quantitative and qualitative predictions of how people will use a proposed system.

A GOMS model is composed of methods that are used to achieve specific goals. These methods are then composed of operators at the lowest level. The operators are specific steps that a user performs and are assigned a specific execution time. If a goal can be achieved by more than one method, then selection rules are used to determine the proper Method.

- Goals are symbolic structures that define a state of affairs to be achieved and determinate a set of possible methods by which it may be accomplished.

- Operators are elementary perceptual, motor or cognitive acts, whose execution is necessary to change any aspect of the user's mental state or to affect the task environment.

- Methods describe a procedure for accomplishing a goal.

- Selection Rules are needed when a goal is attempted, there may be more than one method available to the user to accomplish it.

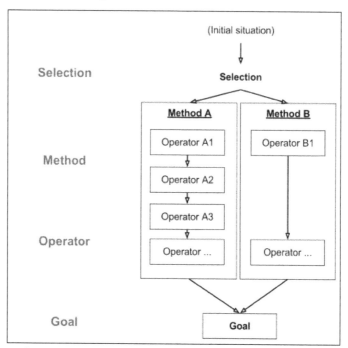

The concepts behind a GOMS model and their relationships.

There are several different GOMS variations which allow for different aspects of an interface to be accurately studied and predicted. For all of the variants, the definitions of the major concepts are the same. There is some flexibility for the designer's/analyst's definition of all of the entities. For instance, an operator in one method may be a goal in a different method. The level of granularity is adjusted to capture what the particular evaluator is examining.

Advantages

The GOMS approach to user modeling has strengths and weaknesses. While it is not necessarily the most accurate method to measure human-computer interface interaction, it does allow visibility of all procedural knowledge. With GOMS, an analyst can easily estimate a particular interaction and calculate it quickly and easily. This is only possible if the average Methods-Time Measurement data for each specific task has previously been measured experimentally to a high degree of accuracy.

Disadvantages

GOMS only applies to skilled users. It does not work for beginners or intermediates for errors may occur which can alter the data. Also the model doesn't apply to learning the system or a user using the system after a longer time of not using it. Another big disadvantage is the lack of account for errors, even skilled users make errors but GOMS does not account for errors. Mental workload is not addressed in the model, making this an unpredictable variable. The same applies to fatigue. GOMS only addresses the usability of a task on a system, it does not address its functionality.

User personalities, habits or physical restrictions (for example disabilities) are not accounted for in any of the GOMS models. All users are assumed to be exactly the same. Recently some extensions of GOMS were developed, that allow to formulate GOMS models describing the interaction behavior of disabled users.

Variations

Basically there are four different GOMS models: the Keystroke-Level Model, CMN-GOMS, NGOMSL, CPM-GOMS, and SGOMS. Each model has a different complexity and varies in activities.

KLM

The Keystroke-Level Model (KLM) is the first and simplest GOMS technique Stuart Card, Thomas P. Moran and Allen Newell created. Estimating an execution time for a task is done by listing the sequence of operators and then totaling the execution times for the individual operators. With KLM the analyst must specify the method used to accomplish each particular task instance. Furthermore, the specified methods are limited to being in sequence form and containing only keystroke-level primitive operators. The biggest difference between GOMS and KLM is how time is assigned to cognitive and perceptual operators when it comes to execution time predictions. Another major difference is that the goal-hierarchy is explicit in GOMS while it was implicit in the KLM. The nature of unobservable operators is another important difference. KLM has a single M operator that precedes each cognitive unit of action. In contrast, GOMS assigns no time to such cognitive overhead. But both models include M-like operators for substantial time-consuming mental actions such as locating information on the screen and verifying entries. Both methods assign roughly the same time to unobservable perceptual and cognitive activities. Also they make different assumptions about unobservable cognitive and perceptual operators and so distribute the time in different ways.

KLM's execution part is described in four physical-motor operators:

- K keystroking/ keypressing.

- P pointing with a mouse to a target.

- H homing the hand on the keyboard.

- D drawing a line segment on a grid.

One mental operator M that stands for the time a user has to mentally prepare himself to do an action, and a system response operator R in with the user has to wait for the system. Execution time is the sum of the times spent executing the different operator types:

$$T\text{execute} = T\text{K} + T\text{P} + T\text{H} + T\text{D} + T\text{M} + T\text{R}.$$

Each of these operators has an estimate of execution time, either a single value, a parameterized estimate.

Touch Level Model (TLM)

GOMS and it variants were designed for keyboard interfaces, nowadays a new type of interface is omnipresent. This addition to the GOMS family, together with updates to the existing KLM operators, is called the Touch Level Model (TLM). Andrew D. Rice and Jonathan W. Lartigue propose this model for the used to model human task performance on a constrained input touchscreen device and, with proper benchmarking, accurately predict actual user performance.

The goal is to provide an instrument for quantitative analysis of touchscreen interfaces. A number of operators are added for touchscreen interactions:

- Distraction (X) a multiplicative operator that is applied to other operators to model real world distractions.

- Gesture (G) gestures are conceptualized as specialized combinations of finger movements across the device's screen.

- Pinch (P) refers to the common two-finger gesture.

- Zoom (Z) the reverse application of the Pinch operator. value in MS = 200 Ms.

- Initial Act (I) KLM assumed the user is prepared to begin an action, touchscreen devices require users to prepare them for use (home button or password).

- Tap (T) operator refers to the physical action of tapping an area on the touchscreen device in order to initiate some change or action.

- Swipe (S) usually a horizontally or vertically swipe like changing the page in a book. value in MS = 70 Ms.

- Tilt (L(d)) used with an interacting with a devices equipped with accelerometers.

- Rotate (O(d)) gesture in which two or more fingers are placed on the screen and then rotated about a central point.

- Drag (D) similar to Swipe, Drag also involves tapping a location on the screen and then moving one or more fingers in specific direction.

CMN-GOMS

CMN-GOMS is the original GOMS model proposed by Stuart Card, Thomas P. Moran and Allen Newell. CMN stands for Card, Moran and Newell and it takes the KLM as its basic and adds subgoals and selection rules. This model can predict operator sequence as well as execution time. A CMN-GOMS model can be represented in program form, making it amenable to analysis as well as execution. CMN-GOMS has been used to model word processors and CAD systems for ergonomic design.The CMN method can predict the operator sequence and the execution time of a task on a quantitative level and can focus its attention on methods to accomplish goals on a qualitative level.

In the example by Bonnie E. John and David E. Kieras a simple CMN-GOMS on editing a manuscript is shown:

GOAL: EDIT-MANUSCRIPT

    GOAL: EDIT-UNIT-TASK ...repeat until no more unit tasks

        GOAL: ACQUIRE UNIT-TASK ...if task not remembered

            GOAL: TURN PAGE ...if at end of manuscript

            GOAL: GET-FROM-MANUSCRIPT

        GOAL: EXECUTE-UNIT-TASK ...if a unit task was found

            GOAL: MODIFY-TEXT

                select: GOAL: MOVE-TEXT* ...if text is to be moved

                    GOAL: DELETE-PHRASE ...if a phrase is to be deleted

                    GOAL: INSERT-WORD ... if a word is to be inserted

    VERIFY-EDIT

NGOMSL

NGOMSL is a structured natural language notation for representing GOMS models and a procedure for constructing them. This program form provides predictions of operator sequences, execution time and time to learn methods. An analyst constructs an NGOMSL model by performing a top-down, breadth-first expansion of the user's top-level goals into methods, until the methods contain only primitive operators, typically keystroke-level operators. This model explicitly represents the goal structure just like the CMN-GOMS and can so represent high-level goals. Shown below is a simple example:

NGOMSL Statements

METHOD for GOAL: MOVE TEXT

    STEP 1: ACCOMPLISH GOAL: CUT TEXT

    STEP 2: ACCOMPLISH GOAL: PASTE TEXT

    STEP 3: RETURN WITH GOAL ACCOMPLISHED

METHOD for GOAL: CUT TEXT

    STEP 1: ACCOMPLISH GOAL: HIGHLIGHT TEXT

    STEP 2: RETAIN THAT COMMAND IS CUT, AND

    ACCOMPLISH GOAL: ISSUE A COMMAND

    STEP 3: RETURN WITH GOAL ACCOMPLISHED

etc.

CPM-GOMS

Bonnie E. John and David Kieras describe four different types of GOMS: CMN-GOMS, KLM and NGOMSL assume that all of the operators occur in sequence and do not contain operators that are below the activity level. CPM-GOMS being the fourth method uses operators at the level of Model Human Processor which assumes that operators of the cognitive processor, perceptual processor, and the motor processor can work in parallel to each other. The most important point of CPM-GOMS is the ability to predict skilled behavior from its ability to model overlapping actions.

Shown below is a simple copy and paste example:

GOAL COPY-AND-PASTE-TEXT

    GOAL COPY-TEXT

      GOAL HIGHLIGH-TEXT

        Operator MOVE-CURSOR-TO-BEGINNING

        Operator CLICK-MOUSE-BUTTON

        Operator MOVE-CURSOR-TO-END

        Operator SHIFT-CLICK-MOUSE-BUTTON

        Operator VERIFY-HIGHLIGHT

    GOAL ISSUE-COPY-COMMAND

      Select:

        GOAL USE-MOUSE

        Operator MOVE-CURSOR-TO-EDIT-MENU

        Operator PRESS-MOUSE-BUTTON

        Operator MOVE-CURSOR-TO-COPY-ITEM

        Operator VERIFY-HIGHLIGHT

        Operator RELEASE-MOUSE-BUTTON

    GOAL USE-KEYBOARD

      Operator PRESS-KEY-STRG

      Operator PRESS-KEY-C

      Operator RELEASE-KEYS

    GOAL PASTE-TEXT[...]

Selection rule for GOAL ISSUE-COPY-COMMAND

if HANDS-ARE-ON-KEYBOARD then

>   select GOAL USE-KEYBOARD

else

>   select GOAL USE-MOUSE

SGOMS

SGOMS stands for Sociotechnical GOMS and was created to allow GOMS to model work in complex sociotechnical systems. GOMS is meant to model an individual user, working in isolation, with no unexpected interruptions, similar to a Cognitive Psychology experiment. This level of analysis is sometimes referred to as *microcognition* to distinguish it from macrocognition, which refers to real world cognition. SGOMS is meant to expand the applicability of GOMS to the macro cognitive level of analysis. To do this, SGOMS adds a high level control structure to GOMS, called the *planning unit*. This allows GOMS to deal with unexpected interruptions.

A planning unit is a list of unit tasks. Planning units can be ordered (the unit tasks must be done in order) or situated (the unit tasks in the list are done as the situation demands). Consistent with CPM-GOMS, SGOMS assumes that the agent can monitor the situation in parallel in order to detect threats (neurophysiologically, this function is associated with the amygdala). Planning units can be interrupted and bookmarked so they can be resumed later. When a planning unit is interrupted the agent considers the situation and can resume the same planning unit or bookmark it and switch to a different planning unit. SGOMS does not prescribe how this choice is made but, if the decision is based on routine expertise, it can be included in the SGOMS model.

Assumptions and Errors

Importance of Assumptions in GOMS Analysis

Accurate assumptions are vital in GOMS analysis. Before applying the average times for detailed functions, it is very important that an experimenter make sure he or she has accounted for as many variables as possible by using assumptions. Experimenters should design their GOMS analysis for the users who will most likely be using the system which is being analyzed. Consider, for example, an experimenter wishes to determine how long it will take an F22 Raptor pilot to interact with an interface he or she has used for years. It can probably be assumed that the pilot has outstanding vision and is in good physical health. In addition, it can be assumed that the pilot can interact with the interface quickly because of the vast hours of simulation and previous use he or she has endured. All things considered, it is fair to use fastman times in this situation. Contrarily, consider an 80-year-old person with no flight experience attempting to interact with the same F22 Raptor interface. It is fair to say that the two people would have much different skill sets and those skill sets should be accounted for subjectively.

Accounting for Errors

The only way to account for errors in GOMS analysis is to predict where the errors are most likely to occur and measure the time it would take to correct the predicted errors. For example, assume an experimenter thought that in typing the word "the" it was likely that a subject would instead incorrectly type "teh." The experimenter would calculate the time it takes to type the incorrect word, the time it takes to recognize that a mistake has been made, and the time it takes to correct the recognized error.

Applications of GOMS

Workstation Efficiency

A successful implementation of CPM-GOMS was in *Project Ernestine* held by New England Telephone. New ergonomically designed workstations were compared to old workstations in terms of improvement in telephone operators' performance. CPM-GOMS analysis estimated a 3% decrease in productivity. Over the four-month trial 78,240 calls were analysed and it was concluded that the new workstations produced an actual 4% decrease in productivity. As the proposed workstation required less keystrokes than the original it was not clear from the time trials why the decrease occurred. However, CPM-GOMS analysis made it apparent that the problem was that the new workstations did not utilize the workers' slack time. Not only did CPM-GOMS give a close estimate, but it provided more information of the situation.

CAD

GOMS models were employed in the redesign of a CAD (computer-aided design) system for industrial ergonomics. An applied GOMS model shows where the interface needs to be redesigned, as well as provides an evaluation of design concepts and ideas. In Richard Gong's example, when GOMS revealed a frequent goal supported by a very inefficient method, he changed the method to a more efficient one. If GOMS showed that there were goals not supported by any method at all, then new methods were added. GOMS also revealed where similar goals are supported by inconsistent methods, a situation in which users are likely to have problems remembering what to do, and showed how to make the methods consistent.

Software Tools

There exist various tools for the creation and analysis of Goms-Models. A selection is listed in the following:

- QGoms (Quick-Goms).

- CogTool KLM-based modelling tool.

- Cogulator Cognitive calculator for GOMS modeling.

Fitts' Law

Fitts's law (often cited as Fitts' law) is a predictive model of human movement primarily used in human–computer interaction and ergonomics. This scientific law predicts that the time required to rapidly move to a target area is a function of the ratio between the distance to the target and the width of the target. Fitts's law is used to model the act of *pointing*, either by physically touching an object with a hand or finger, or virtually, by pointing to an object on a computer monitor using a pointing device.

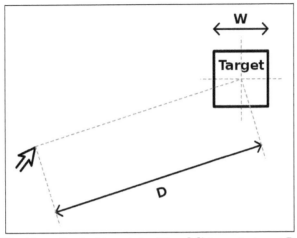

Fitts' Law: Draft of target size W and distance to target D.

Fitts's law has been shown to apply under a variety of conditions; with many different limbs (hands, feet, the lower lip, head-mounted sights, eye gaze), manipulanda (input devices), physical environments (including underwater), and user populations (young, old, special educational needs, and drugged participants).

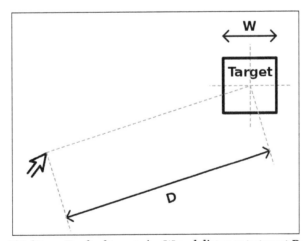

Fitts' Law: Draft of target size W and distance to target D.

The original 1954 paper by Paul Morris Fitts proposed a metric to quantify the difficulty of a target selection task. The metric was based on an information analogy, where the distance to the center of the target (*D*) is like a signal and the tolerance or width of the target (*W*) is like noise. The metric is Fitts's *index of difficulty* (*ID*, in bits):

$$ID = \log_2\left(\frac{2D}{W}\right)$$

Fitts also proposed an *index of performance* (*IP*, in bits per second) as a measure of human performance. The metric combines a task's index of difficulty (*ID*) with the movement time (*MT*, in seconds) in selecting the target. In Fitts's words, "The average rate of information generated by a series of movements is the average information per movement divided by the time per movement". Thus,

$$IP = \left(\frac{ID}{MT} \right)$$

Today, *IP* is more commonly called *throughput* (*TP*). It is also common to include an adjustment for accuracy in the calculation.

Researchers after Fitts began the practice of building linear regression equations and examining the correlation (*r*) for goodness of fit. The equation expresses the relationship between *MT* and the *D* and *W* task parameters:

$$MT = a + b \cdot ID = a + b \cdot \log_2 \left(\frac{2D}{W} \right)$$

where:

- *MT* is the average time to complete the movement.

- *a* and *b* are constants that depend on the choice of input device and are usually determined empirically by regression analysis.

- *ID* is the index of difficulty.

- *D* is the distance from the starting point to the center of the target.

- *W* is the width of the target measured along the axis of motion. *W* can also be thought of as the allowed error tolerance in the final position, since the final point of the motion must fall within $\pm^W\!/_2$ of the target's center.

Since shorter movement times are desirable for a given task, the value of the *b* parameter can be used as a metric when comparing computer pointing devices against one another. The first Human-Computer Interface application of Fitts's law was by Card, English, and Burr (1978), who used the index of performance (*IP*), interpreted as $^1\!/_b$, to compare performance of different input devices, with the mouse coming out on top compared to the joystick or directional movement keys. This early work, according to Stuart Card's biography, "was a major factor leading to the mouse's commercial introduction by Xerox".

Many experiments testing Fitts's law apply the model to a dataset in which either distance or width, but not both, are varied. The model's predictive power deteriorates when both are varied over a significant range. Notice that because the *ID* term depends only on the *ratio* of distance to width, the model implies that a target distance and width combination can be re-scaled arbitrarily without affecting movement time, which is impossible. Despite its flaws, this form of the model does possess remarkable predictive power across a range of computer interface modalities and motor tasks, and has provided many insights into user interface design principles.

Bits Per Second: Model Innovations Driven by Information Theory

The formulation of Fitts's index of difficulty most frequently used in the Human-Computer Interaction community is called the Shannon formulation:

$$ID = \log_2\left(\frac{D}{W} + 1\right)$$

This form was proposed by Scott MacKenzie, professor at York University, and named for its resemblance to the Shannon–Hartley theorem.

Using this form of the model, the difficulty of a pointing task was equated to a quantity of information transmitted (in units of bits) by performing the task. This was justified by the assertion that pointing reduces to an information processing task. Although, no formal mathematical connection was established between Fitts's law and the Shannon-Hartley theorem it was inspired by, the Shannon form of the law has been used extensively, likely due to the appeal of quantifying motor actions using information theory. In 2002, the ISO 9241 was published, providing standards for human-computer interface testing, including the use of the Shannon form of Fitts's law. It has been shown that the information transmitted via serial keystrokes on a keyboard and the information implied by the ID for such a task are not consistent.

Adjustment for Accuracy: Use of the Effective Target Width

An important improvement to Fitts's law was proposed by Crossman in 1956 and used by Fitts in his 1964 paper with Peterson. With the adjustment, target width (W) is replaced by an effective target width (W_e). W_e is computed from the standard deviation in the selection coordinates gathered over a sequence of trials for a particular D-W condition. If the selections are logged as x coordinates along the axis of approach to the target, then:

$$W_e = 4.133 \times SD_x$$

This yields

$$ID_e = \log_2\left(\frac{D}{W_e} + 1\right)$$

and hence

$$IP = \left(\frac{ID_e}{MT}\right)$$

If the selection coordinates are normally distributed, W_e spans 96% of the distribution. If the observed error rate was 4% in the sequence of trials, then $W_e = W$. If the error rate was greater than 4%, $W_e > W$, and if the error rate was less than 4%, $W_e < W$. By using W_e, a Fitts' law model more closely reflects what users actually did, rather than what they were asked to do.

The main advantage in computing IP as above is that spatial variability, or accuracy, is included in the measurement. With the adjustment for accuracy, Fitts's law more truly encompasses the speed-accuracy tradeoff. The equations above appear in ISO 9241-9 as the recommended method of computing *throughput*.

Welford's Model: Innovations Driven by Predictive Power

Not long after the original model was proposed, a 2-factor variation was proposed under the intuition that target distance and width have separate effects on movement time. Welford's model, proposed in 1968, separated the influence of target distance and width into separate terms, and provided improved predictive power:

$$T = a + b_1 \log_2(D) + b_2 \log_2(W)$$

This model has an additional parameter, so its predictive accuracy cannot be directly compared with 1-factor forms of Fitts's law. However, a variation on Welford's model inspired by the Shannon formulation,

$$T = a + b_1 \log_2(D + W) + b_2 \log_2(W) = a + b \log_2\left(\frac{D + W}{W^k}\right)$$

reduces to the Shannon form when $k = 1$. Therefore, this model *can* be directly compared against the Shannon form of Fitts's law using the F-test of nested models. This comparison reveals that not only does the Shannon form of Welford's model better predict movement times, but it is also more robust when control-display gain (the ratio between e.g. hand movement and cursor movement) is varied. Consequently, although the Shannon model is slightly more complex and less intuitive, it is empirically the best model to use for virtual pointing tasks.

Extending the Model from 1D to 2D and other Nuances

Extensions to Two or More Dimensions

In its original form, Fitts's law is meant to apply only to one-dimensional tasks. However, the original experiments required subjects to move a stylus (in three dimensions) between two metal plates on a table, termed the reciprocal tapping task. The target width perpendicular to the direction of movement was very wide to avoid it having a significant influence on performance. A major application for Fitts's law is 2D virtual pointing tasks on computer screens, in which targets have bounded sizes in both dimensions.

Fitts's law has been extended to two-dimensional tasks in two different ways: For navigating e.g. hierarchical pull-down menus, the user must generate a trajectory with the pointing device that is constrained by the menu geometry; for this application the Accot-Zhai steering law was derived.

For simply pointing to targets in a two-dimensional space, the model generally holds as-is but requires adjustments to capture target geometry and quantify targeting errors in a logically consistent way.

Characterizing Performance

Since the *a* and *b* parameters should capture movement times over a potentially wide range of task geometries, they can serve as a performance metric for a given interface. In doing so, it is necessary to separate variation between users from variation between interfaces. The *a* parameter is typically positive and close to zero, and sometimes ignored in characterizing average performance. Multiple methods exist for identifying parameters from experimental data, and the choice of method is the subject of heated debate, since method variation can result in parameter differences that overwhelm underlying performance differences.

An additional issue in characterizing performance is incorporating success rate: an aggressive user can achieve shorter movement times at the cost of experimental trials in which the target is missed. If the latter are not incorporated into the model, then average movement times can be artificially decreased.

Temporal Targets

Fitts's law deals only with targets defined in space. However, a target can be defined purely on the time axis, which is called a temporal target. A blinking target or a target moving toward a selection area are examples of temporal targets. Similar to space, the distance to the target (i.e., temporal distance D_t) and the width of the target (i.e., temporal width W_t) can be defined for temporal targets as well. The temporal distance is the amount of time a person must wait for a target to appear. The temporal width is a short duration from the moment the target appears until it disappears. For example, for a blinking target, D_t can be thought of as the period of blinking and W_t as the duration of the blinking. As with targets in space, the larger the D_t or the smaller the W_t, the more difficult it becomes to select the target.

The task of selecting the temporal target is called temporal pointing. The model for temporal pointing was first presented to Human-computer Interaction field in 2016. The model predicts the error rate, the human performance in temporal pointing, as a function of temporal index of difficulty (ID_t):

$$ID_t = \log_2\left(\frac{D_t}{W_t}\right)$$

Steering Law

The Steering Law is a corollary of Fitts's Law. The Steering Law is an equation that predicts the efficiency of very common interactions; it describes the particular case of path-steering tasks-that is, when a user must move a pointer through a path with boundaries or a "tunnel." The equation is:

$$T = a + b\left(\frac{A}{W}\right)$$

T is the overall movement time, a and b are constants, A is the length of the tunnel, and W is the width of the tunnel.

Most UX professionals will never need to use this equation: the main actionable insight is that long, narrow tunnels take more time to navigate than short, wide tunnels.

The Steering Law predicts the time necessary to steer a pointer (such as a mouse cursor) through a bounded tunnel (such as a menu, a scroll bar, or slider). The steering time depends on the length and the width of the tunnel: the longer and the narrower the tunnel, the more time will be required to successfully steer through it;

According to the Steering Law, a tunnel is any user-interface control that requires the user to move the cursor (or drag a finger on a touchscreen) along a path that has borders. Overstepping the border will have some consequence, though since this is a common user error, the consequences will hopefully be mild, such as having the computer stop paying attention while the pointer is outside the tunnel. Some of the most common UI elements that involve this type of interaction include dropdown menus (particularly hierarchical menus with hover-revealed submenus), parameter-control sliders, scroll bars, video-playback scrubber bars, and video-game elements that require drag and drop in a straight line.

In most cases, moving outside the tunnel boundaries interrupts the user action: for example, in a hierarchical dropdown menu, if the user moves the cursor outside the menu area, the menu disappears (which is a somewhat harsh penalty, if the tunnel breakage was unintentional). That is why the width of the tunnel is important for how easily the user can steer through — a narrow tunnel makes it easy to accidentally exit the tunnel area.

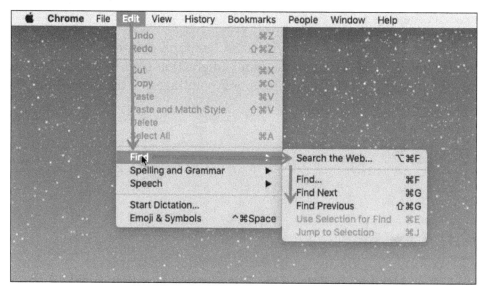

On MacOS, moving the mouse cursor through a hierarchical menu involves a series of linear path-steering tasks separated by 90-degree turns. Within the main menu, submenus open on hover. Note that the second step in this L-shaped sequence (moving from Find to its child menu) involves the narrowest tunnel, which is slow and difficult for users to move through without errors.

Many users will attempt to move diagonally from Find to an item in the child menu, but, because in doing so their mouse will cross the area for Spelling and Grammar, the target submenu will be lost and instead the Spelling and Grammar one will be opened (older versions of MacOS featured a menu designed by NN/g principal Bruce Tognazzini; that menu did not exhibit this behavior, but instead, used a vector-based triangular buffer to allow users to move diagonally. Unfortunately, in the years since, Apple has reverted this excellent bit of interaction design.)

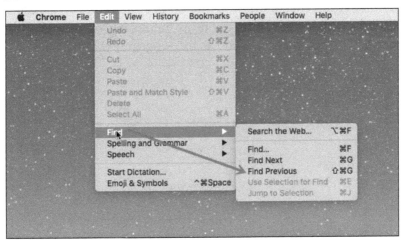

Why people have trouble maintaining the cursor on a straight path has to do with human physiology: the elbow and wrist, which enable the movement of the hand, describe an arc, not a line. Try it yourself: hold your arm out directly in front of you and move your hand from left to right. You'll notice that, even if you attempt to keep it moving in a straight line, your arm will always have a subtle arc in the movement. As a result, using one's hand to move in a long, straight line is physically difficult; the longer the motion, the greater the chance of error. Furthermore, many users (especially older adults and those with disabilities) have unsteady hands, and all mobile users are subject to the bumps and jitters of using a device out in the world.

Making Menus more Steer-friendly

Menus are one of the UI elements most affected by the Steering Law. Here are a few design choices to make them easy to use.

Keep dropdown menus as short as possible. Menus with few choices minimize the time and difficulty of steering through the narrow tunnel, and also reduces the time to visually search through a large number of choices.

Avoid hierarchical menus, particularly hierarchical menus that are more than two-levels deep. Hierarchical menus are inherently a difficult UI to design well due to Steering Law constraints. There will always be a tradeoff between designing the two tunnels associated with a hierarchical menu: the vertical tunnel that corresponds to the main-menu area and the horizontal tunnel, that corresponds to subcategory name that the user has to traverse to open the submenu:

- The vertical tunnel needs to be short, but that means that each of the items in the menu may have to be given smaller height — which leads to narrow horizontal tunnels.

- The vertical tunnel must also be wide, but that leads to longer horizontal tunnels from main-menu option to the corresponding submenu.

This hierarchical menu on Costco.com shows the inherent tradeoff of optimizing a hierarchical menu for Steering Law effects and compromising between the sizes of the vertical tunnel (left) and the horizontal tunnel (right). A wide menu optimizes the vertical tunnel for ease of steering down the menu, especially for menus with many choices. However, by making the menu wide, the length of the horizontal tunnel is increased, and moving across the menu to access the corresponding submenu is more fraught with errors. Note that most menus have not been optimized at all for the Steering Law, as they are simply made as wide as the longest text label.

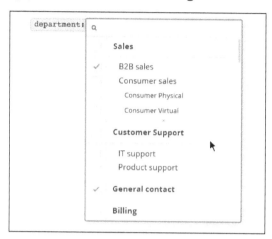

When a hierarchical menu is absolutely necessary, use a short time delay between mouse hover and when reveal of the child menu (or use a vector-based triangular system to allow for some diagonal movement error). Also include as much padding as reasonably possible above and below each menu item, to increase the width of the tunnel for horizontal movement.

For navigation menus, consider mega menus (or square menus) as an alternative to pull-down menus. As mega menus allow for free movement within a wide 2D space, the steering law does not apply (though Fitts's Law still does, so make sure targets are still large).

Sliders, Scrollbars and Scrubbers Need Additional Controls for Precision

When designing other UI elements that involve path-steering tasks, such as sliders, scrollbars, and video playback heads, remember that users will have a hard time achieving precision with such controls. Therefore, for precise tasks, supplement these UI elements with other secondary controls that support precision. When using a slider to select a parameter value, use the slider as a coarse control (for reaching the general desired region), and provide a secondary fine control (such as numeric input box with stepper buttons) to choose a specific value. Also, allow users to click anywhere on the slider to jump to the desired position, rather than requiring them to click and drag; this approach enables a user to move freely in 2D space without needing to steer through the tunnel. On touchscreens, think about the overall target size of the slider knob (it should be at least 1cm x 1cm) and ensure that the user's finger won't obscure the slider (or any labels around it).

Hick's Law

Hick's Law is named after a British and an American psychologist team of William Edmund Hick and Ray Hyman. In 1952, this pair set out to examine the relationship between the number of stimuli present and an individual's reaction time to any given stimulus. As you would expect, the more stimuli to choose from, the longer it takes the user to make a decision on which one to interact with. Users bombarded with choices have to take time to interpret and decide, giving them work they don't want.

The formula for Hick's Law is defined as follows:

$$RT = a + b \log_2(n)$$

Where "RT" is the reaction time, "(n)" is the number of stimuli present, and "a" and "b" are arbitrary measurable constants that depend on the task that is to be carried out and the conditions under which it will be carried out. "A" could be finding the right present online for your mother-in-law; "B" could be an onscreen chat with your mother-in-law in which she reminds you it's her birthday tomorrow.

Generally, the application of Hick's Law is simple – reduce the number of stimuli and get a faster decision-making process – but there are exceptions to the rule. For example, a user may already have made a decision *before* seeing the stimuli. In that instance, the time it takes for him/her to act is likely to be less than if he/she had not already determined a course of action.

The Implementation of Hick's Law

You can find applications of Hick's Law everywhere, not just in web and app design. Hick's Law determined the number of controls on your microwave or your washing machine. A design principle known as "K.I.S.S." ("Keep It Short and Simple") became recognized in the 1960s for its effectiveness in this regard. Echoing Hick's Law, K.I.S.S. states that simplicity is the key for a system to work in the best way. First embraced by the U.S. Navy, the principle of "K.I.S.S." was in general use in many industries by the 1970s. In some environments, K.I.S.S. gets translated as "Keep It Simple Stupid".

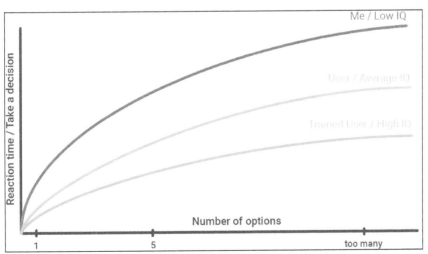

Hick's Law surrounds us. When you go to a high-end restaurant, often whoever has written the menu has used Hick's Law to give you the "right" number of choices. By not getting bogged down in a decision-making process, you're more likely to savor you meal out with the important company joining you. Look at the menu above: what a daunting job to choose a pizza.

Designers don't use Hick's Law in isolation in design. We always combine it with other design principles to make it work effectively. We often have to make compromises with Hick's Law, too – sometimes there is *no avoiding* complexity. This is why a DSLR camera has many more controls and options than a camera on a smartphone. The objective of Hick's Law is to try and simplify the decision-making process, not eliminate that process entirely.

In web and app design, as with other types of product design, we often have several functions and choices to present to the user. Here, we have to take the time to think about how we'll introduce those.

The landing page is the first glimpse your user will have of your site. That's a make-it-or-break-it chance to create an impression using Hick's Law. So, it's particularly important to minimize choices here. Are you promoting a product or a service? If you're selling aquariums, what's your best-selling model? Introduce your company and highlight the model on the landing page, organizing text carefully. Most importantly, draw the user's eye with a well-placed image (remember those sweet spots). They'll see that before they start reading. Make the option you *most* want them to select stand out.

Separating the essential material from the secondary, less-likely-to-be-selected options is vital. On one hand, we may know which, say, aquarium will jump out at most users, and which are the more specialized ones that only expert fish-keepers might want. However, because we have *more familiarity* with such functions and choices, we run the risk of forgetting that our users *won't* have this. They're arriving at the website or examining the product with a fresh perspective. So, understanding this difference, we must stand back and see what we will offer the users to get them to decide their next move. Good designers try to employ Hick's Law to respect their users' time and to ensure a high-quality user experience.

To employ Hick's Law effectively in the design of interactive products, you can consider the following:

Categorizing Choice: You can see Hick's Law in action in the navigation of almost any website. If your menus offered direct access to every link within your site, you could quickly overwhelm the visitor. If Amazon's menus did that, it could take several hours to scroll through a menu! Suddenly, searching for a last-minute birthday present or replacing a printer cartridge becomes a "stressfest".

Happily, designers group menu items into high-level categories instead. These slowly expand as the users select options; the new categories then take users where they want to go. Do you recall Amazon screenshots just above? There's a compromise between offering all functionality and Hick's Law, which pressures the designer to keep things as simple as possible.

With highly complex sites, the use of Hick's Law requires further implementations of choice. As designers, we notice how we can scatter navigation items throughout the design in small, discrete clusters. These help narrow down huge volumes of information without overloading the user.

The card-sorting method is great to find out about the categories that make more sense to your users. You can use card-sorting to define the groupings of the functionalities and also the labels for these categories. You should do this early on in your project, before starting any sketching or wireframe.

As you move on in the design process, you can use eye-tracking to have a heat map of your site. This can help you work out where future design changes might benefit from further applying Hick's Law. Heat maps display areas of a site that users look at most, showing problem areas quickly, too.

Obscuring Complexity: If you have a complex process, you can use Hick's Law to rationalize only presenting specific parts of that process at any one time on the screen. Instead of throwing the entirety of your payment process up in a long, complex form, you can break it down into prompting users to register their e-mail and create a password. Then, you can give them another screen with shopping cart details, then another which collects delivery information and so on.

By reducing the number of options on screen, the payment process becomes more *user friendly*, and it's more likely that the user will reach the end of the process than abandon the cart.

Hints from Analytics

Once your app or website is launched, it is also important to keep an eye on how Hick's law might be affecting your users' experience. Here are some variables that you can use to analyse it:

Time on Site: There is a sweet spot for most websites when it comes to time spent on site. Too little time and the user has likely left without purchasing or registering. Too much time and they may get caught up in information consumption and again fail to make a purchase or register. Just enough time and the majority of users who will make a purchase and register will *do so*.

Once a site is live, you can start to gauge where that sweet spot is and utilize Hick's Law either to increase or decrease the average amount of time spent on site.

While simplifying decision making can extend the time spent on site, it might also reduce it. If the decision making is so simple that users make little progress towards their objectives each time they make a decision, they'll be as likely to leave as users who find a decision-making process impossibly confusing because they've seen too many options at once.

Page Views: Hick's Law can also affect the number of page views that each user carries out. If the navigation menu is too complex, the number of page views is likely to be lower than if users were offered a navigation menu that better met their needs.

Of course, page views are only important if the users are achieving their objectives while on site. It would be easy to construct a very deep menu system of binary choices that required 10 or more clicks to get to the desired information. Unfortunately, were you to design that, you'd almost certainly find that users would abandon the site *long* before getting to the information they needed. This approach might deliver more page views at first, but it is unlikely to deliver the results *required* from your design, either.

References

- Keystroke-Level+Model, definition: definitions.net, Retrieved 26 June, 2019

- Rogers, Yvonne; Helen Sharp; Jenny Preece (2002). Interaction Design. United States of America: John Wiley & Sons. P. 454. ISBN 0-471-49278-7

- Steering-law: nngroup.com, Retrieved 27 July, 2019

- Hick-s-law-making-the-choice-easier-for-users, literature: interaction-design.org/literature, Retrieved 28 August, 2019

6
Applications of Human-Computer Interaction

Human-computer interaction is applied in various fields such as game design, vehicles, wrist watch, etc. It is also used in virtual reality and augmented reality. These diverse applications of human-computer interaction have been thoroughly discussed in this chapter.

Human-Computer Interaction in Game Design

Computer games and video games are one of the most successful application domains in the history on interactive system. This success has appeared despite the fact that games were considered to be different from most of the accepted paradigms for designing usable interactive software. What has made games different is they focus on system performance over consistency; games have always ignored the windowing systems, the standard widget libraries, and the toolkits that define the look and feel of conventional systems which leads to a very different design environment. This environment does not place restrictions on how thing must look or how interaction must be carried out with the user. Instead, it does strongly reward innovation and performance the driving forces in Game Design are user performance, satisfaction and novelty. As a result, games have both become early adopters of new HCI technologies as well as innovators in the area of HCI interaction design.

Key Issues of HCI in Gaming

It is important to understand what Human-Computer Interaction is, and why it is so important in gaming. A relatively new field, HCI was founded in 1983 with the following definition which is still applicable today: The key notion, perhaps, is that the user and the computer engage in a communicative dialog whose purpose is the accomplishment of some task. All the mechanisms used in this dialog constitute the interface: the physical devices, such as keyboards and displays, as well as the computer's programs for controlling the interaction.

Consider every operating system found in the PC whether Windows, Mac or Linux and desktop or notebook which found in millions of homes and offices around the globe. The present PC is more powerful than it used to be; however, the methodology and technology for interacting with the PC remains little changed – a keyboard (based on the 19th Century technology of a typewriter) and mouse for input, and an LCD (or in the past CRT) display combined with speakers for output. These components are still considered as the basic interaction tools for computer games nowadays, especially in the strategy genres. The Total War series, War craft and Star craft are the examples in this case.

Moreover, considering the modern gaming platforms in all their diversity – from the PC, through consoles (the Microsoft Xbox 360, Sony PlayStation 3, and Nintendo Wii), handhelds (Nintendo DS and Sony PSP) and the rapidly growing area of gameplay on mobile phones (best represented by the iPhone and other touch phones). On these platforms, gamers use devices ranging from microphones through touch-screens, accelerometers, cameras, game-pads and remotes to sing, strum, dance, swing, and otherwise conduct a range of physical activities – far richer than those afforded by a keyboard and mouse – in order to play their games. Without a doubt, in the past decade, the game industry has seen a genuine new start in HCI (Human-Computer Interaction) technology with new styles of interaction and play being supported, and these technologies achieving mass market penetration. Furthermore, new technologies such as several Brain Computer Interface (BCI) products have emerged in the past years (the NCI OCZ, the Emotiv EPOC headset) aimed squarely at, and priced for the game market.

What is more, despite the escalating economic importance of the computer and video games, indicated by the rapidly growing revenue within the game industry over the past few decades, it cannot be the sole value in measuring video game cultural value. As the matter of fact, although with some forms of play such as education and communication, computer and video games continue to receive negative recognition from the society. They are still held in rather low value by policy makers. Most schools and organizations have currently banned such form of activities in the class room or at the workplace.

This is intensified by an excess of research writing that over-emphasis the negative effect computer and video games have from various perspectives. At first, it is claimed that the prolonged use of computer games contributes obsessive, addictive behavior, dehumanization of the player, desensitizing of feeling, health problems, and other disorder. Others argue that computer and video games encourage the development of anti-social behavior among game players. In addition, perhaps, the most debated issue concerning games and players, especially teenagers, is their connection to violence. A growing body research is correlating violent computer games play to aggressive cognitions, attitudes, and behaviors. A number of studies have shown a positive association between the amount of video game play and aggressiveness among children, adolescents and even adults.

Consequently, there is an increasing interest in approaching game studies from the perspectives of HCI. Some researchers investigated novel forms of interaction such as tangible interfaces to encourage collaboration and techniques of gathering user requirement for design educational game. While other studies focused on the human behavior and physiological responses such as frustration in order to better understand the interface design toward building affective computer through the study of computer gameplay. In closely with game developers. In addition, to the study of HCI in computer game, is the work of Malone on educational games. Malone in his early work on the motivation of computer game based learning proposes, the Heuristics for Game Designers and researchers. The Heuristics for the fun factor of computer games consists of three main elements that draw largely from Csikszentmihalyi's flow theory: challenge, fantasy and curiosity. Apart from these, there has also been research on the evaluation of the usability of games.

Game user Interface Design

An interface has many pieces; for instance, menus, text, buttons and icons. What is more, the interface is the part of the game that allows the user to interact with the game. Interaction is what makes a video game different from a movie. When playing a video game, the user can make choices and respond to events. An interface is the connection between the user and the game, and a well-designed interface makes the video game experience more fun.

Interface design is a creative, exciting, and challenging subject. However, it is necessary to point out that, too often, video game interfaces are an afterthought. The reason is too many project managers assume the most important part of a software development project is the programming, and then the interface can come later. As the result, insufficient time is assigned for interface design which may leads to a poor quality interface.

All this considered, the visual quality of a game is very important. A poor interface can ruin the entire video game experience. One of the negative example is the user is confused and cannot comprehend how to navigate the menu or if he/she cannot find the information while playing the game. The more the user tries to search for information in order to play, the less enjoyable the game becomes. On the contrary, if the game has a great interface, it can enhance the playing experience. A good-looking interface with a lot of well-designed features can actually be fun to use and even seem like a game itself. But more importantly, great game interface design can boost game sales.

The Game Interface Design Goals

A good way to for a Game Designer to make decisions about features of a game is to have goals. If he understands these goals, it will be much easier for him to make decisions about the interface. It is not always easy to define the overall game goals, but if the Game Designer takes the time to create concise goals for the entire game and clearly understands these, many decisions will be easier to make. In fact, goal oriented design produces great results.

In many cases, the Designer may be wondering, What kind of goals do I need to set when designing an interface? Thus, making the coolest interface ever may be the first thing that comes to mind. This goal sounds great, but it probably should not be the first priority. As much as everyone wants a cool interface, there may be other things that are more important. If making a kids' game; for example, it might be more important that the menu is easy for a six-year old to use than that it looks cool. More importantly, prioritization is the key to using these goals to guide the design.

In addition, below is a list of possible goals that a Designer may have. These goals may not match perfectly with every case, but it is important to understand the goals of the company, and to align these with the user's requirements. This list is by no means a complete list of goals that could ever be used for every Game Design case. In fact, it is a very brief list which meant to simulate thought about the real goals of the Game Designer.

- Promote an existing license or famous personality.

- Capitalize on an existing license or famous personality.

- Meet a particular schedule.

- Reach a particular audience.

- Create something completely unique.

- Outdo a competing game.

- Capitalize on the success of a competing game.

- Continue a successful series.

- Sell another product (other than the game itself).

- Promote a moral issue.

- Create an educational experience.

- Pass the approval process of the console manufacture.

- Please the marketing department.

- Tell a story.

Promoting and capitalizing an existing license or famous personality are the first goal for the Game Designer. It is important to have a good first impression from the users. The second goal is meeting a particular schedule. A game interface design should be treated equally as the other phases in the game development process. Therefore, a sufficient time should be scheduled for the design in order to create a well-made interface that can guarantee meeting the player's expectation. A further goal is reaching a particular audience. A targeted group of customer should be decided first, before starting to create an interface. For instance, different styles of interface will be made based on the information whether the game is for young audiences, or for more mature audiences. Consequently, if the target audiences are students or teachers, creating an education experience should be considered as one of the priority goals. The fourth possible goal is pass the approval process of the console manufacture a game can be developed for playing in many platforms.

Furthermore, for a game manufacture to success in the market, it is essential for the Game Designer to create something completely unique. There is a variety of possible ways to achieve this goal. The Designer can outdo a competing game in features and effects; capitalize on the success of a competing game, continue a successful series or even promote a moral issue. But more importantly, the game should tell a story. For example, the strategy game Total War Shogun promotes the Japan's warfare in the 16th century.

The final goals in this list are the Game Designer needs to please the marketing department and sell another product (e.g. a game is based on a movie or a novel). More innovative ideas can possibly be acquired by the collaboration between different departments. In this case, since the marketing people work closely to the customers, they understand clearly the customer's desires. Additionally, a game may be used in a promotion campaign to boost sale of another product, that is different than game.

What is more, it is essential to mentioned that every Designer should avoid the temptation to set one large goal that is actually several goals in one. This is often the easy way out, since it is more difficult to articulate specific goals than it is to generalize. But in comparison, a goal like make a cool game is not nearly as clear as Add three new and creative features that are not found in competing racing games. The point is to define useful goals that will provide direction during development. As the result, understanding the motive behind the goal is very important.

Basic Design Principles

Every best Interface Designer knows and understands clearly the design principles: In fact, nothing will improve the design skills better than an understanding of basic design principles. Many Interface Designers learn these principles in college or a specialized art school but they forget them later, since it is easy to go out and find a job in the industry, start working on real games, and just gets sort of rusty on design basics. Ignoring or forgetting basic design principles will adversely affect the design ability. Once the Designer has learned basic design principles, it is important to keep using them to evaluate and improve the interfaces. In this subchapter, a number of design principles will be introduced. They are in a form of combination between the design knowledge and the study of Human-Computer Interaction.

Understand the users and support their goals: If a user interface is designed after the fact' it is like designing an automobile dashboard after the engine, chassis, and all other components and functions are specified. If these interfaces are designed after the fact, it is almost impossible for them to be able to meet all the user's goals. In other words, the Designer need to first understand the users (their needs and objectives) in order to create an interface that allows them to effectively access the system's functionality.

Get back to basics using color: Color can be a very powerful design tool. One of the abilities of color is to set a mood; color can express emotion and set an atmosphere. For instance, a design that uses a lot of neutral gray and de-saturated colors can bring the sad feeling. Moreover, one of the major challenges when working with color is finding a set of colors that work well together creating color harmony. Harmonious colors or complementary colors can include colors that are similar to one another like a range of blue colors can look good together.

Make the interface easy to learn and enjoyable to use: This is an important rule that helps the user maintain a sense of spatial orientation and sanity. It is essential to consider how the user will interface with the product before creating it. Additionally, a bonus point for a good interface is creating an interface that is enjoyable to use. The Designer can add a variety of effect like 3D transformation and adding light/shadow, instead of using only plain text and picture, into the design.

Organize the visual: A good rule when creating an interface is to space elements evenly and align them well. It is necessary to paying attention to spacing and alignment results in visual organization. If the elements in the design are scattered and the spacing between them is not consistent, the design will appear unorganized. This is displeasing to the user because most people are attracted to organization. Moreover, if the design calls for objects that are not aligned, then make sure that these elements are not positioned only slightly off-alignment with other objects, in other word, move them far enough out of alignment that there is no doubt that it was intentional. It can be very disconcerting to the user if objects look like they should be aligned but they are not. Many designs can be improved by simply fixing the spacing between objects.

Use Unity and Variation: When creating an interface design, one of the biggest challenges is striking a balance between unity and variation. If the design is composed of a group of unrelated elements, then there is no unity. If all of the elements in the design are a different shape or color, then the composition will appear to be thrown together and it will lack the cohesiveness found in a good design. On the other hand, if all of the colors and shapes in the design are exactly the same, then this design will not be very visually interesting. A little variation is required to make a design pleasing to the eye. The best approach is to start with unity. Everything should feel like it fits together (an application of the Gestalt laws of Perceptual).

Be a problem free: The quickest way to inhibit enjoyment is to create frustration over simple interface and navigation issues. Although, testing is never the most fun part of the process, it is vitally important. In a competitive marketplace, if the game's interface has noticeable bugs it risks losing the users no matter how good the content is. Interface problems can be more than just software bugs, however, as a poorly designed interface is still a major issue. A good way to test an interface is by watching people use this interface a real-world scenario, then arise with some possible questions: Are they able to navigate around and achieve their objectives with relative ease? Is the interface intuitive to both experienced and less experienced game players?

Develop for Console or PC: There are some big differences exist between video game development for consoles and development for PC games. Each platform has its benefits and drawbacks. One of the biggest and most apparent differences between the PC and a console is that they use different input devices. A mouse is very different from a controller. The entire game can change if it is on a console instead of a PC. Understanding these differences can help an Interface Designer create a better interface for either platform.

Methods of Presenting a Game user Interface

All the Game User Interfaces are made of two main elements: text and icon. Therefore, these two elements, in another word, are the two ways of presenting a Game User Interface:

The first element is Text. It is a powerful tool that is often overlooked or at least underestimate by Designer working on game interfaces. The style of text can also set mood of the game as well as color. Each font has a personality. A font that is handwritten and scratched up-looking might be a great choice for an extreme sport game, while a smooth and flowing script font might be great for a horse riding game targeted at young female players. It is also possible to make a great interface design using only text. Font choice, size, placement, color, and type effects can greatly improve the design of an interface.

Nonetheless, in reality, no one likes to read a lot of text when playing a video game. For this reason, text should only be used when it is absolutely necessary. If the information is so important that text must be put in the interface, then it needs to be easy to read. If text is hard to read because it is too small or is not clear enough, the user is likely to ignore it and move on. Additionally, in many cases, it has been proved that text can be used in the background merely as a design element. And the purpose of this background text is to set a mood.

Furthermore, fonts or text styles are an essential element in design text. Fonts can easily be made by using software to manipulate the font design. Most game engines require that an artist create all the fonts. Some advanced engines have tools that can take a standard font and convert it to game format. Even in these cases, it is good to understand how a font works because it is often helpful to edit the font directly. The most common format for a game font is white text placed in a grid. Fonts can also be a great place to put all kinds of images; numbers, dashes, symbols, and icons can all be put into a font file. These icons and images can be used in the game just like a font. A common example of using icons in a font is when creating a console game and small images of the controller buttons are placed in the font.

The second element is Icon. Beside text, it is another important method of communication in an interface. Nevertheless, displaying information graphically is always more interesting than displaying a lot of text. For instance, if an amount of money must be shown, consider using gold coins instead of a number amount. If the amount of energy character has left must be displayed, consider using a fill-bar. So, icons can be used for almost everything in the interface. Although they usually take a lot more time to create than would a paragraph of straight text, they make the game a whole lot more fun to play.

What is more, great icons can accommodate the game to the user without text. Text can used to reinforce an icon, but the better the icons are, the less text will be needed. The key to creating a great icon is choosing the right image to represent the functionality. For example, for a button that allows the player to attack an enemy, a crossed sword icon may be a great solution. Many standard icons, or icons that always mean the same thing, are used in video games. Players already know what these icons mean and can get up to speed more quickly if these standard icons appear in the game. For instance, many game have a save feature, and a common icon for the save feature is a floppy disk. Consequently, it is important to take advantage of player's past experiences by using images that they are familiar with. However, in order to have a better impression from the players, these icons should be customized to fit the look of the game. Moreover, for nongame standard icons; for instance, a symbol used in a bathroom door, a stop icon in music player software, or even a minus and plus sign, these icons can also be used in designing a game icon, since most people can recognize their meaning.

HCI Evaluation Techniques

Evaluation is concerned with gathering data about the usability of a design or product by a specified group of users for a particular activity within a specified environment or work context.

Evaluation can be divided into 2 types: an informal evaluation which only requires a quick feedback of the users, and an evaluation that are much more rigorously planned and controlled (e.g. use laboratory experimentation or large scale surveys). However, regardless of the type evaluation being done, it is important to consider the four aspects: the characteristics of the user who is chosen to participate in the evaluation (e.g. age, gender and experience), the types of activities that the user will do, the environment of the study and the stage of the game that is evaluated (whether it is a demo version or a completed version).

Furthermore, the evaluation methods that are used in game serve three main goals: First of all, it is used to access the functionalities, in the extent of accessibility, that is are provided by the game. Second of all, these methods are used to record the user's reaction and experience when playing the game. And lastly, they are used to identify any specific problem with the game.

So, without evaluation the games reaching consumer would be premature; they would reflect the intentions of the design team but there would be no study of the actual relationship between design and use. As the result, it may lead to the failure of games in the market. For that, there are many evaluation methods can be used in game, however, only the Heuristic Evaluation technique is chosen to present in the next sub-chapter. For the reason, Heuristic Evaluation is one of the most powerful techniques that currently used in the computer game and video game industry; it focuses on evaluating the usability of game interface.

Heuristic Evaluation for Games

Most of video games require constant interaction, so Game Designers must pay attention to usability issues; for example, the degree to which a player is able to learn, control and understand a game. Having failure to design usable game interfaces can interfere with the larger goal of creating a compelling experience for the users, and can have a negative effect on the overall quality and success of a game. Additionally, Game Designers need a method for identifying usability problems both in early designs and in more mature prototypes. However, there are few formal methods for evaluating the usability of game interfaces.

But first, there is a necessity to understand to word Heuristic. It is a set of usability principles that is used by the evaluators to explore an interface. And unlike many common usability inspection techniques which are not appropriate for games since they either rely on formal specifications of task sequence or are oriented around user interface concepts used in desktop applications. Conversely, the Heuristic Evaluation does not make any assumptions about task structure, and it is flexible enough to be adapted to specialized domains.

What more is the Heuristic Evaluation has the potential to improve the Game Design process. Unlike play-testing (one of the most common ways to uncover design problems using playable prototype of a game), it does not require user participation. Instead, Heuristic Evaluation relies on skills of evaluator who inspects the user interface and identifies usability problems. In addition, it is in-expensive and can be carried out in a short amount of time. As the result, Heuristic Evaluation gives the evaluators significant freedom in how they conduct the evaluation, and it also helps the Game Designers find important classes of problems that are not always found with user testing.

One of the first set of Heuristics was developed by Nielsen which is primarily used for desktop applications. It refers to common user interface concepts such as dialogs, undo and redo, and error prevention. However, many of these ideas have limited application in the game context, for the reason, it does not address several important usability issues. An example is the necessity of providing intuitive control mappings when displaying the game world. Similar to the Nielsen case, Feder off and Desurvire et al. also compiled a list of Game Heuristics that concentrates on four areas: game interface, game mechanics, story and playability. Some of the usability issues were mention in both the cases, but they were not described in detail. For instance, Feder off's Heuristics include: −for PC, consider hiding the main interface and the interface should be as non-intrusive as possible , while Desurvire's Heuristics include: players do not need to use a manual to play game and −provide immediate feedback for user action.

Among all, the most appropriated Heuristics, which can be used for the Game Usability inspection, are probably from Pinelle and his associates. What make these Heuristics be different from previous mentioned Heuristics are they consider on the detail of usability. Pinelle and his associate believed that a set of Heuristics that focuses on Game Usability can help improve the video game process. As the result, they created a set of Heuristics to serve as a set of design principle, and to implement the usability inspections at the same time

Provide Consistent Responses to the user's Action

Games should respond to users' actions in a predictable manner. Basic mechanics, such as hit detection, game physics, character movement, and enemy behavior, should all be appropriate for the situation that the user is facing. Games should also provide consistent input mappings so that users' actions always lead to the expected outcome.

Allow users to Customize Video and Audio Settings, Difficulty and Game Speed

The video and audio settings, and the difficulty and game speed levels seen in games are not appropriate for all users. Therefore, the system should allow people to customize a range of settings so that the game accommodates their individual needs.

Provide Predictable and Reasonable Behavior for Computer Controlled Units

In many games, the computer helps the user control the movement of their character, of a small group of teammates, or of a large number of units. Computer controlled units should behave in a predictable fashion, and users should not be forced to issue extra commands to correct faulty artificial intelligence. The game should control units so that path-finding and other behaviors are reasonable for in-game situations.

Provide Unobstructed Views that are Appropriate for the user's Current Actions

Most games provide users with a visual representation (i.e. a −view) of the virtual location that the user is currently occupying. The game should provide views that allow the user to have a clear, unobstructed view of the area, and of all visual information that is tied to the location. Views should also be designed so that they are appropriate for the activity that the user is carrying out in the game. For example, in a 3D game different camera angles may be needed for jumping sequences, for fighting sequences, and for small and large rooms.

Allow users to Skip Non-playable and Frequently Repeated Content

Many games include lengthy audio and video se quences, or other types of non-interactive content. Games should allow users to skip non-playable content so that it does not interfere with gameplay.

Provide Intuitive and Customizable Input Mappings

Most games require rapid responses from the user, so input mapping must be designed so that users can issue commands quickly and accurately. Mappings should be easy to learn and should be intuitive to use, leveraging spatial relationships (the up button is above the down button, etc.) and other natural pairings. They should also adopt input conventions that are common in other similar games (e.g. many first-person shooters and real ime strategy games use similar input schemes). Games should allow users to remap the input settings, should support standard input devices (e.g. mouse, keyboard, gamepad), and should provide shortcuts for expert players.

Provide Controls that are Easy to Manage and that have an Appropriate Level of Sensitivity and Responsiveness

Many games allow users to control avatars such as characters or vehicles. Controls for avatars should be designed so that they are easy for the user to manage, i.e. they are not too sensitive or unresponsive. When controls are based on real world interactions, such as steering a car or using a control stick in an airplane, the game should respond to input in a way that mirrors the real world. Further, games should respond to controls in a timeframe that is suitable for gameplay requirements.

Provide users with Information on Game Status

Users make decisions based on their knowledge of the current status of the game. Examples of common types of information that users need to track include the current status of their character (such as their health, armor status, and location in the game world), objectives, teammates, and enemies. Users should be provided with enough information to allow them to make proper decisions while playing the game.

Provide Instructions, Training and Help

Many games are complex and have steep learning curves, making it challenging for users to gain mastery of game fundamentals. Users should have access to complete documentation on the game, including how to interpret visual representations and how to interact with game elements. When appropriate, users should be provided with interactive training to coach them through the basics. Further, default or recommended choices should be provided when users have to make decisions in complex games, and additional help should be accessible within the application.

Provide Visual Representations that are Easy to Interpret and that Minimize the need for Micromanagement

Visual representations, such as radar views, maps, icons, and avatars, are frequently used to convey information about the current status of the game. Visual representations should be designed so that they are easy to interpret, so that they minimize clutter and occlusion, and so that users can differentiate important elements from irrelevant elements. Further, representations should be designed to minimize the need for micromanagement, where users are forced to interactively search through the representation to find needed elements.

These Heuristics were developed by analyzing PC game review from a popular gaming website, and the review set covered 108 different games divided by 18 for each of 6 major game genres (e.g. action, strategy, simulation, etc.). In the conclusion, Pinelle and his associates believed that the Heuristics that they presented have provided a new way to adapt usability inspection for games, and allow Game Designers to evaluate both mockups and functional prototypes. Moreover, the Heuristics allow –the Game Designers to evaluate Game Usability by applying design principles that are based on design trends seen in recent games, and that are generalized across major genres found in commercial games.

Human-Computer Interaction in the Vehicle

Automobile has become a complex interactive system. Mechanical devices are transformed to the digital realm. It is common that drivers operate a vehicle and, at the same time, interact with a variety of devices and applications. Looking up an address in the map and taking a phone call are such examples that help the driver in driving but also increase the risk on the road. The need to have a car with decent and safer usability from driver drives the researchers and auto companies discover the possibilities of driving with a friendlier and more powerful Human-Computer Interaction interface in the car. As a result, various inventions on usability have been made and they together make the interaction with automobile an easy and safe thing.

The design of usability in automotive domain generally focuses on multiple goals including safety, comfort, enhancement, networking, etc. Actually in some cases the convenience is the same meaning with safety, i.e. the easier the driver finishes one task when driving, the safer he would be. Generally manufacturers improve the feeling of convenience by adding automatic features to devices in the car, a proper example here is power window which greatly reduce the complexity of controlling window in driving. For the need of entertainment, manufacturers usually upgrade the interaction with audio system – more functional buttons, and better effect – since people need to take an eye on the traffic but their ears are available.

Beyond the basic enhancements in HCI in automobile, recent years manufacturers are trying to integrate some more amazing features into the car by providing a powerful microcomputer and a central console with touch screen named vehicle telematics. These novel features include navigation system, auto drive and remote control etc.

Imagine this scenario: you start a new day with a cup of coffee in the car, watching the morning news from holographic projection that projected on the windshield. Following the presetting route, the car drives you to office after sending your children to school. You have a quick review on the whole day agenda while the car looks for a best place to park. After the car is parked, you leave it without locking with a key – the car will unlock itself when sensing your biometric identification around. Some parts of this fantastic scenario have been realization by the cutting edge technologies in automotive usability aspect.

Safety

Automobile safety is the study and practice of design, construction, equipment and regulation to minimize the occurrence and consequences of automobile accidents. Road traffic safety more broadly includes roadway design. One of the first formal academic studies into improving vehicle safety was by Cornell Aeronautical Labs of Buffalo, New York. The main conclusion of their extensive report is the crucial importance of seat belts and padded dashboards. However, the primary vector of traffic-related deaths and injuries is the disproportionate mass and velocity of an automobile compared to that of the predominant victim, the pedestrian. In the United States a pedestrian is injured by an automobile every 8 minutes, and are 1.5 times more likely than a vehicle's occupants to be killed in an automobile crash per outing.

Improvements in roadway and automobile designs have steadily reduced injury and death rates in all first world countries. Nevertheless, auto collisions are the leading cause of injury-related deaths, an estimated total of 1.2 million in 2004, or 25% of the total from all causes. Of those killed by autos, nearly two-thirds are pedestrians. Risk compensation theory has been used in arguments against safety devices, regulations and modifications of vehicles despite the efficacy of saving lives.

Two Systems

Technology is increasingly being seen to have a critical role to play in alleviating the negative aspects of road transport, such as congestion, pollution and road traffic accidents. Many technological initiatives are considered under the umbrella term, Intelligent Transport Systems (ITS), where "ITS provides the intelligent link between travelers, vehicles, and infrastructure". In this respect, in-vehicle computing systems are an important facet of ITS. Specifically, there are two core types of computing and communications systems which are either being implemented or developed for use in vehicles:

Information-based systems: Which provide information relevant to components of the driving environment, the vehicle or the driver. Examples of systems include navigation (facilitating route planning and following), travel and traffic information (traffic conditions, car parking availability, etc.), vision enhancement (providing an enhanced view of the road ahead, when driving at night, in fog or in heavy rain), driver alertness monitoring (informing the incapacitated driver if they are unfit to drive) and collision warnings (presenting warnings/advice regarding hazards). Typically all lamps in panel should be classified into this kind of system. These lamps can warn you whether your car is in a good condition, is there something wrong with your engine. Also, when you leave your car with door opened, you will be warned by hearing continues sound. Information-based systems can improve safety for you and your car.

Control-based systems: Which affect the routine, operational elements of the driving task. Examples of systems include adaptive cruise control (where the car is kept at a set time gap from a lead vehicle), speed limiting (the car speed cannot exceed the current limit), lane keeping (the driver's vehicle is kept within a given lane), self parking (vehicle automatically steers in low speed operation to position itself within a selected parking space) and collision avoidance (the vehicle automatically responds to an emergency situation). Clearly, such systems fundamentally change the nature of what we consider to be 'driving'.

Safety Equipments

These two systems are major implications for safety. Then we will introduce specific facilities of automobile to keep safety.

Driver Assistance

A subset of crash avoidance is driver assistance systems, which help the driver to detect obstacles and to control the vehicle. Driver assistance systems include:

- Automatic Braking systems to prevent or reduce the severity of collision.
- Infrared night vision systems to increase seeing distance beyond headlamp range.
- Adaptive headlamps control the direction and range of the headlight beams to light the driver's way through curves and maximize seeing distance without glaring other drivers.
- Reverse backup sensors, which alert drivers to difficult-to-see objects in their path when reversing.
- Backup camera.
- Adaptive cruise control which maintains a safe distance from the vehicle in front.
- Lane departure warning systems to alert the driver of an unintended departure from the intended lane of travel.
- Tire pressure monitoring systems or Deflation Detection Systems.
- Traction control systems which restore traction if driven wheels begin to spin.
- Electronic Stability Control, which intervenes to avert an impending loss of control.
- Anti-lock braking systems.
- Electronic brakeforce distribution systems.
- Emergency brake assist systems.
- Cornering Brake Control systems.
- Precrash system.
- Automated parking system.

Crashworthiness

Crashworthy systems and devices prevent or reduce the severity of injuries when a crash is imminent or actually happening. It includes:

- Seatbelts limit the forward motion of an occupant, stretch to absorb energy, to lengthen the time of the occupant's deceleration in a crash, reducing the loading on the occupants body. They prevent occupants being ejected from the vehicle and ensure that they are in the correct position for the operation of the airbags.

- Airbags inflate to cushion the impact of a vehicle occupant with various parts of the vehicle's interior. The most important being the prevention of direct impact of the driver's head with the steering wheel and door pillar.

- Laminated windshields remain in one piece when impacted, preventing penetration of unbelted occupants' heads and maintaining a minimal but adequate transparency for control of the car immediately following a collision. It is also a bonded structural part of the safety cell. Tempered glass side and rear windows break into granules with minimally sharp edges, rather than splintering into jagged fragments as ordinary glass does.

- Crumple zones absorb and dissipate the force of a collision, displacing and diverting it away from the passenger compartment and reducing the deceleration impact force on the vehicle occupants. Vehicles will include a front, rear and maybe side crumple zones (like Volvo SIPS) too.

- Safety Cell: The passenger compartment is reinforced with high strength materials, at places subject high loads in a crash, in order to maintain a survival space for the vehicle occupants.

- Side impact protection beams, also called anti-intrusion bars.

- Collapsible universally jointed steering columns, along with steering wheel airbag. The steering system is mounted behind the front axle - behind and protected by, the front crumple zone. This reduces the risk and severity of driver impact or even impalement on the column in a frontal crash.

Pedestrian Protection Systems

Padding of the instrument panel and other interior parts, on the vehicle in areas likely to be struck by the occupants during a crash, and the careful placement of mounting brackets away from those areas.

Cargo barriers are sometimes fitted to provide a physical barrier between passenger and cargo compartments in vehicles such as SUVs, station wagons and vans. These help prevent injuries caused by occupants being struck by unsecured cargo. They can also help prevent collapse of the roof in the event of a vehicle rollover.

However, can we say that with all these safe systems, we can assure safety on the road and never got car accident? The answer is no.

All of our proud, graphically oriented screen devices, especially those with touch-sensitive screens and a paucity of physical controls, may be delightful to use while in a comfortable environment, but they become safety hazards when also attempting to drive a car. If the eyes of the driver are off road for two seconds, studies show a dramatic rise in accident rate. Can you try programming a street address into a navigation system in less than two seconds? Impossible, you need more time.

Moreover, because the driver is attention switching, not only must the eyes shift from road to device, and back again, but all the context must be restored: memory structures, intentions, planned activities. Task switching lengthens the time to do each task considerably, thereby magnifying the danger.

The way to alleviate dangerous while you are driving is using acoustic warning system instead of visual warning system. New car should have sound to report current speed coordinates with speed panel. Thus when driver drives on a speed limit road, driver only need focus on front views and see if other cars runs in left or right lane, acoustic warning system will report whether the car is surpassing speed limit.

Comfort

Original Entertainment Equipments

More and more people not only care about the driving experience of a car, but also care about the comfort of a car, this is the reason why more and more advertisement focusing on interior trim. With CD/FM becomes the common equipment in a car, more and more people treat car as a "small home", not only a driving tool.

Of course if you want to pay more money, you can have more entertainment equipment in your car. In-Car Entertainment is a collection of hardware devices installed into automobiles, or other forms of transportation, to provide audio and/or audio/visual entertainment, as well as automotive navigation systems (SatNav). This includes playing media such as CDs, DVDs, Free view/TV, USB and/or other optional surround sound, or DSP systems. Also increasingly common in ICE installs are the incorporation of video game consoles into the vehicle.

In-Car Entertainment systems have been featured TV shows such as MTV's Pimp My Ride. In Car Entertainment has been become more widely available due to reduced costs of devices such as LCD screen/monitors, and the reducing cost to the consumer of the converging media playable technologies. Single hardware units are capable of playing CD, MP3, WMA, DVD.

New Facilities

As the time change, In-Car Entertainment systems also involved new features, such as AUX, heat seat and Internet. When you get tired of listening FM music and tired of changing CD one by one. You can just link iPod or MP3 into your car by AUX. Then you can listen all music in that iPod or MP3. For heat seat, imagine this, in a cold winter, you got up really early and you saw snow covered everything near you. Is there something better than seating into a warm seat while driving to company? Internet is an increasingly popular option in cars. According to a study by market researcher Invensity that by the year 2013 every new car built in Europe will be equipped with Internet connection.

Comfort of car may make us love to drive, however, it also bring negative effect to our safety while driving. It is important to note that there is actually a third category of incar computing system, include those systems which do not provide any functionality to support the driving task. These systems are an important consideration though, as they can negatively influence safety, particularly through the potential for distraction. Such systems may aim to enhance work oriented productivity whilst driving (e.g. mobile phones, email/internet access) or be primarily conceived for entertainment/comfort purposes (e.g. music/DVD players, games).

Enhancement

Modern world has completely changed our lives by providing us with new technology and advancements. Automobiles possesses an important place in everybody life. Even though there are lots of types of cars that serve different purposes of various customer groups, the very basic functionality of automobiles is always driving. As automobile industry is such a large and profitable industry, manufacturers make every effort to research and apply new technologies to enhance people's driving experience. Automatic transmission has made driving an easy task to almost every person. Other techniques like cruise control and auto-piloting aims at continuing save people further from driving control. Indeed, an age of driverless car is approaching to totally free users from driving.

Automatic Transmission

Automatic transmission is one type of motor vehicle transmission that can automatically change gear ratios as the vehicle moves, freeing drivers from having to shift gears manually.

Besides automatics, there are also other types of automated transmissions such as a continuously variable transmission and semi-automatic transmissions, which free the driver from having to shift gears manually, by using the transmission's computer to change gear, if for example the driver were redlining the engine. Despite superficial similarity to other transmissions, automatic transmissions differ significantly in internal operation and driver's feel from semi-automatics and continuously variable transmissions.

A conventional, 5-speed manual transmission is often the standard equipment in a base-model car. Manual transmissions, generally, offer better fuel economy than automatic or continuously variable transmissions. However, the disparity has been somewhat offset with the introduction of locking torque converters on automatic transmissions. For most people, there is a slight learning curve with a manual transmission, which is likely to be intimidating and unappealing for an experienced driver. And because manual transmission require the operation of an extra pedal, and keeping the car in the correct gear at all times, they require a bit more concentration, especially in heavy traffic situations. The automatic transmissions, on the other hand, simply require the driver to speed up or slow down as needed, with the car doing the work of choosing the correct gear.

Automotive Navigation System

An automotive navigation system is a satellite navigation system designed for use in automobiles. Many modern vehicles are equipped with in-vehicle navigation systems that utilize global positioning systems (GPS), digital maps, and automatic route calculation. An navigation system typically uses a GPS navigation device to acquire position data to locate the user on a road in the unit's map database. Using the road database, the unit can give directions to other locations along roads also in its database. Just entering a destination will typically generate an accurate route that is displayed to the driver. Although the activity of entering a destination is not easy, especially while driving, voice activated systems are bringing to the market to solve this problem. These systems can greatly improve the driving experience by helping drivers navigate in unfamiliar setting and reduce the mental load of remembering where to go.

Navigation systems rely on good human-computer interaction. A quality design here helps drivers find their location and directions easily. As the driver approaches a change in direction, the application warns him in advance of an upcoming change. These systems typically include calculations and displays of time and range to destination. It would be easy to ignore safety issues by pointing out the troubles with driving and looking at a paper map.

The introduction of information systems into vehicles is a growing trend that can provide drivers with useful tools for navigation, communication, and exploration. However, invehicle information system (IVIS) cannot be allowed to distract users from the demanding task of driving. Among these IVIS, car navigation systems have been among the most widely adopted technologies. The decision to open up the map is the driver's own. However, car navigation system manufacturers have a responsibility to society to produce safe systems in addition to possible liability caused by their systems facilitating accidents. There are lot of research focusing on exploring the safest ways to present navigational vehicles.

Cruise Control

Cruise control, sometimes known as speed control or auto cruise, is a system that automatically controls the speed of a motor vehicle. The system takes over the throttle of the car to maintain a steady speed as set by the driver.

Modern cruise control was invented in 1945 by the inventor and mechanical engineer Ralph Teetor. His idea was born out of the frustration of riding in a car driven by his lawyer, who kept speeding up and slowing down as he talked. Daniel Aaron Wisher invented Automotive Electronic Cruise Control is 1968. His invention was the first electronic gadgetry to play a role in controlling a car and ushered in the computer-controlled era in the automobile industry. Two decades lapsed before an integrated circuit for his design was developed and as a result, cruise control was eventually adopted by automobile manufacturers as standard equipment.

Cruise control is really useful for long drives, in which it helps reduce driver fatigue, improve comfort by allowing positioning changes more safely, across highways and sparsely populated roads. This also results in better fuel efficiency. Besides, a driver who tends to unconsciously increase speed over the course of a highway journey may avoid a speeding ticket by using cruise control.

The advantage of electronic speed control over its mechanical predecessor, which was featured on luxury models but never gained wide acceptance, was that it could be easily integrated with electronic accident avoidance and engine management systems.

Some modern vehicles have adaptive cruise control systems, which is a general term meaning improved cruise control. These improvements can be automatic braking, which allows the vehicle to keep pace with the car it is following, or dynamic set-speed hype controls which uses the GPS position of speed limit signs to dynamically control speed.

Autopilot

When it comes to driving, human beings have an appalling safety record. With motor-vehicle accidents claiming more than a million lives worldwide annually, car companies are pushing the development o technology that increasingly borrows control from erratic human beings allowing the car to drive itself.

An autopilot is a mechanical, electronically, or hydraulic system used to guide a vehicle without assistance from a human being. An autopilot usually refers specifically to aircraft, self-steering gear for boats, or auto-guidance of space craft and missiles. But because of its technical constraints and great expenses, autopilot has been evolved to common motor vehicles until the recent years. However, low-level autonomous safety features have been around in various forms for decades.

Antilock brake systems, which automatically sense when a wheel is skidding and reduce brake pressure, were introduced back in 1971. In 1997, General Motors introduced an Electronic Stability Control system that can sense the difference between the direction a car is going and the angle of the steering wheel, and then pump the brakes to keep the car on course. These safety features are so commonplace today that federal legislation requires they be installed on all new cars, along with airbags and seatbelts.

The current set of semi-autonomous safety features can quickly combine into something more. For example, a car could use Lane Keep Assist and Adaptive Cruise Control together to drive itself under highway conditions, sticking to one lane and not hitting the car in front. The next step is to expand these capabilities. Adaptive Cruise Control currently works only over 25 mph, but the next version (called Full Speed Range ACC) lowers that number to zero so that cars can begin to handle traffic jams in the city.

Driverless Car

Fully autonomous vehicles, also known as robotic cars, or driverless cars, already exist in prototype, and are expected to be commercially available around 2020. According to urban designer and futurist Michael E. Arth, driverless electric vehicles—in conjunction with the increased use of virtual reality for work, travel, and pleasure—could reduce the world's 800 million vehicles to a fraction of that number within a few decades. This would be possible if almost all private cars requiring drivers, which are not in use and parked 90% of the time, would be traded for public self-driving taxis that would be in near constant use. This would also allow for getting the appropriate vehicle for the particular need—a bus could come for a group of people, a limousine could come for a special night out, and a Segway could come for a short trip down the street for one person. Children could be chauffeured in supervised safety, DUIs would no longer exist, and 41,000 lives could be saved each year in the US alone.

Networking

Before the computer technology evolved to be good enough, manufacturers brought the usability of automobile to customers with a focus mostly on driving itself. The traditional solution were consist of a bunch of on-board embedded electronics systems that performing various operational functions focusing on different purposes, such as seat heating for comfort, cruise control for enhancement, parking sensor for safety, etc. While these helpers are already utilized in most of today's modern vehicle, new need on networking is raising recent years due to the development of Internet digit devices such as tablet and smart phone. Seeing this potential usability area, manufacturers begin to research and install more and more in-vehicle embedded system that focus on providing better functionalities, robust operation and higher degree of convenience to the in-vehicle users in the networking level. Within this trend, advance of wireless communication and information technology in the digital era has promoted new killer applications to the in vehicle drivers and occupants. Among these advanced killer applications, services provided in the area of the telematics and information/ entertainment have attracted most attention in the automotive industry.

Telematics Service

Telematics were considered as the system that provides location-based services for mobile vehicles over wireless communication networks. Typical example of automotive telematics services includes emergency call system, which instantly connects vehicle users to a service center for emergency assistance or roadside services while automatically reporting the vehicle's position. Normally, the emergency call system requires a wireless transceiver for voice and data communication and an on-board GPS receiver for positioning. Telematics system was considered as the core technology in an Intelligent Transportation System (ITS) and applications of telematics services to ITS have been proposed and developed in some countries. An integrated positioning system were developed to realize an efficient and cost-effective GPS based electronic road pricing system by He, Law, and Ling. In, the importance of "situational awareness" in conveying the state of the automobile to other parties across a communication link was addressed and a novel interactivity environment for integrated intelligent transportation and telematics systems was proposed.

Information/Entertainment Services

As more and more people are traveling with Internetenabled information appliances (IA) such as laptops, tablets, smart phones, digital cameras, MP3 players, etc., there is a desire to connect to the Internet permanently from anywhere, at any time, without any disruption of service, particularly for those people who spend a significant amount of time in mass transportation systems in weekdays or in their own vehicle during weekend. In order to access the Internet, an in-vehicle local area network or personal area network environment must be established, and the in-vehicle embedded system shall become the mobile gateway for these Internet-enabled IA. Ernst, Uehara, and Mitsuya, detailed the networking requirements for connecting vehicles to the Internet by displacing an entire IPv6 network and network mobility support in the InternetCAR project. The software and hardware requirements in designing humancomputer interface for an in-vehicle information system were proposed such that the safety of the in-vehicle drivers is discussed. A distributed service-based architecture were proposed to provide fault tolerant application services to remote in-vehicle computers and mobile devices, such as Wifi-enabled tablet and smart phone. It seems that research trend has shifted to providing an infotainment server system for the in-vehicle users such that the network-enabled IA can access the information from the in-vehicle network and also obtain the entertainment services from the entertainment server.

Products in Practice

A well-known example of telematics system is GM's OnStar service which provides multiple emergency services. Typically the OnStar in installed in the bottom of rearview mirror. The OnStar service relies on CDMA mobile phone voice and data communications well as location information using GPS technology. Drivers and passengers can use its audio interface to contact OnStar representatives for emergency services, vehicle diagnostics and directions. The OnStar service allows users to contact OnStar call centers during an emergency. In the event of a collision, detected by airbag deployment or other sensors, Advanced Automatic Collision Notification features can automatically send information about the vehicle's condition and GPS location to OnStar call centers. This Advanced Automatic Collision Notification service is designed to assist emergency response efforts.All OnStar equipped vehicles have Stolen Vehicle Tracking, which can provide the police with the vehicle's exact location, speed and direction of movement.

User Interfaces for Applications on a Wrist Watch

A wrist watch is an attractive form factor for a wearable computer. It has the advantage of always being with you; and it can be instantly viewed with the flick of the wrist. By comparison, devices such as pagers, cell phones and PDAs are typically worn on belts or kept in pockets, and need to be picked up and opened first before they can be accessed. Table summarizes a study we did on various objects that people tend to carry with them. The study included about fifty researchers at IBM and technical visitors.

As we see from Table, a wrist watch is a very attractive form factor into which one can pack a significant amount of computer power into. One of the reasons a wrist watch is attractive is that a large fraction of the population is already accustomed to wearing wrist watches. Further, people generally keep watches on their wrists, and watches are less likely to be misplaced compared to phones and pagers. For example, a hip holster is not the best place to keep a cellular phone while sitting in a car, and so people tend to keep them in the car seat and forget them when they leave the car in the parking lot.

Another significant advantage of a wrist watch is that it is much more accessible than many of the other devices one may carry. It is often said that one of the reasons for the initial success of the Palm was its moving to an instanton paradigm, i.e. eliminating the long boot up time associated with laptops. Wrist watches move us to the next step; to an instantly-viewable paradigm.

The watch form factor requires a relatively small screen size, and there is not much room for input devices or batteries. The value of a wristwatch platform depends on finding good solutions to these issues. To interact with the watch, we need both hands since the hand on which the watch is worn is practically useless for controlling input devices on the watch, unless the hand wearing the watch is used to manipulate some other input device.

Several smart watches are available commercially today. Personal Information Management (PIM) applications are provided on the Seiko Ruputer, the onHand PC, the Casio PCUnite and the Timex DataLink. These watches pack an impressive amount of function but have low resolution displays. This limits the amount and type of data that can be displayed on their screens. The Casio WMP-1V is a wearable MP3 player, the Casio WQV-1 is a wearable digital camera, with a 1206120 display, the Casio BP 100 measures blood pressure and the Casio Satellite Navi provides GPS on a watch.

The Timex Beepwear watch has a built in pager. The Swatch Access watch has an RF id tag which can be used as a ski pass at some ski resorts. Swatch is also working on a cell phone in a watch called Swatch Talk. The NTT PHS Personal Handy Phone System and the Samsung Watchphone Anycall are watches with a telephone. Polar produces heart rate monitor watches (Smart Edge, Beat, Protrainer NV, Lady Beat Target, Pacer).

Table: Comparison of the devices we carry.

Is this device with you?	At Work	At Home	In Car/ Train	Play	In Bed	In Shower	Notes (Y=Yes, N=No, M=Maybe)
Wallet	Y	N	Y	M	N	N	Wallet probably on dresser at home, Not easily accessible while driving.
Keys	Y	N	Y	M	N	N	In the car but stuck in steering wheel.
Pen	Y	N	Y	M	N	N	How many days has it been since you lost one? Maybe in the briefcase.
Badge	Y	N	Y	N	N	N	Maybe in the briefcase. Maybe clipped to shirt and winter jacket on top may prevent access to display.
Pager	Y	Y	Y	Y	N	N	
Credit card sized PDA	Y	M	Y	Y	N	N	Is extremely portable, but tend to put it in wallet making it not instantly accessible.
Cell phone	Y	N	Y	M	N	N	Generally too big to have on you all the time.
PDA	Y	Y	Y	N	N	N	Generally too big to wear.
Coat/Shirt	Y	Y	Y	N	N	N	Need all clothes to be wired, can't wear same coat everyday!
Eyeglasses	Y	M	Y	Y	N	N	Only 50% need glasses. May not wear at home depending on defect, and increasing trend towards laser eye surgery may eliminate glasses.
Shoes	Y	N	Y	Y	N	N	Different shoes for different occasions.
Ring	Y	Y	Y	Y	Y	Y	A ring is too small.
Watch	Y	Y	Y	Y	Y	M	Maybe in shower if waterproof, One handed operation is not possible.

There is plenty of interest in adding function to watches in the industry. Our interest is not in so much in providing a watch, as in providing an open, extensible computing platform in a small form factor. Our objective is to understand the challenges in packaging, hardware design, power management and embedded software.

Wrist Watch Computer

The IBM wrist watch computer is a wearable personal information access and alert notification device with both short range and long range RF wireless connectivity. The first version that we built had a 966120 pixel monochrome reflective Liquid Crystal Display (LCD), and is shown in fig. In the second version shown in figure below we moved to an ultra high resolution (741 dpi) monochrome direct view Organic Light Emitting Diode (OLED) display jointly developed with eMagin Corporation. These display and communication capabilities could make the wrist watch computer the preferred viewer for other devices that are around you and for your electronic agents running on web, business or e-commerce servers on the intranet or the Internet.

The OLED display is a high contrast emissive display which can even be viewed under direct sunlight. It also supports a wide viewing angle far superior to LCDs. The power dissipated by the OLED is proportional to the number of pixels that are turned on. In addition, there are controls that allow us to trade off power consumption for the average brightness of the OLED.

Wrist watch computer with low resolution liquid crystal display.

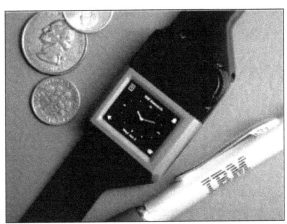

Wrist watch computer with high resolution organic light emitting diode display.

The applications and user interfaces described in this paper were prototyped for both the high resolution OLED display and the low resolution LCD display. The pixel pitch of the LCD (approximately 250 microns) is comparable to the pixel pitch on a laptop LCD. So the initial prototypes of the LCD user interface was done on a laptop. The pixel pitch of the OLED is much finer (34.3 microns), and we prototyped the OLED user interface on a commercially available backlit VGA resolution LCD display from Epson which was a little bit larger than our OLED. This meant that the pixel pitch of our prototyping set up (around 42 microns), was not as fine as the OLED but was close enough to permit us to understand the tradeoffs and design for the OLED. Researchers began the application prototyping exercise the actual watch hardware was not available. Now that we have both the LCD and OLED versions available.

At the core for the wrist watch computer is an ARM 7 based low-power system board that runs the Linux operating system and X11 graphics. The system board uses state of the art technology such as Surface Laminar Circuit (SLC). It is 34.7627.563.0 mm in size. Additional communication cards are used to support short range wireless protocols such as Bluetooth. Figure shows the circuit boards that are inside the watch. The wrist watch with the low resolution display has a Bluetooth communication card inside it. Researchers have not built a prototype of a watch with the high resolution display and Bluetooth as of yet. Power is supplied by a rechargeable lithium polymer battery.

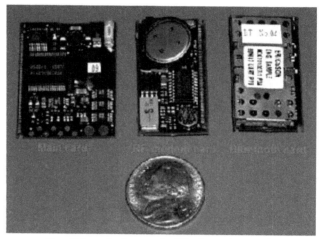

Circuit boards that are inside the wrist watch.

The watch must be viewed as a companion to some other key devices such as a PC in an office, a cell phone in a bag, or a wireless beacon in a building. So the watch need not do all the functions a user wants but must communicate and cooperate with other devices so that the strengths of each device can be exploited to the maximum.

Selection of Input Devices

The choice of input mechanisms is critical for ease of use. In our effort to find the right input devices for the wrist watch computer, Researchers first studied the advantages and disadvantages of input devices on a few research projects such as the ParcTa and Itsy and a set of commercially available products including the Palm Pilot, Psion Series 5, HP Jornada and other handheld PDAs, the RexPro 5-DS, RIM Interactive Pager 960, Hertz NeverLost car navigation system, several digital cameras, remote controls, smart watches and cell phones. The pros and cons of several choices for input devices are described below:

Keyboards: though useful for entering large amounts of text, watches do not have the surface area and volume needed for hardware switches such as keyboards. Even if we were able to fit a tiny keypad with a limited number of keys on the wristwatch, it would be difficult to use for most people. Predictive keyboards such as the Reactive Keyboard could help mitigate this problem. T9 from Tegic Communications is another predictive keyboard that uses a standard phone keypad for text entry, but appears to put too much of a cognitive load on the user. Recent innovations in text entry include Thumbscript, which uses a small nine button keypad, but does not appear to be intuitive. Researchers could consider using one of these schemes by simulating a limited keypad on the touch screen, if there is a pressing need from the user community.

- Touch Screen: a touch sensitive screen can be used on the wrist watch computer to provide for soft switches and character input. The relative sizes of a watch face and a human finger limit the number of distinguishable touch zones to four or five, although a stylus could be used on the watch face to accept fine grained input gestures such as Unistroke or variants such as graffiti used on the PalmPilot. Although the LCD watch is larger than the OLED watch and its touch screen therefore larger in area, we felt that restricting the touch zones to four was appropriate in both versions. It was clear to us through experimentation with the Casio VDU 200B watch that touch screens frequently showed screens other than the desired time screen due to accidental activation every now and then. Despite this shortcoming we felt that a touch screen would be a good input mechanism to support on a wrist watch since it was more versatile and more elegant compared to buttons. And for usability reasons, we limit the number of distinguishable zones to four – one for each corner.

- Scrolling: a touch screen provides a good selection mechanism but does not perform too well as a scrolling mechanism. The Itsy used accelerometers to implement their rockand-scroll mechanism. Since researchers did not have accelerometers on our watch, this was not an option open to us. The options we considered were a rocker switch, a rotating bezel, and a roller switch. The rocker switch rocks up or down. It can be pushed in to select. The roller wheel and the bezel allow complete revolutions to scroll up or down. The roller wheel may be pushed towards the center to select and the bezel may be pressed down to select. Initial user tests revealed that a rocker switch (fitted on a RexPro 5-DS by our colleagues) was superior to touch screen actions, but a roller or bezel that allowed complete rotations seemed easier to use and more natural. Since our present watch is rectangular, we chose a roller wheel over the rotating bezel.

We positioned the roller wheel to minimise the chance of accidental activation by bending the wrist. The user has to push in the southwest direction to select.

As shown in Figs 1 and 2, the wheel is also positioned in the northeast corner to accommodate both left- and right-handed users. Righthanded users anchor their thumb to the bottom left corner of the watch and use their index finger to roll the wheel, moving the index finger north to south, or vice versa, depending on the desired direction of rotation. Left-handed users who wear the watch on their right wrist tend to anchor their thumb in a similar fashion, but move their index finger along the upper boundary of the watch, in an east-west or westeast direction. Therefore, placing the wheel at the northeast corner of the watch was desirable.

Alternatively, for left-handed users we could build a mirror-image watch, where the watch could be reversed so that the roller wheel appears in the northwest corner instead of the northeast corner. However, in this case there would be two distinct types of watches: left-handed and righthanded ones.

- External I/O: external input/output devices can interact with the watch over wireless standards such as IrDA and Bluetooth. For example, one could bring the watch near a Bluetooth connected keyboard, perhaps a Twiddler, or a Palm portable keyboard, to enter information into the watch. Other bodyworn input devices such as Dataglove, FingeRing, or GesturePad may be used if the user is willing to wear such devices.

- Voice recognition: the wrist watch computer includes a microphone and speaker, so that speech based interfaces are possible. Researchers have found that current technology limits extensive use of this concept, although the capability can be improved using a wireless connection to an adjunct device with more computing power that can be used for doing part of the voice recognition.

Application and Interaction Design

The primary applications of a watch are related to time. Watches started with the ability to tell time. Then alarms were added to help people wake up. The next generation of smart watches will extend this concept by allowing people manage their time, provide personal information management (PIM) functions and also save time in their jobs by receiving just in time information on their wrists by leveraging short range wireless connectivity.

Before designing the applications for the watch, we spent a great deal of time trying to simplify the user interface by taking advantage of the high resolution display and the chosen input devices.

Researchers started a study of existing devices which suggested we focus on navigation between functions. After some study, we settled on the following requirements for navigation between screens on the watch:

- A quick return to the watch face from any application.

- A time-out to the watch face from any function.

- One touch deactivation of alarms.

- Direct access to the main list of applications.

- User programmable touch screen areas that could be used to access the user's most important applications.

- User ability to perform most of the common actions without lifting finger off the wheel.

- The ability to easily return to the previous screen. (Our studies indicated that people had become familiar with the browser model and the concepts of following hyperlinks and going back in the browser history stack. Therefore extending the concept of a browser back button to every watch face screen was desirable).

We wanted the usage of the wrist watch computer to be obvious, and avoid the need for a thick user manual for the watch. We started with Human-Computer Interaction (HCI) concepts from familiar computing environments such as web browsers, etc., and then employed a user-centered design process to tune the environment.

From our user study that included several of our colleagues, visitors to IBM Research, attendees at trade shows and conferences where we have extensively demonstrated the wrist watch prototypes, in all several hundred people, we determined users were typically not aware that the screen was touch sensitive or that the roller could be pushed in to generate a selection. So some documentation to make the users aware of these features was useful.

With the basic input mechanisms on the wrist watch computer, and the four zone limitation we have placed on the touch screen, the following input options are available on the watch.

- Press any of the four regions on the touch screen.

- Roll the roller wheel clockwise.

- Roll the roller wheel counterclockwise.

- Push the roller wheel in the SW direction to select.

To facilitate a quick return to the watch face, we decided to dedicate a touch on the top left corner to go back to watch face, irrespective of what the watch face is currently displaying. There is one exception to this rule, however; if the watch face is already displaying the time a top-left tap takes the watch to the main-menu screen.

The top-left zone was chosen for this returnto-home function, since a right-handed user's right index finger (who wears his watch on the left hand) will almost completely cover the wrist watch computer display when this zone is being pressed. Obscuring the screen in this fashion is not desirable if the user needs to remember some information on the current screen. However, since a top-left tap results in a complete switch to a well-known screen the user is least concerned with the current contents of the display being obscured in this fashion.

To support a consistent page-back mechanism, we decided to dedicate the bottom left zone to the go-back function – in this case 75% of the screen is visible for the right-handed user.

The two right zones are under the control of the application that currently has control of the screen. The application may decide to use them to go to the next page or previous page, or to invoke a list of menus for a hyperlink or an application, or for other purposes.

For left-handed users the conventions of functions mapped to the left and right zones may be reversed in software. This is another advantage that results from the use of a touch screen.

The above conventions are suspended when an alarm sounds. In this case the alarm is quickly silenced by pressing any zone on the watch display.

By asking people we determined that many found it easier to set time on an analogue watch using the watch stem than it was to set time on digital clocks with buttons. Since, this design is for a high resolution display where the hands of the watch could be displayed in an analogue fashion, we use a circular metaphor and analogue representations in our screens whenever desirable. The circular metaphor on the screen works well with the roller wheel.

Rolling the wheel also causes a scrolling action when textual content is displayed on the screen. Clicking the wheel causes a selection action similar to a mouse click. For instance, in the case of setting time, rolling the wheel moves the hands and clicking the wheel sets the time to the current time displayed by the hands.

The availability of the back button provides a quick way to undo tasks or revert to previously computed screens, and is very convenient and saves time in many instances. For example, Researchers found that some users were looking for a person's phone number and then would quickly want to check what time it was at the person's location and would go back to the clock, and in the meanwhile forget the phone number they just looked up. Researchers solve situations like this by allowing the user to jump to the watch face with one touch and then get back to the previous screen with another touch.

The history stack maintained for the back button functionality does not preserve every screen; only a few canonical screens are preserved for any application. So, for example, it would be quite useless to preserve every screen update that was made during a stopwatch application that counted milliseconds.

We found that touch screens on watches are also activated accidentally by people trying to keep their watch screens clean. To address this, we use a variable time-out mechanism that returns the watch to the time screen from any screen after a time-out interval. Furthermore, the time-out period is initially set to a small value and increased gradually till it reaches an upper limit if the user is actively using the applications. For instance, the time-out interval starts at 10 seconds. After the first interaction with the watch (tap on screen/activation of wheel) the watch will time out to the clock face in 10 seconds if there is no further interaction. If there is a second interaction within the 10 seconds the time-out is increased to 20 seconds and so on till it reaches, say, one minute. If at any point the watch times out to the clock face, the time-out interval is reset to 10 seconds. This mechanism ensures that accidental activations quickly revert the watch to the clock without annoying the user with spurious time-outs when the watch is being used actively.

Data Model

Since the wrist watch computer does not have a keyboard, textual content will most likely be created on other devices, such as PCs, and transferred to the watch. One interesting issue is how to represent this textual content on the wrist watch computer to make it most accessible to the user.

We expect a compact form of XML to be a standard format for publication of content for small form-factor devices like cellular phones, and hope to be able to use such content on the watch without change. When we started our application prototyping, Wireless Markup Language (WML) appeared to be a good choice, since it was an emerging standard that was expected to be widely accepted. We therefore chose to use WML as the text format on the watch. Besides, WML supports the notion of hyperlinks, and had an intuitive and well accepted navigation model.

All textual information on the wrist watch computer such as list of appointments, todo lists, email messages, etc., are stored as WML cards. Typically such information will be resident on a PC or other servers. As part of the synchronization software that extracts this information and sends it into the wrist watch computer, the information will be transcoded into WML along with the appropriate hypertext links. For example, a calendar entry can be scanned for people's names and the names are turned into WML hyperlinks that point to the corresponding cards in the address book. In addition, each calendar entry is automatically linked with the previous and next entries to aid in the navigation.

When the watch displays WML content, rolling the wheel causes the current highlight to jump from hyperlink to hyperlink in the appropriate direction. Clicking the wheel in causes an activation of the hyperlink, i.e. navigation to the card pointed to by the hyperlink.

Applications

We surveyed prospective wrist watch computer users (typically those who carried PDAs and cell phones), who told us they would like to see watch functions, Personal Information Management (PIM) applications (calendar, phone book, to dos), games, and an MP3 music player, on the wrist watch computer. Access to data from the web was cited as an important application as well. This included alerts, stock quotes, sports scores, email headers, headline news, weather and traffic reports, etc.

Researchrs have implemented an prototype application environment for the wrist watch computer and have created several of the requested applications. The following sections discuss some of the above applications. With the power of such a device, one can easily imagine more applications, some highly personalized, some customized to games and trivia, etc.

Clock Face

The primary display on the wrist watch is a clock face showing current time and date. On the high resolution OLED display the clock hands appear smooth and the stair steps due to pixelation is not perceptible. Also due to a wider viewing angle on the OLED it is easier to tell the time on the OLED watch. In the low resolution LCD display, one can see the jagged edges of the hands quite easily and we have made the hands wider and triangular (as in the xclock application) to make the jagged edges seem less obvious.

This clock display is the default screen to which we come back to when the return-to home function is invoked by tapping on the top left zone on the touch panel.

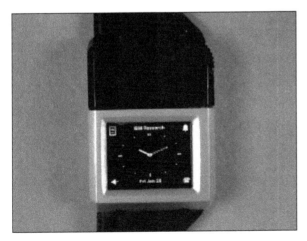
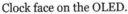

| Clock face on the OLED. | Clock face on the LCD. |

On the clock face screen we decided that the top right touch zone should provide access to alarms, and the bottom right region should access the phone book, since these are likely to be the most common applications. As discussed earlier, the top left zone in this screen will present the main menu or the application launch pad. Rolling the roller wheel will cycle through the days schedule. Pressing the roller wheel will provide access to the quiet time function. This allocation allows one action access to key functions of the device – calendar, phone book, alarms, and turning off alarms.

Icon ring – Application Selector

The set of applications on a watch is expected to be quite small for any given person, perhaps of the order of a dozen or so. In keeping with the circular metaphor and using the roller wheel for most interactions, we chose to represent the application menu by means of icons that we position around a circle as shown in fig. for the OLED display.

The user can roll the wheel clockwise or counterclockwise to move the selection from one icon to another. Once the desired icon is selected, the user clicks the roller wheel in to launch the application.

It is quite difficult to create culture-neutral, self-evident icons that unambiguously convey functional purpose. The small size and limited color depth of the wrist watch computer display makes this even more difficult. Icon design is more of a challenge for the low resolution LCD display since the number of pixels available is also small. In the OLED version since the pixel pitch is high, better icons can be designed. In addition, dithering can be used to create a three dimensional effect. Nevertheless, it is generally quite difficult to design such icons unless one has color pixels and a reasonable physical area for the icons. As a result, it is important for functional icons to have captions that explain their function.

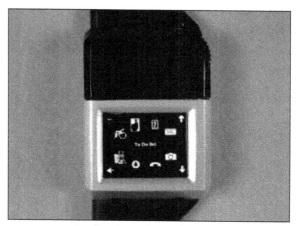

Application selector (OLED).

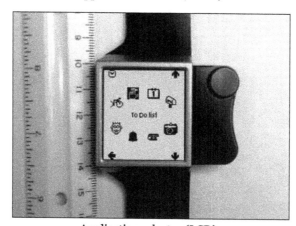

Application selector (LCD).

Users will initially rely on the caption, but gradually become familiar with the icons and use them directly. Since the screen dimensions are small, we cannot show all icons and their captions at the same time. Though icons can be small, the caption font has to be proportionally quite large to be legible. Therefore, we chose to display just the caption for currently highlighted icon in the center of the icon ring. As the user rolls the wheel to move the highlight, the caption changes accordingly.

Based on user experiments, we restricted the number of icons shown on a screen to eight. If there are more than eight applications, we can place them on consecutive menu pages that one can access by touching the top right or bottom right zones of the touch screen to go to the previous page or next page of applications, respectively.

Initial experience with this environment leads us to believe that users will be able to navigate to the right application page by tapping in corners of the wrist watch computer without looking at the display. For instance if a user has two application screens and knows that the application of interest is in the second page a top left tap followed by a bottom right tap will get the user to the appropriate menu page.

Once in the right page, the user will have to look at the display while he selects the application icon by rolling the wheel and launches it by clicking the wheel. On any menu screen we put the most commonly used application in that screen as the default highlighted item. In this case, the user does not even have to look at the screen to launch his application, he just has to count the number of screen taps and follow it with a wheel click.

Alarms

An alarm can be associated with a specific time, a calendar entry, a to do entry, and to software agents either running on the watch or remotely. Alarms associated with time can be set by adjusting the hour first and then adjusting the minute hand. Alarms can be set relative to the current time or on an absolute basis. For example, relative alarms are useful to remind people to shut the stove off in twenty minutes. A bell is displayed on the screen at the time for which the alarm is set, e.g. an alarm for 7 AM will be represented by a bell at the 7 AM position on the clock face.

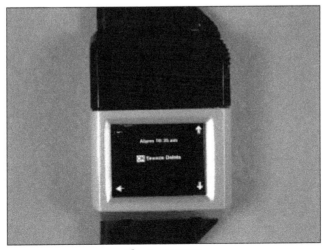

Alarm message.

When an alarm is activated the wrist watch computer plays a sound on the speaker and presents the associated message title if any, on the display. In addition to the message title, options to acknowledge, snooze, and delete, are depicted as shown in Fig. The "acknowledge (OK)" option is highlighted when the alarm rings. Simple text messages like those shown in Fig. can be easily shown on the LCD display, so long as one chooses an appropriately sized font.

When the alarm is ringing, the user can silence it by touching any part of the touch screen or by rotating the roller wheel or even by pressing in the roller switch. The focus here is to quickly silence the alarm since this is the first thing that the user would want to do.

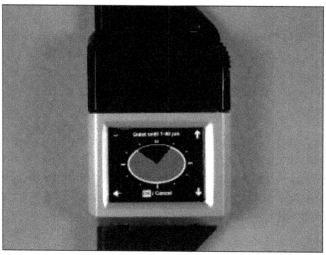

Quiet time.

After the alarm has been silenced the watch will continue to display the message title associated with the alarm for some time interval, say 30 seconds. If the user taps on the touch screen again within these 30 seconds, the user acknowledges the alarm and the alarm is canceled. Once an alarm is cancelled, the message is removed from the screen and the watch reverts back to showing the current time.

If the user does not tap the alarm a second time within the specified duration, and does nothing, the alarm message title disappears and the alarm is automatically snoozed, i.e. the alarm will ring again after a snooze interval.

The user also has the ability to proactively snooze the alarm without waiting for the timeout by rolling the wheel to highlight the snooze option and clicking the wheel to select it. The alarm text may also have hyperlinks to other pieces of information (for example a name in the message text may be a hyperlink to the person's phone number) that the user may navigate to by selecting the link and clicking the wheel.

The salient part of this user interface to alarms is the consistency and simplicity of actions the user needs to take to silence, snooze or view the details for the alarm. A single tap silences the alarm, a double tap cancels the alarm, a single tap and time-out snoozes the alarm.

Single or double taps on the watch face do not require the user to even look at the watch and can be done while doing other things such as engaging in a conversation, reading a newspaper, etc. Using a tap followed by a roller wheel and click can launch other actions, but in this case the user needs to pay more attention to the watch, i.e. look at it. Still if the list of possible options is small the amount of user distraction is minimal.

Quiet Time

We allow the user to set a quiet time from the clock face screen. It is activated by pressing the roller wheel. This application quickly allows the user to turn off audible alarms until a specified time as shown in Fig. When audible alarms are turned off, if an alternative tactile method of alerting the user is available, it will be used. The time is specified by rolling the wheel to the desired time and pressing the roller wheel. Once the quiet time elapses the alarms are re-enabled automatically and any pending alarms are sounded.

Alphabet Selector

Since the wrist watch computer has no keyboard, text must be entered with either the roller wheel or the touch screen. We do not expect the user to enter much text, but some will be required. Researchers are testing one text input model as part of the name and address book application.

In these situations all textual input must be accomplished using the roller wheel or the touch screen.

When the user needs to look up a phone number the user is presented with a screen that looks like the one shown in figure. The letters from A through Z are presented in a pair of concentric circles. We had to put the letters in two circles since putting them all on one circle made it look very cluttered and hampered readability. Since, the size of the LCD display was only slightly larger than the OLED, the above comment regarding the pair of concentric circles also applies to the LCD. Again, we use a different font that is suitable for the pixel pitch of the LCD to display the text as shown in figure below.

Alphabet selector (OLED).

As the user rolls the wheel the selection cursor moves from character to character.

Once the user has the highlight on the right character, pushing in the roller wheel causes phone numbers corresponding to all names that begin with that letter to be displayed. These can then be scrolled though with the roller wheel. The advantage of placing the letters in this fashion is that the user can quickly select the desired character without much difficulty. The user can perceive at a glance where the desired character is located and simply roll the wheel, peripherally observing the highlight till it gets into the vicinity of the desired character. At this point, a marginally higher level of concentration is required to match up the highlight with the desired character.

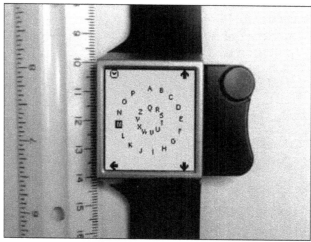

Alphabet selector (LCD).

The same scheme could be used to provide longer input strings to the watch that consist of say alphabets, numbers and a limited set of punctuations (to enter a phone number for example).

Calendar

The high resolution display allows a complete month view to be displayed on the watch as shown in Fig. Even on the low resolution display one can display the calendar for a complete month, but it looks much more cluttered and not as elegant. Scrolling past the last day of the month gets you to the next month and scrolling past the first day of the month gets you to the previous month. The next month and previous month hyperlinks get you there as well. Upon selection of a particular day, the day view shown in figure is displayed below. Zoomable interfaces such as the Pad, though impractical due to the limited compute power available on the current watch, may be considered in the future.

Calendar month view (OLED).

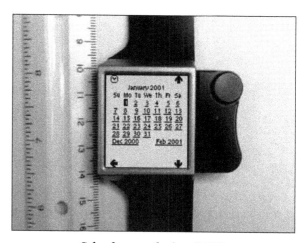

Calendar month view (LCD).

Calendar day view (OLED).

To do List

To do lists can be shown on the OLED. They can also be shown on the LCD since what is displayed is simple text. These to do lists are typically created on a PC or other device. Items can be checked off by pushing the roller wheel after positioning the highlight on the right item. It would be simple to have a predefined set of to dos in the watch and then allow the user to create a list from the pre-defined list. The predefined list could be personalised and downloaded in to the watch.

Images

Since, researchers are designing for a high resolution display, we can easily display images on the watch, such as photographs of one's family members for example. We do not support gray scale or colour in the initial versions of the watch, however, it is quite easy to simulate grey scale using spatial dithering on the OLED watch. Since the display has a very fine dot pitch, the graininess associated with dithering is normally not perceptible to the human eye. If we apply the same spatial dithering to the image and try to display it on the LCD watch, the picture looks very grainy, somewhat similar to a picture one may see in a newspaper under a magnifying glass.

In addition to photographs, one can easily load images such as cartoon strips into the OLED watch and read them for amusement. This is not feasible on the LCD watch, since the resolution is not sufficient to display even the simple line graphics that cartoonists create. It is conceivable that special cartoons may be designed for the LCD watch, but that may prove difficult given the low display resolution.

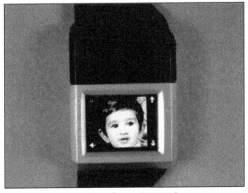

Family photo (OLED).

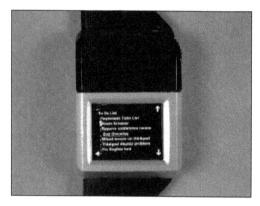

To do list.

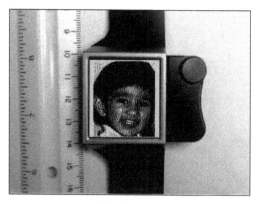

Family photo (LCD).

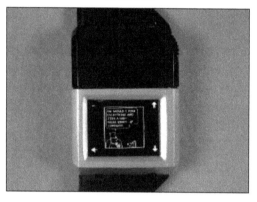

Cartoon strip (OLED).

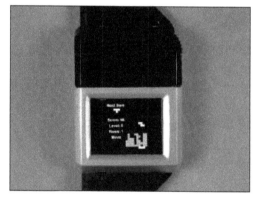

Tetris on OLED.

Games

It was interesting to see if we could use the limited input function on the wrist watch computer to support a game. We found a public implementation of a game similar to Tetris and found we were able to map it to the wrist watch computer controls. To play a game like Tetris one needs to be able to both move as well as rotate falling pieces. In addition, players like the ability to drop a falling piece quickly once it is in the correct position and orientation. The ability to pause and resume the game is also an important requirement.

Given the limited input capabilities of the watch, it is a challenge to accomplish all of the above controls. The way we solved this problem is to map movement and rotation to the roller wheel and pause/resume and drop functions to the touch screen. Since, Tetris only uses rectangular shapes, this is a game that can also be played on the LCD watch and the shapes do not look odd even though many of shapes are comprised of a very small number of pixels. A similar game, hextris, that uses hexagonal blocks may be harder to implement on the LCD watch.

The roller wheel can be in one of two modes, rotate or move. If it is in the rotate mode turning the wheel rotates the piece in the direction the wheel was rotated. If the wheel is in the move mode, turning the wheel moves the piece to the left or right. One can switch the mode of the wheel between rotate and move by clicking it in. When a new piece starts falling the wheel always reverts to the rotate mode, since in our observations of Tetris players we noticed that they first oriented the piece the right way, then moved it and usually dropped it. However, this is not always true, and sometimes one rotates the piece moves it and then changes ones mind, rotates it again to a new orientation and may move it again. For this reason, till the piece actually hits the bottom one is allowed to alternate modes by clicking the wheel in. Admittedly this is a bit more cumbersome than having separate controls for rotate and move, but as we pointed out earlier, we are constrained in our input capabilities due to requirements.

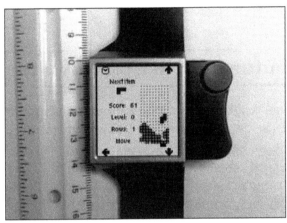

Tetris on LCD.

Another game that is reasonably easy to play using the roller wheel is the 15 tile puzzle where one has to arrange 15 numbered tiles in the correct order using one empty slot. At any stage in the game, any tile that is adjacent to the empty slot (in the North/South/East or West) directions can be moved into the empty slot. In other words, at any stage in the game there are at most four tiles that are valid selections for a move. We use the wheel to move between these selections, i.e. by rolling the wheel either clockwise or counter-clockwise, the user can move the selection to the next valid tile in the respective direction. Clicking the wheel in, moves the tile into the empty slot. After the move, the selection automatically jumps to the tile that is in the same relative position to the empty slot. In other words, if the selected tile was to the right of the empty slot, clicking the wheel moves the tile to the left, and the selection jumps to the tile that is now to the right of the empty slot. This simplifies a common operation where one wants to move a linear set of tiles together; one rolls to the first tile in the set and repeatedly clicks as many times as the number of tiles that need to be moved.

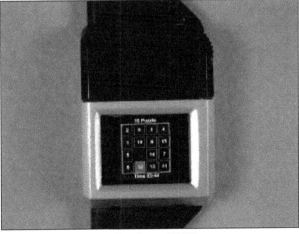

15 Puzzle on OLED.

Finally, after completing the arrangement, one taps on the touch screen to end the game at which point, the watch displays the time taken and displays the fastest six times. Tapping on the screen will start a new game after randomising the board.

Since, this game just consists of rectangles and text as far as the display is concerned, it maps quite well to the LCD watch as well.

Human-Computer Interaction in Virtual Reality

Many people associate virtual reality and computer simulations with science fiction, high-tech industries, and computer games; few associate these technologies with education. But virtual reality and computer simulations have been in use as educational tools too. Although they have mainly been used in applied fields such as aviation and medical imaging, these technologies have begun to edge their way into the primary classroom. There is now a sizeable research base addressing the effectiveness of virtual reality and computer simulations within school curriculum.

Why is it Important?

Computer-based virtual reality has been a common part of modern popular culture and technology for decades now. It is used both as a tool and also for entertainment purposes. The technology has many applications, although its importance may occasionally need some clarification. Following is a small part of the motivation for this report:

- Architectural visualization is one of the applied uses of virtual reality today. A virtual walk-through of a building design, prior to its construction, can actually help architects and their clients better understand what the building will actually be like to inhabit once built.

- The training of pilots for the aviation industry is another popular use of virtual reality today. This is especially beneficial to airline pilots flying simulated commercial jetliners, as it offers the ability to practice something that is relatively risky and costly with an actual plane.

- There is certainly a wide array of possible applications for virtual reality in science. One interesting way virtual reality is already being used is for the design of molecular compounds. Scientists wear a virtual reality control glove which allows them to position molecules in a virtual space.

- Industrial designers can easily manipulate and shape the models they design through the use of a virtual reality display. Some computer graphics cards have outputs specifically for use with stereoscopic headsets for this kind of application

The history of VR has been recent and sudden. While components have been in development for nearly forty years, working VR systems have only recently appeared on the scene. According to Chesher, "Virtual Reality developed from fiction in 1984 to a rich discourse and a marketed technology by 1992". Although, the popular fascination with VR has existed for less than a decade, VR has already gained importance from educational areas to military training, from social interaction to media.

Not only VR offers us a new way to interact with computer but also it enables us to experience a (virtual) world that is impossible in real world.

With its undeniable services at easing human tasks, VR is changing our lives and eventually VR will increasingly become a part of our life.

> "Facts as facts do not always create a spirit of reality, because reality is a spirit." - G. K. Chesterton, On the Classics

The role of perception in defining reality raises interesting issues of psychological, sociological, philosophical, and cognitive origins. Just how real, for example, are mental constructs or even sensory perceptions? In Heidegger and Virtual Reality: The Implications of Heidegger's Thinking for Computer Representations, Richard Coyne addressed the two different approaches that Human-Computer Interaction (HCI) and VR researchers have taken to explain perception; the "data-oriented" and the "constructivist views." According to Coyne, the data-oriented view assumes that the achievement of immersive VR is accomplished by increasing the quantity and quality of data streams to the human sensory organs. Those holding to the constructivist position would argue that immersion can be accomplished with much more limited sensory input, as long as the mind is engaged in the process of "constructing" the reality. Because the reality created by VR is based on the transmission of symbols in an interactive environment, symbolic interactionism may provide a useful schema for its analysis.

According to Brenda Laurel, "Reality has always been too small for the human imagination. We're always trying to transcend". Since the beginning of time people have transcended time and space with little more than their imaginations. Artificial experiences have long relied on the generative ability of the human imagination.

The Technology of VR

"The input and output points of contact define the human-computer interface. If an interface is defined as where two different worlds meet, it would appear that the more dissimilar the two worlds the greater the need for a well-designed interface."

Interface tools used for interactive media include the keyboard, mouse, touch screen, and joystick. For more advanced applications, such as VR, the technology becomes more complicated. The hardware that makes immersive VR, as it is generally understood, possible includes; a head-mounted display (HMD that presents a wide-angle stereoscopic visual environment) an audio system that provides threedimensional sound, and a data glove and body-suit and tracking device to gather input data from the user. Other options for input devices include the wand and 3D mouse. At this level, the interface begins to change the nature of user involvement. Sensory data gathered from and provided to the user creates an operating environment that masks the underlying technology.

VR is principally about getting human data into and out of a computer with as little distortion as possible. The most transparent, but still futuristic, approach is the one described by William Gibson in his 1984 novel Neuromancer. In this cyberpunk novel, information cowboys "jack-in to the Matrix" using a wetwired neural implant to bypass the external sense organs altogether.

The HMD, since its first prototype in the 1960s, has continued to evolve. Increasing in resolution and picture quality and decreasing in size and weight, the HMD presents a stereoscopic view of the computergenerated scene that fills the viewers' field-of-view. The display typically includes electromagnetic coils that provide tracking information. This allows the computer to continually update the scene to reflect changes in the position and angle of the user's head.

The development and increased capacity of computer processing technology has made computer-generated imagery possible on a level necessary for true VR. Photorealistic texture-mapped 3-D imagery that responds with minimal lag time to the users gaze or gestures has been possible for only a short time, and affordable for an even shorter time. The computer chips necessary to perform such feats becomes smaller, more reliable, and less expensive every year. At the same time, 3-D audio systems have advanced to bring the same level of realism to the auditory dimension.

The data glove is an input device that is worn on the hand and that allows the user to gesture, point, motion, or even "pick up" virtual objects. Fiber optic sensors measure the position and flex of the hand and supply this information to the computer. As with all VR hardware, early versions of the devices were costly.

Another sense that has been the target of VR research has been that of touch. Haptic interfaces that provide information to the fingertips and other sensitive areas are used to give the user a sense of the tactile qualities of the virtual world. Force feedback systems take this a step further by providing realistic information about the behavior of the virtual device. For example, the joystick used to fly a plane or the steering wheel used to direct a car should transmit information back to the operator for a fully realistic experience. Motion platforms, used both by NASA and by immersive amusement park VR rides, convey a sense of bodily motion with "carefully calibrated movements, vibrations and jolts".

VR Applications

The concept of VR has captured the imaginations of people from a diverse spectrum of modern culture. Diverse cultures ranging from cyberpunk to the military collaborated in bringing VR to life. From this perspective, VR is really about providing an alternative to our mundane, everyday reality. On the other hand, VR applications for business and commercial purposes are promoted for very different purposes. These apparently distinct views of VR, the first as an environment that will allow us to modify our mental or emotional state and the second as an environment that will allow us to manipulate our physical environment, suggest very different uses for VR development.

Military Applications: The military origins of VR are evident on numerous fronts. The Defense Department's SIMNET project allows participants to "practice" war by linking simulators around the country, and even around the world. Learning sophisticated aircraft systems has been at the forefront of military research.

Military uses of VR involve problem solving and experimentation that is more efficient and less costly when performed virtually. Flight training for air combat, missile launches, and other high-risk activities can be practiced in relative safety and at less expense on virtual battlefields. However, simulation is not the only military application of VR technology. C. J. Keep, describing the "Super Cockpit" program of the US Air Force, pointed out an important difference between this technology and the flight simulators that have gone before. "In the hyperreal Super Cockpit, the work performed in the virtual space is also work done in the real world; when the 'young fighter jock' downs a 'bandit' by pushing 'a phantom button on a virtual display screen,' then it is not a virtual person but a real person who dies in the bright light of a real air-to-air missile".

Commercial Applications: Businesses with an interest in VR include architecture, medicine, travel, and science. Taking a virtual tour through a building still in the process of architectural design is just one example of the practical application of VR research. A slightly different proposed application is for the visualization of and navigation through data in three-dimensional space. Elizabeth Weiss envisions an application for VR in "The cybergym; Virtual reality in the health club." Weiss envisions a time when one will be able to, "cross-country ski across a mountain, row across a lake, or even bike across America. But gone are any unpleasant snow moguls, the irregular currents of a lake, or those unpredictable hills in nature".

Such utopian visions of a future where family time and togetherness are facilitated by VR technology appear to me to run counter to the lessons of history and ignores the reality of human nature.

Virtual Sets: Another commercial application of VR technology is not one you'll find on your desktop computer, but rather one that may become increasingly visible on your television receiver. "Virtual set" technology makes possible computer generated sets that replace the conventional sets found in the typical television studio. Instead of sets manufactured from wood and paneling, virtual sets are computer generated. When combined with live-action elements, such as actors and props, they allow a studio production to appear as though it is taking place in any real or imaginary location of the producer's choosing. The "virtual" nature of the technology, and what sets it apart from more traditional blue-screen or chroma-key effects, is that the computer generated background is constantly updated to account for any movement of the studio cameras. The position of the camera in the virtual set sends data to the computer which is used to render the appropriate graphic background.

Alternative Applications of VR Technology

The immersive VR that has been described so far has largely been the playground of researchers and scientists who have had big budgets and powerful computers. However, the current trend in VR for the masses has been made possible by a different Defense Department computer project-the Internet. The sudden growth and popularity of the Internet and the graphically-rich World-Wide Web (WWW) has resulted in a new computer-mediated medium. It should come as no surprise that VR enthusiasts have rushed to take advantage of the possibilities presented by this new medium.

VRML: The programming language of the WWW is Hyper Text Markup Language (HTML) a subset of Standard Generalized Markup Language (SGML). In early 1994 Mark Pesce added to these Virtual Reality Markup Language (VRML), for authoring and navigating through virtual graphical worlds on the web. VRML is a computer language that allows users to create virtual objects and spaces that can be explored by anyone connected to the Internet who has the required VRML-capable browser software. VRML has the potential to turn the flat, two-dimensional graphics and information on the WWW into threedimensional spaces for interactive navigation.

QuickTime VR: Another variety of VR on the WWW is provided by Apple Computer's QuickTime

VR. QuickTime VR takes advantage of Apple's QuickTime technology to create virtual worlds that are created from a series of still photographs. Photographs are scanned and then "stitched" together by the authoring software. The final product appears to be a seamless three-dimensional photograph that the viewer can move through, in and around.

The Social uses of VR

In some VR environments interaction is provided by another human who is occupying the same virtual space. In others, such as single player games, all or nearly all of the interaction is supplied by the many lines of computer code that make up the program. Even then is important to understand that this programmed interaction is a product of human invention by a software engineer. Every virtual world has a human creator. While some VR critics warn of the dangers of isolation for those who spend extended lengths of time alone in virtual worlds, others envision a new social context for communication in which global virtual communities are formed around shared interests.

Text-Based VR: The fantasy role-playing game 'Dungeons and Dragons' is widely understood to be the inspiration for computer fantasy worlds called MUDs. MUD at one time stood for Multi-User Dungeon, but now more commonly means Multi-User Domain. Text-based MUDs have evolved to become objectoriented MOOs (MUD, Object-Oriented), moving closer to the concept of VR. In both MUDs and MOOs, participants create a persona or avatar, contribute to building a simulated environment, and interact with other participants.

In contrast to the immersion VR systems described thus far, text-based VR facilitates the construction of virtual worlds with readily available materials-a computer keyboard and a willing mind. These virtual worlds are created in cyberspace and are populated by computer enthusiasts seeking to engage in mediated human interaction. As physical spaces become increasingly dangerous and uninhabitable, virtual spaces of our own construction become increasingly attractive. Virtual realities allow us to modify our identities, improve our appearance, and control our interactions with others. As users of MUDs and MOOs have known for some time, creating an avatar to operate in a fictive dimension is an intoxicating experience.

These virtual worlds are real in so far as they represent the interactions of humans in real-time. The creation of reality in this case is a social construction, rather than the biological, sense-based artificial reality of what is traditionally known as full-immersion VR. One could argue that this socially-constructed, text-based VR experience is immersive in a different sense of the word. Reports of "addictive" behavior have been attributed to MUDDing and related activities.

Human-Computer Interaction with Augmented Reality

People today are used to the WIMP (Windows Icons Menus Pointing) paradigm to interact with a computer. This is the conventional desktop UI metaphor that we find in almost all operating systems. But with augmented reality, we can not use this paradigm as it wouldn't make sense to have windows floating in the reality. Even though this paradigm is not relevant any more, we still need to manipulate objects, thus the need for a way to select, drag, resize, remove, add etc. objects. Indeed, Augmented Reality is per definition interactive, so we need a way or multiple ways to interact with it. User Interfaces and inputs are used to change the system state and thus interact with it. In, the researchers are categorizing interfaces into 7 different groups. They have Tangible UI and 3D pointing, Haptic UI and gesture recognition, Visual UI and gesture recognition, Gaze tracking, Aural UI and speech recognition.

To have a better idea of the different possibilities to interact with augmented reality, here is an overview of the different HID. Table presents different techniques to interact with virtual reality depending on their mobility and the way of interacting with them. The references are referring to the cited solutions in the same order they appear on their respective lines. Nowadays, any computer with a web-camera or phone with an image sensor can be an AR device. Especially smartphones, which have cameras along with a touchscreen and other sensors such as a gyroscope, compass, GPS or accelerometer. That's why most of the AR systems make use of a touch-screen. This area is evolving and we can see today projects such as ATAP Project Tango from Google trying to integrate a depth sensor into mobile devices. For Project Tango, the main goal is not direct interaction from the user (i.e. using it to "see" his hands) but to create a map of the environment. Mapping the user's environment in 3D allows for a better integration of virtual object.

Tangible UI and 3D Pointing

The first step toward a more natural user interaction is to have something both tangible and registered in 3D to manipulate for the user. This way the user is not lost with abstract concepts and can relate to already existing concepts. The Studierstube project by Szalav´ari et al. implemented this principle by having a pen and panel being tracked by their system. The user sees the layer of augmented reality with his see-through glasses. The pen is used to do any 3D manipulation, with 6 degrees of freedom, and the panel is here to display information, menus or options that would other be a problem to integrate with reality. The system "projects" information on the panel, as if it was a 2D display. This system makes collaboration relatively easy. Users can manipulate a 3D model with their respective pen and will share the view of this 3D model. Their goal is to have naturally integrated displays, represented by the panel, and enabling the users to independently control the 3D model from their viewpoint. Their experiment showed that this kind of system is ideal to work collaboratively on synthetic data, such as 3D curves.

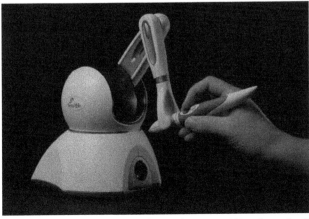

SensAble/Geomagic PHANTOM Omni Haptic Device1, providing force feedback to the user.

More recently, we have seen this kind of user interface with video games and the Nintendo Wii, where the user has a "remote" integrating an accelerometer and infra red camera. This system enable the gaming console to track the gesture of the user precisely while the user still has a concrete object in his hand. Feedback can be given to the user with either vibrations or sound, also integrated in the controller.

Haptic UI and Gesture Recognition

To have a better feedback and a more realistic feeling when interacting with augmented reality, Haptic user interfaces have been introduced. The difference with these category of interfaces is that the force is not only from the user to the device, but also from the device to the user. This interfaces are usually arm robots, for instance the Phantom by SensAble, see figure, which is a popular device for research purpose.

Hayward et al. list and review Haptic interfaces and devices. One of them is a joystick by Rosenberg et al, used in their study to rate the user preferences on haptic virtual surfaces. To do so they had a joystick with two degrees of liberty manipulated by the user. They simulated different kind of feedback, either having a damper or a spring wall model. This kind of studies shows that no aspect should be neglected when working to build a more natural user interface. Indeed, every detail can make the user experience better.

Gloves have also been used with an added haptic feedback, for instance the buzzing gloves of Buchmann et al. but Haptic UI in general is usually bulky and difficult to use for augmented reality, especially for mobile systems.

Table: User Interfaces Categories.

	Fixed	Handheld	Wearable
Tangibl	Studierstube, PlayStation 3		
Tactile		Smartphones	
Visual 2D	PlayStation 2 and 3	Smartphones	
Visual 3D	HoloDesk, Studierstube MirageTable	Tango	Digits
Gaze	FreeGaze		Occulus Mod, Google Glass
Hybrid	Sublimate	KITE, 3DTouch & Homer-S	Google Glass

Tactile UI

Touch-screens with vibration could be considered the poor man's Haptic UI. This kind of input is only 2D, and the haptic feedback is determined by whether or not the device is integrating a vibrator. But this has the advantage of having the input right in front of the display, making it easier to interact with virtual elements than with a traditional haptic device, such as a Phantom. Touch-screens are part of the broader category of Tactile UIs.

This area could itself be split in several categories, it has already been done in a survey, but we are not going to spend that much time talking about them in the present paper. We will only have an overview of what is existing. Human finger tips contain many sensitive nerves, this is only logical tu use this to give feedback information to the user. Most of the tactile interfaces use an array small actuators to "touch" back the user's finger. Only the mechanical principle changes between the different devices, with motors, electrostatic or piezoelectric technology, pneumatic, electrical etc. to give sensation to the user's fingertip. Of course tactile interfaces can be used for blind people to read in Braille. This is a nice way to have augmented reality for blind people along with Aural UI. Arrays with taller actuators are also used to produce a plane which can be deformed. This is the case with MATRIX (A Multipurpose Array of Tactile Rods for Interactive eXpression) and more recently with Sublimate. The latter combines an array of actuator with a see 3D see-through display, thanks to a half-silvered mirror and shutter glasses. They also use a "wand", a Tangible UI, thus making this system a Hybrid UI. The actuators are both used to give the user a feedback and to be manipulated by the user. The user can move the actuators to change the shape of the surface. They also have a collaborative work use-case with a "Multi-user geospatial data exploration", where they use tablets in addition to the rest in order to extend the active workspace, interact and add layers of data. Tactile UIs are not limited to fingertips, and some devices to substitute vision have been developed, they are placed on the tongue are allowing disabled people to see again.

Visual UI and Gesture Recognition

When leaving the Haptic feedback aside, less cumbersome user interface can be achieved. Visual UI for instance, tracks the hands of the user. It can be done with a camera, when doing so, the user's hand are free and don't have to manipulate any device. The camera can be placed at different places. Externally, filming the user, around the neck of the user, oriented toward his hands or around his wrist, has been demonstrated with UbiHand.

MATRIX, Multipurpose Array of Tactile Rods for Interactive eXpression, an array of tactile actuators.

This category can be split in two, the 2D and 3D devices. Smartphones really often use their camera for gesture recognition but are limited to 2D whereas a device such as UbiHand or Digits can model in 3D the hand of the user. The latter aims to be used with mobile devices whereas it is not especially the case for UbiHand. However, both aim at being low cost. Digits wants to be reproducible using only off-the-shelf components. The advantages against 3D depth cameras is that depth cameras are not yet precise enough to track our finger, but we use our fingers every day to do complicated things. For this reason using fingers to do gestures, and not only the arm or hand, is viable. Digits is really precise and permits to do fine work on virtual objects.

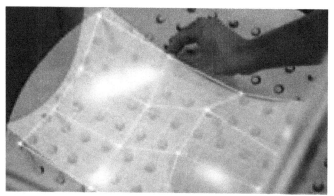

Sublimate, 3D interactive plane with actuators.

Systems such as HoloDesk or Mirage Table both have demonstrated that the recognition accuracy is much better in 3D than in 2D. The latter makes use of a depth camera, 3D glasses and a beamer to view the scene in 3D whereas HoloDesk also makes use of a depth camera but projects the image aligned with reality on a see through mirror. Although, aligning the virtual layer with reality can be an immersive experience for the user, having this layer in 2D can introduces problems, for instance the Dimension Gap of which we will talk later. For this reason, usage of a 3D display, for instance in Mirage Table, can result in a better accuracy when manipulating virtual objects. This solution has the advantage of being gloveless and blurs the line between the real and virtual world, but the user doesn't have any feedback when his hand is touching a virtual object, in a similar fashion to Haptic UIs. To lessen this inconvenience, Benko et al. have what they call a "mirror view", where real object are duplicated in front of the user, replicating the experience of a real mirror. This way, the user doesn't have a projected virtual object on his hand when trying to manipulate it.

Gaze Tracking

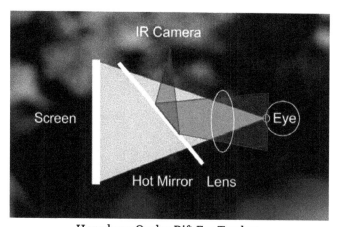

Homebrew Oculus Rift Eye Tracker.

Gaze tracking can be one of the most powerful user interface but also one of the most difficult to implement. Our gaze often reflects what we are thinking about in the real world. When we look at something we certainly have an intention with this object. For this reason, by following the gaze of the user, we can obtain information about what he wants to achieve. Gaze tracking is done by having tiny cameras filming the user's pupils. The difficulty is to calibrate it correctly and to filter out involuntary eye movements. Google has a very simple gaze tracking technology in his Google Glass where the screen activates only when the user is looking at it. But this can be much more powerful, as it has been demonstrated with FreeGaze by Oh no et al, where a non-intrusive, fast calibrating (only two points) gaze tracking system is used for an everyday use. Their study shows that the system is viable and accurate.

James Darpinian recently built his own Oculus Rift Eye Tracker. The Occulus Rift is a 3D head mounted display usually used for Virtual Reality, but which can also be used for Augmented Reality. The problem when using a device such as this is that the user face is not visible, making usual eye tracking with a system such as FreeGaze impossible. James Darpinian resolves this problem by cutting a hole on top of the left eye socket in the Occulus Rift and by placing there a PlayStation 3 Eye Camera. He place a hot mirror, a mirror reflecting only infra-red light, in the Occulus to reflect the picture of the eye to the camera. The principle is illustrated in figure. This way of integrating an eye tracker with a head worn display could also work with see through display usually used in augmented reality. By using OpenCV, the pupil can be extracted in about 6ms per frame for a precision of 1/4 of a pixel. The user can stare at something displayed by the Occulus Rift with a precision of 2 pixels. Although, the Occulus Rift is fixed to the user's head, James Darpinian still encounters problems with calibration, as when moving his head rapidly or when changing facial expression, the Occulus slightly changes position and the calibration is not good anymore.

Aural UI and Speech Recognition

Another natural way of interacting, especially between human, is by talking. Therefore, Aural user interfaces are today more and more used, especially with connected object which can process the voice recognition in the cloud. For instance, Google and Apple use speech recognition on their mobile operating systems, the voice of the user is recorded, sent to servers on the internet and the result comes back to the smart-phone. On a hardware standpoint, only a cheap microphone is needed.

Papers often make examples with an industrial application. For instance with a maintenance engineer using AR to work more efficiently. That's also the case for Goose et al. who is suggesting to use a Aural UI for maintenance technicians. This application is a good example for the usage of speech recognition. Indeed, factory workers or maintenance technicians often have their hands occupied as they have to work with them. Interacting with their hands is not a solution. Their example is using a head-worn eye screen and camera along with a headset with microphone. They have specialized algorithms to recognize the equipment being maintained, for instance pipes, and the worker can manipulate the software via the Aural UI. The technician can for instance ask the system to enlarge a specific part of the picture or to recognize it and display it rotating in 3D. All those actions can help the technician, without having him to even use his hands.

Difficulties arise when working in a noisy environment, which can happen often when doing maintenance in a factory. Fortunately, noise cancellation techniques do exist, using a second microphone to capture only the noise and removing it from the first microphone audio. The main difficulty may be when using speech recognition with augmented reality. Indeed, when a human talks about an object, ambiguity can arise.

Hybrid UI

Most important of all, Hybrid UI is not a category in itself but a combination of categories. Indeed, what can be better against ambiguity when verbally describing an object than to point a finger at it? This is the principle of multi-modal interactions.

This type of UI has been very well illustrated with KITE. which has three different types of input. Their device is made of a Windows tablet with a touch-screen, a Razer Hydra magnetic tracker and Primesense Carmine short range depth camera, see figure. This camera is the same technology embedded in the Kinect or Google's project Tango. This setup is not really viable for a Handled one as it is heavy. User complained about its weight in the study. However, the goal was to demonstrate that such a Hybrid device could be possible to do with consumer devices. If it were to be integrated, it could be better done and weight less. They found out that the magnetic tracker is very accurate with a less than 1 mm error and less than 1 degree for orientation when being within 1.5 m from the transmitter. This transmitter is a huge drawback of the solution, as it transforms a potentially hand-held device to a fixed device. The benefits of the magnetic tracker is not only the accuracy but also a very reasonable processing requirement. This is especially true when comparing it to a visual tracking solution, such as the Primesense depth camera. They only achieved a processing speed of less than 10 fps while working with 640x480 pixels, and this is with an Intel Core i5 and 4GB of memory. Tablets usually have a lot less processing power, being equipped with low power ARM CPUs. Although, the system is not perfect, the user experience was much better than when using only one input. This permitted to have a car racing game taking in the real world. This is the kind of capabilities, which has a gyroscope, accelerometer, magnetometer and depth sensor. Although the Razer Magnetic Sensor is much more accurate than a gyroscope and magnetometer combined, this makes it very similar to KITE.

KITE Platform, hand-held AR device made with off-the-shelf hardware.

Problems While Interacting with Ar

All those interfaces aim at providing a better control over AR applications. Unfortunately, three sorts of problems, among others, can appear when using such a system.

Dimension Gap

AR is usually three dimensional and require six degrees of freedom while most of the HID are two dimensional. A touch-screen, camera or mouse only have X and Y coordinates, while the interaction might need a Z coordinate, for the depth. This problem has been demonstrated in. In this paper, users are asked to grab a virtual object integrated to the scene captured by the camera, as illustrated in figure. They have markers on their fingers so that the mobile device can track them. It appeared to be more difficult to grab the object this way than by touching it on the touch-screen, because of the lack of depth with the camera. Trying to interact with a 3D space through a 2D camera is the same as trying to put the cap back on your pen with only one eye open. This is frustrating for the user as he has try again multiple times before succeeding.

Object Selection and Screen Concealment

Another concern when using AR applications with a touchscreen, especially with mobile devices, is that the user usually has to put his hand or finger on the screen thus covering the object of interest or other important elements. This also has been demonstrated in. When the object the user wants to manipulate is hidden, it makes it more difficult to move it to a desired position, scale it or rotate it for instance. One loses precision as one has to guess where the object is.

Lack of Haptic Feedback

This problem has been clearly identified by Hurst et al. When the user tries to grab a virtual object through a camera view on the device, either 3D or 2D, in reality there is only air. This makes the confirmation of grabbing an object we usually have in real life non existent here.

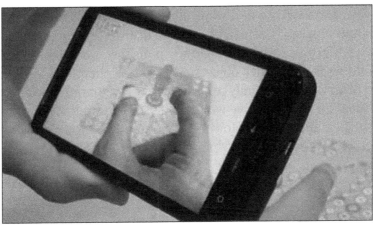

A green marker (thumb) and a red one (index finger) are used to track
fingers and manipulate virtual objects on the board game.

Solving the Problems

3D Interface Interaction

First of all, the lack of dimension problem can be tackled with a 3D sensor, instead of using a simple 2D camera, some use a depth sensor, demonstrated by Hilliges et al. with HoloDesk. This camera will generate a cloud of points, spread in the three dimensions. Using this we can know exactly where the hand of the user is or map the environment more precisely. For instance, when the user wants to grab a virtual object, like in, a depth camera will enable the device to draw the virtual object in front of or behind the hand of the user. Also, the user will not need to wear markers on his fingers. With the depth, we can detect more reliably the shape of the fingers, thus detecting easily when they are moving. In addition, when displaying a virtual object, the device can integrate it more realistically in the environment with the help of depth information. With conventional cameras, AR software usually require to have a square marker on the surface we want to "project" the virtual objects, to be able to calculate the perspective. This requirement doesn't exist with depth sensors as the sensor gives information about the plane the device is looking at. Like demonstrated in, this makes blending virtual object with real objects much more easy.

The usage of a back camera can be a solution to the screen concealment problem, however the depth remains important even when we don't need it to grab an object. Indeed, it has been shown by a user study in that the user experience is better when displaying the user's finger on top of the virtual button, for which we didn't specially need depth information. According to the study, it makes the button pushing experience feel more realistic. We can easily see here the use of depth information from a sensor to draw correctly the finger on top or under a button, thus saving computing power for other tasks.

The usage of a depth sensor may be nice, but this is not the only solution for a 3D interface interaction. Experimentations have been made with gloves and more recently with a gloveless wearable sensor. The advantage of this solution is a much more accurate tracking of the users finger as well as the possibility to have his hand wherever he wants and not in front of a sensor. But the drawback is that the AR application needs to draw a 3D hand on screen to represent the user's hand, as we don't have a camera.

For head worn displays and working in a somewhat fixed fashion, Schmalstieg et al. propose an interface with a pen and a panel. The pen allows the user to do any movement and operation a 3D mouse supports. They project, with the head worn display, information both on the panel and everywhere else, blending it with other objects. The goal of the panel is to have a surface when manipulating text or other data we usually use with the WIMP paradigm. This combination of pen and panel makes it ideal for collaborative work. The user can interact in 3D and use a paradigm he already knows (the pen and paper). However its limitation shows up when the user wants to manipulate an object with its own hands, which are no tracked. The system will not not the user's intention.

Alternatives

Backside Touch-panel and Dual Screen

An answer to the screen concealment problem can also be a backside touch-panel. By moving the touch surface to the back of the device, the fingers no longer the screen and the user can see everything that is on screen. This king of usage has been demonstrated by Sony with the PlayStation Vita and the mini game "Rolling Pastures" in "Little Deviants". In this game, the player can bump the ground in the game by placing his finger on the rear touchpad and by moving it. This way, the player can still see the whole screen while playing. Nintendo previously implemented another solution on the Nintendo DS4 by both having two screen, one touchscreen and one regular screen, and by using a stylus instead of a finger. The stylus being much thinner than a finger, the user can see more of the screen and can also select an object more precisely. Those two examples may not be used for AR, but we can easily imagine it.

Haptic UI and Tactile UI

Another type of touchscreen with haptic feedback could be used to partially solve the problem of screen concealment. Like some devices described in, it could have a different texture when the user has his finger on something interesting, for instance, the object he tries to move. This way, even when the screen is occulted, the user can still feel what is under his fingertip. But the limitation is that the user can not read what is under his fingertip and that any part of the screen that is not visible but also not touch will remain equally occulted as before.

Of course, this goes without saying that both Tactile UIs and Haptic UIs solve the lack of haptic feedback problem. This is self-explanatory for Haptic UIs and as for Tactile UIs, the texture of the tactile surface can be changed when an object is selected, confirming the selection to the user.

Another alternative to solve the screen concealment and a few other problems is to have a Aural UI and speech recognition. By giving orders, the users doesn't need to use his hands at all, which comes very handy in some situation, for instance in the maintenance field where a technician needs his hands. However, the compute power needed to understand speech is much bigger than what is required even for a depth sensor. Also, human languages are often ambiguous, making it more difficult for a computer to understand us. Finally, it may be socially unacceptable to be apparently speaking alone in a public space and private informations could end in the wrong ears.

Fixed System

Of course, on fixed AR systems, the problem of screen concealment is less noticeable as screens are bigger than for mobile systems. But another problem for fixed systems is the need to be near the display to interact with it, as those display are not moveable. A solution is also to have a depth sensor, such as the Kinect 5, so that the user can interact at any distance from the display. Also, a lot of fixed system use a half-silvered, for instance Sublimate or HoloDesk. The consequence is that they usually have the user manipulate under the half-silvered mirror, resulting in having the augmented reality layer on top of the user's hand. This can be disturbing if the system is not blending the virtual objects correctly (i.e. if the part of the object under the user's hand is displayed). However, this solves the screen concealment problem.

Visual Help

An additional and artificial visual help can improve the user experience in most of the problem. For instance, for the lack of haptic feedback problem, Hurst et al. have ¨ implemented a system indicating the interpenetration of two objects and a visual confirmation of the selection. In their study, with a visual confirmation, the selection of an object reportedly takes less time than without.

To help resolve the screen concealment problem, some systems use a deported view of what is under the user's finger. This is also used in non AR applications on smart-phones when precision is required.

3D Touch and Homer-S

Without adding any hardware to an existing smart-phone or tablet, Mossel et al. propose a novel way to interact with 6 degrees of freedom with AR. This is done while using the device one handedly, which can appear impossible at first. Solution to manipulate the third dimension with a 2D touch-screen usually make use of multi touch gestures, but those are difficult to do one using the device with only one hand. Here, what is proposed is to take into account the current position of the device, changing the meaning of the same gesture when the device is not in the same position. For instance, when the user slides his finger on the screen, it will translate the object along the x or y axis. But if the device is lying on its back, then it will move along the z axis, like if the user was watching the virtual object from the top through a window provided by the device. This has some advantages but it also has drawbacks. For instance, while with the usual AR interfaces the user can manipulate objects without moving, here the user needs to move around the virtual objects he his manipulating. Indeed, if he wants to move the object closer to him, he has to place his device on top, under or on next to the virtual object. He can then proceed to translate it. This technique is only viable for small objects and small AR environment, or if the user is willing to move around a lot.

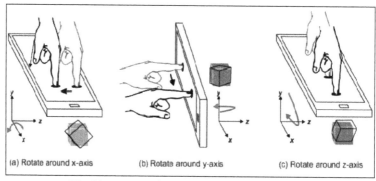

The Homer-S technique for rotating an object.

To rotate objects, they have a technique called Homer-S which seems more viable. It is a complicated to describe gesture which combines touching the screen and moving the device. The gesture is illustrated in figure. In their study, user were more efficient when using Homer-S, it took them less time to complete the same tasks compared to 3DTouch, but almost only for a specific task, which was to let a barrel down an inclined platform. In average, there is no significant difference in performance among a broad type of tasks.

Permissions

Index

Printed in the USA
CPSIA information can be obtained
at www.ICGtesting.com
JSHW051417221024
72173JS00006B/1371